Race, Sex, and Segre[Colonial Latin America

MW00975782

This book traces the emergence and early development of segregationist practices and policies in Spanish and Portuguese America—showing that the practice of resettling diverse indigenous groups in segregated "Indian towns" (or *aldeamentos* in the case of Brazil) influenced the material reorganization of colonial space, shaped processes of racialization, and contributed to the politicization of reproductive sex.

The book advances this argument through close readings of published and archival sources from the 16th and early 17th centuries and is informed by two main conceptual concerns. First, it considers how segregation was envisioned, codified, and enforced in a historical context of consolidating racial differences and changing demographics associated with racial mixture. Second, it theorizes the interrelations between notions of race and reproductive sexuality. It shows that segregationist efforts were justified by paternalistic discourses that aimed to conserve and foster indigenous population growth, and it contends that this illustrates how racially qualified life was politicized in early modernity. It further demonstrates that women's reproductive bodies were instrumentalized as a means to foster racially qualified life, and it argues that processes of racialization are critically tied to the differential ways in which women's reproductive capacities have been historically regulated.

Race, Sex, and Segregation in Colonial Latin America is essential for students, researchers, and scholars alike interested in Latin American history, social history, and gender studies.

Olimpia E. Rosenthal is Assistant Professor of Spanish and Portuguese at Indiana University. Her main research areas include colonial Latin American literary and cultural studies, postcolonial theory, and visual culture. She has published in prestigious journals worldwide and has organized various conferences, including one at IU's Gateway Center in India.

Early Modern Iberian History in Global Contexts: Connexions

Series Editors: Harald E. Braun (University of Liverpool) and Pedro Cardim (Universidade Nova de Lisboa)

Race, Sex, and Segregation in Colonial Latin America
Olimpia E. Rosenthal

For more information about this series, please visit https://www.routledge.com/Early-Modern-Iberian-History-in-Global-Contexts/book-series/EMIHIGC

Race, Sex, and Segregation in Colonial Latin America

Olimpia E. Rosenthal

Routledge
Taylor & Francis Group

NEW YORK AND LONDON

First published 2023
by Routledge
605 Third Avenue, New York, NY 10158

and by Routledge
4 Park Square, Milton Park, Abingdon, Oxon, OX14 4RN

Routledge is an imprint of the Taylor & Francis Group, an informa business

© 2023 Olimpia E. Rosenthal

The right of Olimpia E. Rosenthal to be identified as the author of this work has been asserted in accordance with sections 77 and 78 of the Copyright, Designs and Patents Act 1988.

Library of Congress Cataloging-in-Publication Data
Names: Rosenthal, Olimpia E., author.
Title: Race, sex, and segregation in colonial Latin America / Olimpia E. Rosenthal.
Description: New York : Routledge, 2023. | Series: Early modern Iberian history in global contexts | Includes bibliographical references and index. Identifiers: LCCN 2022036733 (print) | LCCN 2022036734 (ebook) | ISBN 9780367702403 (hardcover) | ISBN 9780367702410 (paperback) | ISBN 9781003145196 (ebook)
Subjects: LCSH: Indians, Treatment of—Latin America. | Spain—Colonies—Latin America—History. | Portugal—Colonies—Latin America—History. | Segregation—Latin America—Sources. | Race—Political aspects—Latin America—Sources. | Sex—Political aspects—Latin America—Sources. | Latin America—Race relations—Sources. | Latin America—History—To 1830.
Classification: LCC F1411 .R783 2023 (print) | LCC F1411 (ebook) | DDC 305.80098—dc23/eng/20220816
LC record available at https://lccn.loc.gov/2022036733
LC ebook record available at https://lccn.loc.gov/2022036734

ISBN: 978-0-367-70240-3 (hbk)
ISBN: 978-0-367-70241-0 (pbk)
ISBN: 978-1-003-14519-6 (ebk)

DOI: 10.4324/9781003145196

Typeset in Sabon
by codeMantra

This book is dedicated to my parents, Maureen and Steve Rosenthal, for their guidance and unwavering support, and to Diego Amaru, for the joy you bring to my life.

Contents

Acknowledgments

As I complete this book in a context of an ongoing global pandemic, I feel a heightened sense of gratitude for the people and institutions that have fostered my intellectual and personal development over the many years it took to get here. As a graduate student at the University of Arizona, I had the fortune of having two exceptional mentors: Kátia Bezerra and Laura Gutiérrez. Both granted me the leeway to explore the conceptual questions that guided this project initially, and they continue to be inspiring role models as accomplished feminist academics. Bram Acosta and Mónica Morales likewise played a decisive role in shaping my intellectual trajectory by introducing me to the two main analytical fields that inform this book: colonial and postcolonial studies in Latin America. I am also grateful for the community in Tucson that made my experience in graduate school as enjoyable and intellectually stimulating as it was, including Sara Beaudrie, Ana Carvalho, Will Costley, Joan Gilabert, Andrés Guzmán, Beatriz Jiménez, Daniela Johannes, Luciana Luna Freire, José Promis, Andrew Rajca, Eliana Rivero, Eva Romero, and Jamie Wilson. Thanks also to the Louise Foucar Marshall Foundation Dissertation Fellowship for supporting my work, and to the Mellon Foundation for funding a summer workshop in Spanish paleography.

At Indiana University, I have the privilege of working in a supportive and dynamic department. I am indebted to *each* of my colleagues in the department of Spanish and Portuguese for their support and camaraderie. I especially want to thank Alejandro Mejías-López for his invaluable mentorship, Kathleen Myers and Patrick Dove for their guidance, Manuel Díaz-Campos for his support, and Andrés Guzmán for priceless insight on many of the key arguments I develop in this book. Anke Birkenmaier, Deborah Cohn, Melissa Dinverno, Laura Gurzynski-Weiss, Kathleen Myers, Luciana Namorato, Estela Vieira, and Reyes Vila-Belda have also been welcoming and supportive colleagues who kindly shared their experiences and helped me navigate pregnancy and the early years of motherhood, and from whom I continue to learn, both personally and professionally. Indiana University has also generously supported my work and fostered my intellectual development, including through grants by the New Frontiers in the Arts &

Humanities-New Currents award, the Ostrom Grants Program, and the College of Arts and Humanities Institute Conference Grant. These grants, in addition to others from the Antipode and Mellon Foundations, helped me establish meaningful and productive academic relations that enhanced my commitment to comparative interdisciplinary scholarship. The faculty writings groups, and the many women from whom I learned in that setting, were also essential for the completion of this project.

The community of colleagues, graduate students, and friends I have had the joy and privilege to interact with in Bloomington, Eronga, and beyond have also shaped and enriched this project. Personally and intellectually, I am indebted to Majed Akhter, Penelope Anderson, Ishan Ashutosh, Orlando Betancor, Hall Bjornsatd, Purnima Bose, Andrés Guzmán, Pedro Machado, Daniel Nemser, Micol Seigel, Jessie Speer, and Shane Voegel. I also want to acknowledge other friends who have encouraged and guided me at different points in this long trajectory, including Abdul Aijaz, María de los Angeles Barbosa Gaona, Benjamin Jaramillo Gaona, Gaelle Le Calvez, Israel de la Luz, Shane Green, Nishanie Gunawardane, Gwen Kirk, Meredith Lee, Massiel Maldonado Mendiola, Mintzi Martínez-Rivera, Gabriel Mendoza Chavez, Akwasi Obempe, Anthony Palacios, Javier Robledo Jacobo, Judith Rodriguez, Olga Rodríguez-Ulloa, Michael Schultz, Mónica Solorio Cervantes, Esperanza Solorio Herrera, Alejandro Viveros, and Mareike Winchell. I extend my special thanks to Anna Macango and Elizabeth Schechter for our conversations and evening walks that were always something to look forward to and helped ground me in challenging times. I also especially thank Ishan Ashutosh, for our enduring friendship, and Mónica Solorio Cervantes, for her lifetime coaching. I also had the pleasure of teaching and mentoring exceptional graduate students whose ideas have shaped my own and whose developing work I look forward to reading, including Stephanie Estrada, Ollin García Pliego, Gabriela Kolman, Daniel Runnels, José Luis Suárez Morales, and Nilzimar Vieira.

I also wish to acknowledge my family, without whose support, the development of this book would not have been possible. My mother, Maureen Rosenthal, read multiple iterations of this project and always offered me sharp editorial and content comments; she also kept me accountable while helping me prioritize work-life balance. My father, Steve Rosenthal, celebrated some of the milestones with me, brought critical perspective, and indulged me in long conversations. The book was completed in the span of my son Diego's lifetime, and though I realize I might have talked too much about the book (he knew by the time he was two that Chapter 3 is about Guaman Poma), his joyful presence continuously propels me forward. I also want to acknowledge my sisters, Ariel and Ondine Rosenthal, for always being there for me, and my nephews, Alek and Kai Fliess, for constantly making me smile. I also extend my special thanks to Thomas Fliess for helping me with formatting and to Miguel Maldonado for the fun conversations. I am also so grateful for the positive influence and support

I have received from Aaron, Alex, Sander, Greg and Steve Dawson; Anita Rosenthal; and Karen Truax. I am especially indebted to Aaron Dawson for the multiple ways in which he supported this project. I want to also acknowledge and thank Andrés Guzmán, for everything we have shared and continue to share, and Marco, Tatiana, Paulina, Rudy, and Sofia Bohorquez; Christian, Cristina, Gabriel, and Mateo Yen; and Francisco Guzman, for the ways in which they have enriched my life. I am especially thankful to María Eugenia Guzmán Freire for her wisdom and positive impact.

Finally, I want to thank the anonymous reviewers who read the manuscript and my editors at Routledge, Harald Braun, Pedro Cardim, and Max Novick. As the pandemic disrupted the timeline I envisioned at the beginning of 2020, their patience, encouragement, and support meant more to me than they can ever imagine. Thank you all!

Introduction
Theorizing Race as a Border Concept

Race is not reducible to any prior or preexisting identity. It is not a starting point but an end product, the result of a process called racialization. The racialization processes that began with the Spanish colonial project were routed through a politics of space.

Daniel Nemser.[1]

Race, of course, has always been formulated alongside and within the biopolitics of sexual reproduction: its regulation, its proliferation, its restrictions, and its social implications.

Joshua Lund.[2]

Race as a concept has always been about constructing borders.

Robert Bernasconi.[3]

Placed in dialogue, the elements of each of the theorizations of race advanced in the epigraphs help illuminate how the history of segregation in colonial Latin America shaped the development of processes of racialization across the region.[4] Daniel Nemser's account offers a genealogy of spatial practices of concentration in colonial Mexico, which, as he shows, decisively influenced the composition of differentiated groups that, over time, became naturalized. In his study, Nemser specifically traces how categories like *indio/a* and *mestizo/a* gradually consolidated as meaningful markers of group identity, largely as a result of the material practices sanctioned by the Spanish Crown as part of the transition toward the segregationist dual republic model, and he shows how this gradually led to the homogenization of diverse indigenous groups as *indios/as*, and contributed to the progressive differentiation of *mestizos/as* as a distinct socio-racial category.[5] Race, as he argues, "is not reducible to any prior or preexisting identity, but is rather the product of a process called racialization."[6] In Nemser's theorization, the material reorganization space is thus presented as a key analytical component to understand processes of racialization.

DOI: 10.4324/9781003145196-1

Joshua Lund similarly advances the claim that theorizations of race must account for the way in which notions of racial difference inform, and are naturalized by, the production and reorganization of space.[7] In his earlier work, Lund also points to the inextricable relation between the development of race relations and the biopolitical regulation of reproductive sex. As he argues, the history of reproductive sexuality "between Africans, Amerindians, and Europeans," has a long tradition in the Ibero-American world in the language of mestizaje, and it offers a unique insight to trace "the interactions between discourses of race, gender, and social reproduction."[8] Indeed, the history of mestizaje in colonial Latin America can be described as a history of racialized sexuality—a term first coined by Abdul Jan Mohamed to describe "the point where the deployment of sexuality intersects with the deployment of race"[9]—and it is critical to understand the development of processes of racialization in the region. Mestizaje, however, tends to be invoked by scholars to challenge the fixity of socio-racial categories and to dismiss the effectiveness of segregationist efforts in colonial Latin America.[10] This position is largely premised on the assumption that notions of racial mixtures work to disrupt fixed notions of race, but, on this point, Lund offers a productive way to rethink the issue, for, as he contends, "*mestizaje* as the exception to racial purity ultimately makes possible, legitimates, and reconfirms that purity."[11] From this perspective, the fact that segregationist projects in colonial Latin America developed in a context in which reproductive sex between differently racialized peoples was commonplace becomes all the more meaningful.[12] Not only does Lund's argument destabilize the idea of "pure" races prior to "mixture," but it also compels us to think about the way in which the regulation of reproductive sex informs how populations are racialized.

Robert Bernasconi's theorization of race is likewise grounded on an argument about space, but it also compels us to consider how notions of racial borders are articulated in relation to sex, and, more specifically, to reproductive, heteronormative sex. On the one hand, Bernasconi's claim that "race as a concept has always been about constructing borders" is developed to account for the relation between race and geography. As he states, "the division between the races frequently coincided with geographical borders."[13] On the other hand, he argues that the notion of racial borders is fundamentally tied to perceived sexual transgressions, particularly since the legal and social status of a child born of such "transgressions" has been historically shaped by the different ways in which said individuals are classified within particular racial formations.[14] In other words, for Bernasconi, racial borders must first be crossed or transgressed before they can be policed and regulated, including through segregationist policies and systems of classification.[15] This is why, for him, the concept of racial mixture is critical to understand the historical development of notions of race, since, as he argues, "races are identified only through race mixing."[16] Moreover, as Bernasconi suggests, although it is sometimes claimed that the introduction of a mixed race category can disrupt or serve to overturn the racial system because of its resistance to the dominant racial binary of black and white, it is hard to find any historical support for this view.[17]

According to Bernasconi, race is better theorized as a border concept in the sense that notions of racial difference have been historically premised on the creation of borders, both geographical and sexual.[18] Yet, as he stresses, in dialogue with Ann Laura Stoler, the operations of race are never actually reliant on fixed essentialisms, but rather, as Bernasconi puts it, "the recognition of the fluidity of racial terms provides an unexpected insight into how racism functions."[19] While Bernasconi does not develop these arguments specifically in relation to Latin America, his conceptual framework is nevertheless highly productive for tracing processes of racialization in the region.

As a conceptual framework to think about the history of segregation in colonial Latin America, the theorizations of race outlined above offer a productive way to reframe ongoing scholarship on the topic. On one level, the systematic concentration of diverse indigenous groups in segregated communities offers incisive insight to understand the way in which spatial borders helped solidify the conceptualization of *indios/as* as a racialized collectivity. Indeed, the segregationist policies and practices that were introduced in the course of the 16th century in both Spanish and Portuguese America were premised on the assumption of *indios/as* as a distinct and identifiable population group, and, over time, these contributed to the homogenization of diverse indigenous groups as a distinct socio-racial category.[20] Segregation also implied the delimitation of territorial and jurisdictional borders—which tied geography to law—[21] the physical transformation of the built environment—including, in some cases, through the construction of walls intended to separate differentiated groups—[22] and the regulation of people's movement based on racial ascription and gender considerations—as illustrated, for instance, in laws that sought to ensure that childbearing indigenous women remain in segregated communities.[23] The reorganization and regimentation of colonial space sanctioned by segregationist policies and practices are thus critical to understand how emerging notions of racial difference developed as material spatial borders were being erected and policed.

On another level, the history of segregation in colonial Latin America offers a unique insight to trace the intersections between notions of race, gender, and sexuality; particularly since segregationist efforts developed in a context in which reproductive sex between differently construed groups of people became increasingly subject to political reflections and regulations. This context is generally described by scholars by appealing to concepts like mestizaje, racial mixture, and miscegenation, and, as mentioned, it tends to be invoked to dismiss the effectiveness of segregationist efforts in the region.

This framing, however, precludes us from understanding how notions of racial mixture work to reify, rather than undermine, ideas about racial difference. For instance, when Ben Vinson argues that "Africans, Asians, Native Americans, and Europeans comprised the foundation upon which New World racial mixture would occur,"[24] he appeals to continental-scale geographical borders to describe the reproductive practices between the diversity of peoples that Iberian colonization brought together. Though Vinson acknowledges that there are significant national, cultural, and ethnic differences among the four groups that he lists, the processes of racial mixture that he traces in his book—and which he describes as "a hallmark feature of the region's demography"[25]—takes the categories of Africans, Asians, Native Americans, and Europeans as self-evident rather than inquire into the processes of differentiation through which those categories emerged as meaningful markers of group identity. This process of differentiation, I argue, is critically tied to the way in which reproductive sex between these groups was politicized and regulated by the nascent Iberian colonial states, and it sheds light not only on the way in which the foundational categories on which narratives of mestizaje are premised were historically produced but also on a much broader restructuration of power that can be productively analyzed by considering Michel Foucault's theorization of biopower.

Populations and Races

For his projected sixth volume on the *History of Sexuality*, Foucault envisioned a study focused on the topic of "Population and Races," as advertised on the back cover of the first French edition of Volume I.[26] He never pursued the project in any significant way, however, partly, as Ann Laura Stoler argues, because after 1977 he abandoned his investigations on race altogether—a close associate of Foucault's later suggested that the critic was "deadlocked on thinking about race."[27] Still, Foucault's theory of biopower offers critical insight to understand the conceptual links he started to trace between race, sex, and reproduction. In the last part of *The History of Sexuality. Volume I*, Foucault discusses the shift from sovereign power to biopower. He argues that during the classical age, which he dates from the middle of the 17th to the end of the 18 century, a major shift occurred in the mechanisms of power over life. Prior to the classical age, he argues, one of the sovereign power's characteristic privileges was the right to decide life and death.[28] As Foucault puts it

> the sovereign exercised his right of life only by exercising his right to kill, or by refraining from killing…The right which was formulated as the 'power of life and death' was in reality the right to *take* life or *let* live.[29]

He argues, however, that "since the classical age the West has undergone a very profound transformation of these mechanisms of power." In his words: "the old power of death that symbolized sovereign power was now carefully supplanted by the administration of bodies and the calculated management of life."[30] Foucault summarizes the shift of power's hold over life by suggesting that "the ancient right to *take* life or *let* live was replaced by a power to *foster* life or *disallow* it to the point of death."[31]

According to Foucault, moreover, the type of power over life which he describes as "marking the beginning of an era of 'biopower,'" developed in two basic forms.[32] As he argues:

> starting in the seventeenth century, this power over life evolved in two basic forms; these forms were not antithetical, however; they constituted rather two poles of development linked together by a whole intermediary cluster of relations. One of these poles—the first to be formed, it seems—centered on the body as a machine, its disciplining, the optimization of its capabilities, the extortion of its forces, the parallel increase of its usefulness and its docility, its integration into systems of efficient and economic controls, all this was ensured by the procedures of power that characterized the *disciplines*: an *anatomo-politics of the human body*. The second, formed somewhat later, focused on the species body, the body imbued with the mechanics of life and serving as the basis of the biological processes: propagation, births and mortality, the level of health, life expectancy and longevity, with all the conditions that can cause these to vary. Their supervision was effected through an entire series of interventions and *regulatory controls: a biopolitics of a population*. The setting up, in the course of the classical age, of this great bipolar technology—anatomic and biological, individualizing and specifying, directed toward the performances of the body, with attention to the processes of life—characterized a power whose highest function was perhaps no longer to kill, but to invest life through and through.[33]

As evinced, biopower is conceived by Foucault as encompassing both disciplinary technologies centered on the individual body—what Foucault terms "an anatomo-politics of the human body"—and regulatory controls aimed at the population as a whole—or what he calls "a biopolitics of a population." As Stoler suggests, what makes biopower unique is precisely the fact that it "joins two distinct technologies of power operating at different levels; one addresses the *disciplining* of individual bodies, the other addresses the 'global' *regulation* of the biological processes of human beings."[34]

Within this framework, Foucault theorizes the interconnections between race and sexuality. Foucault maintains that sexuality, being an eminently corporeal mode of behavior, is a matter for individualizing disciplinary controls that take the form of permanent surveillance. Yet, because sexuality has procreative effects as well, it is also inscribed in broad biological processes that concern not the bodies of individuals but rather the perceived unity of the population.[35] In the latter case, his theorization of sexuality is specifically focused on reproductive sex, but Foucault does not consider what this implies for thinking about the historical regulation of women's embodied role in reproduction.[36] Like sexuality, Foucault contends that racism involves both disciplinary controls aimed at producing docile bodies, as well as regulatory mechanisms targeting the population as a whole. On this point, though, Foucault theorizes racism's relation to the power over life almost exclusively in terms of death, arguing, for instance, that "[o]nce the State functions in the biopower mode, racism alone can justify the murderous function of the State."[37] As Paul Rabinow and Nikolas Rose point out, however, while exceptional forms of biopower can indeed lead to a type of thanatopolitics or necropolitics, its characteristic function entails a relation between "letting die" and "making live," that is to say, strategies for the governing, not taking, of life.[38] The undertheorized quality of some of Foucault's insights on this matter seems to typify the kind of conceptual deadlocks that he was encountering in his theorization of race, and it is precisely such gaps that justify going beyond the temporal and geographic delimitations of his work.

As described above, for Foucault, the regulatory controls that he describes "a biopolitics of a population" are a later historical development. Yet, on this point, his work has been both critiqued for not paying sufficient attention to the colonial context, and productively expanded to think precisely about said context, as Stoler, Jennifer Morgan, and Silvia Federici do, in different ways, in their work.[39] In Stoler's case, she argues that Foucault systematically bypasses crucial colonial discourses on racialized sexuality.[40] By doing so, she maintains that his analysis of how biopower was deployed during the 18th and 19th centuries around the issues of sexuality and race overlooks a key site: the colonial context. Stoler's intention is not to question the validity of Foucault's assertions, but rather she seeks to demonstrate how, by reconfiguring Foucault's chronology and displacing his focus to the colonies, we can engage in a more profound inquiry into the historical articulations of race and sex. In her work, she focuses on Dutch colonialism in the East Indies in the early modern period, and she shows that the management of sex was repeatedly and explicitly discussed among high metropolitan officials and colonists, specifically, since sex was regularly linked to the potentialities of colonial settlement and to the reproduction of populations loyal to the emerging colonial state.[41] Her conceptual framework is nevertheless intended as a broader interpretive framework to think about these issues in different colonial settings. She rightly insists, for example, "that the discursive management of sexual practices of colonizer and colonized was fundamental to the colonial order of things."[42] Moreover, she contends that "an implicit racial grammar underwrote the sexual regimes of bourgeois culture in more ways than Foucault explored" and she urges scholars to go beyond his work to further elucidate precisely the conceptual links between race and sex.[43] By bringing these issues to the fore,

Stoler thus reconfigures Foucault's periodization by tracing some of the key problematics he discusses in relation to earlier colonial discourses about sex and their articulation to notions of racial difference.

In a similar vein, in her most recent work, Jennifer Morgan critiques Foucault's theory of biopolitics for failing to consider the significance that the Atlantic slave trade has for tracing the politicization of life at the level of racialized collectivities.[44] She also engages with his work on the topic of populations to productively rework his periodization.[45] Specifically, she develops two key arguments. First, she shows that reproductive sex was politicized in early modern discourses by, among others, lawmakers in Virginia who "faced the quotidian consequences of sex between free subjects and those who were or could be enslaved."[46] She also contends that the politicization of sex, and more specifically of reproduction, had particular meanings and implications for enslaved women who were "locked into a juridical category of perpetual servitude," and whose bodies were used to determine the heritability of enslavement.[47] As she clarifies in her earlier, groundbreaking analysis, of the Roman legal principle of *partus sequitur ventrem* (literally meaning 'offspring follows womb'), Atlantic slavery rested on a notion of heritability that made maternity a key vehicle through which racial meaning was concretized since the principle established that the legal status of enslaved children followed that of their mothers.[48] For Morgan, moreover, slavery does not represent a "residual form of emergent capitalism, nor are reproductive capacities and the gendered meanings attached to them residual to the emergence or early modern racial formations."[49] In her work, she thus calls for a reassessment of political economy that pays greater attention to how motherhood has been historically linked to economic processes, particularly in relation to what she terms "racialized maternity."[50]

A second, crucial argument that Morgan develops in her recent work pertains to her revision of the periodization offered by Foucault in relation to the notion of populations. According to Morgan, "the concept of populations came into being for early modern thinkers as a new way of considering community in relationship to governance."[51] As she shows, the topic of populations was a major focus of 16th- and 17th-century English discourses; particularly, in relation to concerns over depopulation, the potential success of colonial ventures, and in response to the massive movement of people across oceans brought about by the Atlantic slave trade.[52] She also foregrounds the burgeoning interest in quantification that is reflected in discourses on populations, and she contends that reproduction was a major object of political reflection.[53] Morgan builds from this framework to offer a theory of racialization that begins by historicizing the notion of race as "a system of thought" that, for her, is grounded in medieval Europe.[54] She also considers how emerging notions of race were tied to reflections about population—specifically, to processes of differentiation tied to classification and adscriptions of racial difference— and she argues that "the work of differentiation was so often accomplished through the bodies of women."[55] Though Morgan does not use this terminology, her work helps establish that early modern discourses about sex were not merely about disciplinary technologies centered on the individual body but rather about broader regulatory controls more akin to what Foucault describes as "a biopolitics of a population."

Silvia Federici likewise offers an important reassessment of Foucault's theory of biopolitics. On the one hand, she reworks his periodization to account simultaneously for the population crisis in Europe—which she associates with the processes of accumulation by dispossession that characterized the transition to early capitalism— and for the demographic impact of Iberian colonization on different population groups.[56] On the other hand, Federici highlights the way in which Foucault's theory of biopolitics elides the question of social reproduction, and, specifically, what this implies for thinking about how the politicization of life at the level of collectivities affected women differentially.[57] Federici's work thus highlights the way in which women's embodied role in reproduction was transformed into a state matter. As part of this process, as Federici argues, a series of power dynamics coalesced around the interrelated objectives of attempting to dispossess women of their knowledge and authority over their own bodies and of transforming them into a naturalized site of reproductive labor.[58]

The types of questions that guide this project are informed by the different ways in which Foucault's account of biopolitics has been expanded to think about the colonies, and this framework decisively informs the arguments that I develop in this book. While Stoler's and Morgan's arguments are not grounded specifically on the colonial context in Latin America, both of their conceptual frameworks point to broader patterns of colonial governance that are highly productive to analyze the said context.

Race, Sex, and Segregation

Race, Sex, and Segregation in Colonial Latina America traces the emergence and early development of segregationist policies in Spanish and Portuguese America. It shows that segregationist measures influenced the material reorganization of space, shaped colonial processes of racialization, and contributed to the politicization of reproductive sex. The book advances this argument through a series of close readings of published and archival sources from the 16th and early 17th centuries, and it is informed by two main conceptual concerns. First, it considers how segregation was envisioned, codified, and enforced in a historical context of consolidating racial differences and changing demographics associated with mestizaje. Though mestizaje is regularly invoked to dismiss the effectiveness of segregationist efforts in colonial Latin America, I complicate this common assumption by showing that negative views about *mestizos* and other mixed-ancestry groups are actually crucial to understand the evolution of segregationist laws and the increasing regimentation of space. Second, the book theorizes the interrelation between race, sex, and segregation. It traces how concerns about reproductive sex were articulated in relation to spatial segregation, and it considers how this affected women differentially because of putative views about social reproduction, feminized notions of racial purity and impurity, and legal codes like the Roman legal principle of *partus sequitur ventrem*.[59] As interlocking concepts, race, sex, and segregation function as the main analytical framework for this monograph, and together they provide a new approach for thinking about racialization in colonial Latin America.

In Spanish America, efforts to segregate diverse indigenous groups were first rehearsed in the early 1530s as part of the transition to the dual republic model. The two-republic system was based on the creation of two separate commonwealths, one Spanish and one Indian, and it implied physically separating diverse indigenous groups from the rest of colonial society. As part of the segregationist model, indigenous communities were also granted limited autonomy, which reshaped native power structures and led to the consolidation of two primary administrative units and jurisdictions: the Republic of Spaniards and the Republic of Indians.[60] The dual republic model was thus both a spatial project with concrete material effects and a juridico-political framework that operated on the basis of bounded notions of territory. By the second half of the 16th century, moreover, millions of indigenous subjects were resettled as part of the policy of *congregación* or *reducción*, and this practice of spatially concentrating diverse indigenous groups played a major role in shaping processes of racialization across the region.[61]

The laws codifying segregation in Spanish America also offer insight to understand how the politicization of life, and, more specifically, the politicization of racially qualified life, became an object of political reflection and intervention. For one, segregationist projects were justified from the beginning through rhetoric that explicitly emphasized the need to foster the demographic growth of *indios/as*, and this formulation was both adapted and expanded in juridical discourses on the topic. These discourses were largely a response to the devastating impact that colonizing violence and disease had on diverse native groups, but they also bring into focus the way in which the topic of population *as such* begins to be registered as a political and economic problem. Moreover, segregationist laws point to a growing regulation of people's movement based on racial ascription, and they reflect the way in which reproductive sex between differently racialized groups started to be regulated. One way this gets expressed, for instance, is in the laws that promoted marriages among enslaved Africans and their descendants, while at the same time forcefully discouraging reproductive relations between enslaved African men and indigenous women, partly, because once indigenous slavery was prohibited in 1542, the principle of *partus sequitur ventrem* had direct implications for the legal status of the children born of such relations.[62] These legal discourses illustrate not only how reproductive sex was politicized, but they also evince how this politicization helped solidify racializing distinctions between increasingly homogenizing conceptions of Africans, indigenous, and Europeans as distinct population groups.

Another way in which the monograph contributes to scholarship on race during the colonial period is by considering these issues from a comparative perspective that highlights common patterns of colonial governance that developed in colonial Brazil. Though segregationist policies and practices in Brazil differed from what we find in Spanish America, the policy of indigenous *aldeamento* can be situated as part of the same genealogy of spatial concentration that informs the policy of *congregación* or *reducción*. Both projects decisively transformed prior models of socio-spatial organization, both were premised on a segregationist logic that differentiated between different groups of people, and both contributed, in different ways, to the gradual homogenization of *indios/as* as a meaningful category of group identity.[63] In Brazil, moreover, the perceived need to populate the colony helped sanction a series of biopolitical measures designed to foster the growth of the Portuguese population. Specifically, a series of institutional practices developed to facilitate the transportation of Portuguese penal exiles and female orphans to the colonies as a means to meet the populating needs of empire building while simultaneously taking care of—and making productive use of—the increasing number of destitute individuals in Portugal.[64] These practices, I argue, foreground the way in which Portuguese women's reproductive capacities were explicitly instrumentalized by nascent colonial states as a means to foster racially qualified life, and they bring into focus a broader pattern of colonial governance increasingly staked on the regulatory management of life.

The book is divided into four chapters whose progression is meant to highlight a consistent pattern in the discursive articulation and material implementation of segregation. With varying degrees of emphasis, all chapters demonstrate that segregation was never strictly conceptualized in terms of space or jurisdiction, but also in relation to the regulation of reproductive sex. The timeframe covered is determined by the discursive analyses I offer of key figures who shaped segregationist policies and practices, as well as the juridical discourses that were used to justify them, and it covers primarily the 16th and early 17th centuries. Geographically, the book begins in colonial Mexico, then moves to consider legal codes that were applied throughout Spanish America, shifts to consider the Andean context, and ends with a discussion of Brazil. The overall cohesion of the book is provided by the common analytical framework that I use to analyze the different cases, which posits race, sex, and segregation as interlocking concepts.

Chapter 1 examines Vasco de Quiroga's foundation of two segregated indigenous communities in Mexico that were inspired by Thomas More's *Utopia* and that served as future models for the dual republic model. I begin by analyzing how segregation was first envisioned and justified by Quiroga, and I consider how his writing helped change prevailing assumptions about socio-spatial organization. I further contend that Quiroga's discourse allows us to identify some of the ways in which reproductive sex between Spaniards and indigenous is problematized as part of his appeal for spatial separation, and I trace how he develops this issue while largely disavowing the context of mestizaje in which his project is inscribed. I also offer a reflection on the ways in which indigenous life is politicized in Quiroga's discourse, I show that Quiroga strengthened his plea for segregation by referencing the demographic collapse of indigenous groups caused by colonizing violence, and I contextualize his views and their implications by reconsidering More's influence from a historically grounded interpretation of *Utopia* that foregrounds the crisis of depopulation at the core of the narrative.

Chapter 2 offers a reevaluation of the dual republic model's presumed failure by considering how the project of indigenous segregation was codified in the context of mestizaje. Rather than assume that mestizaje undermined segregationist efforts, I show that segregationist laws actually account directly for processes of racial mixture, including by becoming progressively focused on regulating the movement of *mestizos* and other mixed-ancestry groups. Moreover, I argue that the sense of spatial and sexual boundaries between the Indian and Spanish Republics that were instituted through the dual republic framework was not initially based on fixed or essentialized notions of racial difference. Instead, the boundaries between republics were acknowledged as breached from the beginning because of mestizaje, but, not only did this not deter segregationist efforts, it actually contributed to the gradual consolidation of distinct socio-racial categories as colonial authorities were compelled to make ever-exacting distinctions between different groups of people in order to regulate their circulation within the dualistic system.

In Chapter 3, I offer a contextualized analysis of Felipe Guamán Poma de Ayala's endorsement of segregationist policies and practices in the Andes. Guaman Poma's illustrated manuscript offers an extensive textual and visual commentary on the project of indigenous segregation, and, I argue, it provides incomparable insight to understand its uneven implementation and multilayered implications. In the chapter, I show that Guaman Poma's conceptualizes boundaries in terms of space, jurisdiction, and reproductive sex between differently racialized groups. I further contend that his comments evince the fact that, while the author recognized that mestizaje was a central feature of colonial society, he nevertheless insisted on the viability of indigenous segregation by forcefully discouraging further reproduction of mixed-ancestry groups, and by insisting that the latter live and labor among Spaniards. I also highlight Guaman Poma's consistent emphasis on fostering indigenous population growth. I show that his endorsement of segregation was articulated as a plea for the preservation of racially qualified life, and I consider the implications that this formulation has for how the author politicizes and seeks to regulate indigenous women's reproductive capacities.

In the final chapter, I turn to Brazil to show that the policy of indigenous *aldeamento* can be productively analyzed in relation to the dual republic framework. I offer an account of how Manuel da Nóbrega influenced the reorganization of colonial space and paved the way for the policy of indigenous *aldeamento*. I also emphasize that Nóbrega's arrival in the colony was part of a much broader shift in colonizing tactics introduced by the Portuguese Crown to secure its territorial control and ensure long-term population growth. As part of this, I examine Nóbrega's repeated requests that Portuguese women be sent to the colony. I begin with a discursive analysis of Nóbrega's letters on the topic, and I show that his repeated request for Portuguese women is part of a broader concern with the regularization of reproductive relations between differently racialized groups. I further discuss the network of institutions that were set up in Portugal to temporarily house and ultimately ship the women overseas, I consider the disciplinary regulations and gender assumptions on which these institutions were premised, and I contextualize how some of the major shifts that were happening in Portugal in regard to poverty and how to make productive use of the increasing number of destitute and economically "surplus" populations influenced the system of forced and state-sponsored colonization. Finally, I consider the conceptual implications of this case, both for thinking about how the politicization of life at the level of collectivities influences processes of racialization, and how this intersects with the ways in which differently racialized women's reproductive capacities have been historically regulated and instrumentalized.

Notes

1 Daniel Nemser, *Infrastructures of Race: Concentration and Biopolitics in Colonial Mexico* (University of Texas Press, 2017), 4.
2 Joshua Lund, *The Impure Imagination. Toward a Critical Hybridity in Latin American Writing* (Minneapolis: University of Minnesota Press, 2006), 132.
3 Robert Bernasconi, "Crossed Lines in the Racialization Process: Race as a Border Concept" *Research in Phenomenology* 42 (2012): 211.
4 In this monograph, I draw and build from current scholarship that emphasizes the importance of Iberian colonization for thinking about the development of notions of race. In particular, I draw from studies that consider how notions of purity of blood influenced colonial processes of racialization, as well as scholarship that considers how debates over the "nature" of the indigenous and the institutionalization of African slavery shaped these processes. For more on this, see Francisco Bethencourt, *Racisms: From the Crusades to the Twentieth Century* (Princeton University Press, 2013); Angela Barreto Xavier, "Purity of Blood and Caste Identity Narratives among Early Modern Goan Elites," in *Race and Blood in the Iberian World*, edited by Max S. Hering Torres, María Elena Martínez, David Niremberg (Lit Verlag, 2012), 125–149; George M. Fredrickson, *Racism: A Short History* (Princeton University Press, 2002);

David Theo Goldberg, *Racist Culture* (Blackwell, 1993); Max S. Hering Torres, "Purity of Blood. Problems of Interpretation," in *Race and Blood in the Iberian World*, edited by Max S. Hering Torres, María Elena Martínez and David Niremberg (Lit Verlag, 2012), 11–38; María Elena's Martínez *Genealogical Fictions: Limpieza de Sangre, Religion, and Gender in Colonial Mexico* (Stanford University Press, 2008); David Niremberg, "Race and the Middle Ages. The Case of Spain and Its Jews," in *Rereading the Black Legend. The Discourses of Religious and Racial Difference in the Renaissance* Empires, edited by Margaret R. Greer, Walter D. Mignolo, Maureen Quilligan (University of Chicago Press, 2007), 71–87; Verena Stolke, "O enigma das interseções: classe, 'raça,' sexo, sexualidade. A formação dos impérios transatlânticos do século XVI ao XIX," *Estudos Feministas* 14, no. 1 (2006): 15–42.

5 Daniel Nemser, *Infrastructures of Race*, 4–5, 59, 67–68. Though Nemser uses the term "racial" rather than "socio-racial" to describe these processes of racialization—largely to draw a difference between his work and that of scholars who appeal to notions of racial fluidity to, as he says, "downplay the structural character of race," I use the term "socio-racial" throughout the book as a recognition of the fluidity of racial terms and the way they are informed by cultural notions of difference. I also affirm, however, in line with Nemser's argument, that race is a critical concept to think about colonial Latin America. For Nemser's discussion on the term "socioracial," see *Infrastructures of Race, 9.*

6 Daniel Nemser, *Infrastructures of Race*, 4. Patrick Wolfe makes a similar argument about how race is not an ontology but rather a process of conflictual differentiation. See *Traces of History: Elementary Structures of Race* (Verso, 2016), 18, 29.

7 See Joshua Lund, *The Mestizo State. Reading Race in Modern Mexico* (University of Minnesota Press, 2012), 75. It is also important to note that Nemser himself acknowledges and draws from Lund's arguments in *The Mestizo State*, but he also productively reconfigures his timeframe to account for earlier colonial processes of racialization.

8 Joshua Lund, *The Impure Imagination*, x, 4–5.

9 Abdul Jan Mohamed, "Sexuality on/of the Racial Border: Foucault, Wright, and the Articulation of 'Racialized Sexuality'," in *Discourses of Sexuality: From Aristotle to AIDS*, edited by Domma Stanton (Ann Arbor: University of Michigan Press, 1993), 94. For more recent scholarship on racialized sexuality, see "Introduction," in *Connexions: Histories of Race and Sex in North America*, edited by Jennifer Brier, Jim Downs, and Jennifer Morgan (University of Illinois Press, 2016), E-book.

10 See, for example, Robert Schwaller, *Géneros de Gente in Early Colonial Mexico: Defining Racial Difference* (Norman: University of Oklahoma Press, 2016), 8; Joanne Rappaport, *The Disappearing Mestizo: Configuring Difference in the Colonial New Kingdom of Granada* (Duke University Press, 2014), 6. For arguments about the dual republic's failure because of mestizaje, see Kathryn Burns, "Unfixing Race," in *Rereading the Black Legend: The Discourses of Religious and Racial Difference in the Renaissance Empires*, edited by Margaret R. Greer, Walter D. Mignolo, Maureen Quilligan (Chicago: University of Chicago Press, 2007), 191; Karen Vieira Powers, "Conquering Discourses of 'Sexual Conquest': Of Women, Language, and Mestizaje," *Colonial Latin American Review* 11, no. 1 (2002): 15; Vieira Powers, *Women in the Crucible of Conquest: The Gendered Genesis of Spanish American Society, 1500–1600* (Albuquerque: University of New Mexico Press, 2005), 72; Ben Vinson, *Before Mestizaje: The Frontiers of Race and Caste in Colonial Mexico* (Cambridge: Cambridge University Press, 2018), 6; Magnus Mörner, *La Corona Española y los foráneos en los pueblos de indios de América* (Madrid:

Ediciones de Cultura Hispánica, 1999), 11. Daniel Nemser also discusses how mestizaje is invoked to dismiss segregationist efforts, but he problematizes this argument, see *Infrastructures of Race,* 130–131.

11 Joshua Lund, *The Impure Imagination,* 15.

12 I use the Spanish term mestizaje here, given that the first three chapters of the book talk about the context of Spanish America, but, as in Chapter 4, I use the Portuguese equivalent, *mestiçagem,* to reflect the Portuguese context while not drawing any conceptual distinction between these two words.

13 Robert Bernasconi, "Crossed Lines in the Racialization Process," 211, 213.

14 Robert Bernasconi, "Crossed Lines in the Racialization Process," 215–216.

15 Robert Bernasconi, "Crossed Lines in the Racialization Process," 216.

16 Ibid.

17 Robert Bernasconi, "Crossed Lines in the Racialization Process," 211.

18 Abdul Jan Mohamed similarly argues that "the racial border...is in fact always a sexual border," see "Sexuality on/of the Racial Border," 109. Likewise, Joane Nagel contends that racial boundaries are always/already also sexual boundaries which must be patrolled, policed, and protected, see "Ethnicity and Sexuality," *Annual Review of Sociology* 26 (2000): 107.

19 Robert Bernasconi, "Crossed Lines in the Racialization Process," 208.

20 For more on this, see Daniel Nemser, *Infrastructures of Race,* 25–64. Maria Regina Celestino de Almeida also makes a similar claim about the homogenization of *indios* in Brazil, see *Metamorfoses indígenas: identidade e cultura nas aldeias coloniais do Rio de Janeiro* (Arquivo Nacional, 2003), 136.

21 For more on the associations between law and geography and its implications for thinking imperial sovereignty, see Lauren Benton, *A Search for Sovereignty: Law and Geography* in *European Empires 1400–1900* (Cambridge: Cambridge University Press, 2014).

22 In Lima, for instance, colonial authorities built a walled neighborhood known as Santiago del Cercado, which was officially inaugurated by viceroy Francisco de Toledo in 1571. For more on this, see Karen Graubart, "Containing Law within Walls: The Protection of Customary Law in Santiago del Cercado, Peru," in *Protection and Empire: A Global History,* edited by Lauren Benton, Adam Clulow, Bain Attwood (Cambridge University Press, 2017), 34.

23 See Law 6, Title 17, of Book 6, Law 14, Title 13, of Book 6, and Law 13, from Title 17, of Book 6 of the *Recopilación de Leyes para las Indias, 1681.* Content downloaded from https://home.heinonline.org. I also offer an analysis of these laws in Chapter 2.

24 Ben Vinson, *Before Mestizaje: The Frontiers of Race and Caste in Colonial Mexico* (Cambridge: Cambridge University Press, 2018), 8.

25 Ben Vinson, *Before Mestizaje,* 15. Magnus Mörner makes a similar point in his classic study *Race Mixture in the History of Latin America* (Boston: Little Brown, 1967), 2, 4. Lund also makes a similar claim when he describes the concept of hybridity (in which he includes mestizaje) as "the generic mark of Latin America's geocultural singularity." See Joshua Lund, *The Impure Imagination,* x.

26 Ann L. Stoler, *Race and the Education of Desire. Foucault's History of Sexuality and the Colonial Order of Things* (Duke University Press, 1995), 21.

27 See Ann L. Stoler, *Race and the Education of Desire.,* 25.

28 Michel Foucault, *The History of Sexuality: An Introduction, Volume I.* Trans. Robert Hurley (Vintage Books, 1990), 135.

29 Michel Foucault, *The History of Sexuality: An Introduction, Volume I,* 136.

30 Michel Foucault, *The History of Sexuality: An Introduction, Volume I,* 140.

31 Michel Foucault, *The History of Sexuality: An Introduction, Volume I,* 138.

32 Michel Foucault, *The History of Sexuality: An Introduction, Volume I,* 140.

33 Michel Foucault, *The History of Sexuality: An Introduction, Volume I*, 139.

34 Ann L. Stoler, *Race and the Education of Desire. Foucault's History of Sexuality and the Colonial Order of Things* (Duke University Press, 1995), 33.

35 Michel Foucault, *Society Must Be Defended. Lectures at the Collège de France, 1975-76*. Trans. David Macey (Picador, 2003 [1997]), 251–252.

36 Ladelle McWorther argues, similarly, that the central intersection between race and sex that Foucault identifies emerges when major goals for populations are concerned. Like Foucault, though, she does not develop the issue of what this implies for theorizing the regulation of women's reproductive bodies. See McWorther, Ladelle "Sex, Race, and Biopower: A Foucauldian Genealogy," *Hypatia* 19, no. 3 (2004): 54.

37 Michel Foucault, *Society Must Be Defended*, 256.

38 See Paul Rabinow and Nikolas Rose, "Biopower Today," *BioSocieties* 1 (2006): 195. Achille Mbembe also develops and expands the focus on death at the core of Foucault's theory in his writing on necropower. See Mbembe, *Necropolitics*, trans. Steven Corcoran (Duke University Press, 2019), particularly pp. 71 and 92.

39 See Ann L. Stoler, *Race and the Education of Desire*, 5–16; For more on Foucault and colonialism see Robert C. Young, "Foucault on Race and Colonialism," *New Formations* 25 (1995): 57–65. Daniel Nemser also productively engages with, and reworks, Foucault's genealogy of biopower to advance a theory of racialization, but here I focus on more explicitly feminist critiques and reworkings of biopolitics. For more on Nemser's account, see *Infrastructures of Race*, 12–16, 63. Giorgio Agamben's reformulation of the notion of biopower in *Homo Sacer: Sovereign Power and Bare Life* (Stanford University Press, 1998) is also productive insofar as it questions the chronological specificity of Foucault's conceptualization. Yet, as Leland de la Durantaye, Michael Dillon, and Judith Butler argue in different ways, there are important limitations with Agamben's work, including the problem of ahistoricity, and the fact that he does not sufficiently consider how race functions to differentiate populations. For more on these critiques, see Judith Butler, *Precarious Life: The Powers of Mourning and Violence* (Verso, 2004), 68; Michel Dillon, "Cared to Death. The Biopoliticised Time of your Life," *Foucault Studies* 2 (2005): 37–46; and Leland Durantaye, *Giorgio Agamben: A Critical Introduction* (Stanford University Press, 2009), 210.

40 Ann L. Stoler discusses the term racialized sexuality in *Race and the Education of Desire*, 21–22, 47, 97.

41 Ann L. Stoler, *Race and the Education of Desire*, 40.

42 Ann L. Stoler, *Race and the Education of Desire*, 4.

43 Ann L. Stoler, *Race and the Education of Desire*, 12.

44 Jennifer Morgan, *Reckoning with Slavery: Gender, Kinship, and Capitalism in the Early Black Atlantic* (Duke University Press, 2021), 42. She also critiques Giorgio Agamben's notion of bare life for the same reason.

45 Jennifer Morgan, *Reckoning with Slavery*, 89–104.

46 Jennifer Morgan, *Reckoning with Slavery*, 5.

47 Jennifer Morgan, *Reckoning with Slavery*, 7.

48 Jennifer Morgan, "Partus sequitur ventrem: Law, Race, and Reproduction in Colonial Slavery," *Small Axe* 22, no. 55 (2018): 1, 12.

49 Jennifer Morgan, *Reckoning with Slavery*, 16

50 Jennifer Morgan, *Reckoning with Slavery*, 20, 22.

51 Jennifer Morgan, *Reckoning with Slavery*, 13, 89.

52 Jennifer Morgan, *Reckoning with Slavery*, 89, 93.

53 Jennifer Morgan, *Reckoning with Slavery*, 94.

54 Jennifer Morgan, *Reckoning with Slavery*, 59.

55 Jennifer Morgan, *Reckoning with Slavery,* 12, 102, 103.
56 Silvia Federici, *Caliban and the Witch* (New York: Automedia, 2004), 63.
57 Silvia Federici, *Caliban and the Witch,* 8, 38, 86, 89. Judith Butler also elaborates on the question of gender in Foucault. She argues, for instance, that regulatory power has certain broad historical characteristics and operates on gender as well as other kinds of social and cultural norms; as she puts it, gender is "but an instance of a larger regulatory operation of power" and "gender requires and institutes its own distinctive regulatory and disciplinary regime." See Butler, *Undoing Gender* (Routledge, 2004), 41.
58 Silvia Federici, *Caliban and the Witch* (Automedia, 2004), 16, 86–89, 181.
59 Jennifer Morgan, "Partus sequitur ventrem," 1, 12.
60 Yanna Yannakakis and Martina Schrader-Kniffki, "Between the 'Old Law' and the New: Christian Translation, Indian Jurisdiction, and Criminal Justice in Colonial Oaxaca," *Hispanic American Historical Review* 96, no. 3 (2016): 521. See also Ben Vinson, *Before Mestizaje,* 3.
61 Daniel Nemser, *Infrastructures of Race: Concentration and Biopolitics in Colonial Mexico* (University of Texas Press, 2017), 26, 37.
62 For more on indigenous slavery in Spanish America, see Nancy Van Deusen, *Global Indios: The Indigenous Struggle for Justice in Sixteenth-Century Spain* (Duke University Press, 2015); Lewis Hanke, *The Spanish Struggle for Justice in the Conquest of* America (Little Brown and Company, 1965); Kathleen Myers, *Fernández de Oviedo's chronicle of America: A New History for a New World* (University of Texas Press, 2007), 116. For more on free the womb principle in Spanish America, see María Elena Martínez, "Space, Order, and Group Identities in a Spanish Colonial Town: Puebla de los Ángeles," in *The Collective and the Public in Latin America: Cultural Identities and Political Order,* edited by Luis Roniger and Tamar Herzog (Sussex Academic Press, 2000), 29. For more on slave marriages, also see Michelle A. McKinley, "Such Unsightly Unions Could Never Result in Holy Matrimony: Mixed-Status Marriages in Seventeenth Century Colonial Lima," *Yale Journal of Law and the Humanities* 217 (2010).
63 Maria Regina Celestino de Almeida, *Metamorfoses indígenas: identidade e cultura nas aldeias coloniais do Rio de Janeiro* (Arquivo Nacional, 2003); Charlotte de Castelnau-L'Estoile, *Operários de uma vinha estéril: Os Jesuítas e a conversão dos índios no Brasil 1500–1620* (Editorial da Universidade do Sagrado Coração, 2006).
64 It is important to also stress that, starting in 1549, Brazil was prioritized as a destination for Portuguese penal exiles, and, in particular, for female convicts (or *degredadas*), who were increasingly sent to the colony. For more on this, see Timothy Coates, *Convicts and orphans. Forced and state-sponsored colonizers in the Portuguese Empire, 1550–1755* (Stanford University Press, 2001), 63, 85.

1 Vasco de Quiroga's Utopian Communities

The Contradictory Foundations of Segregation

Vasco de Quiroga (ca. 1480–1565), is a renowned and omnipresent figure in the Mexican state of Michoacán. A petition to beatify him is currently underway in Rome, and there are countless schools, streets, and statutes in his honor, including in the city named after him. He first arrived in Mexico as a judge for the Second Audiencia, after serving in a similar legal capacity in modern-day Algeria, and was eventually named bishop of Michoacán in 1538.[1] In popular discourse, he is widely regarded as a benevolent figure who advocated against indigenous slavery, and he is still commonly referred to as "Tata Vasco," an endearing term that in P'urhépecha means father and that aptly captures the paternalistic influence he had on shaping indigenous relations in the region. Quiroga is also particularly well known for founding two communities inspired by Thomas More's *Utopia*.

Quiroga established the first Utopian community, Santa Fe de los Altos, in 1532 in an area known as Acatxóchitl, which is today considered part of metropolitan Mexico City. He founded a second community in Michoacán in 1533, which he named Santa Fe de la Laguna.[2] As Silvio Zavala shows in his oft-cited study from 1937, Quiroga organized these communities (known as hospital towns) by adapting the three key principles of order that are described in *Utopia*'s Book Two: that is, a communal association based on usufruct rather than ownership of goods, a system of labor centered on practical trades and 6 hours of communal work, and a political system based on elections and hierarchical family discipline.[3] Zavala's study is based on his analysis of a 1518 Latin copy of *Utopia* that scholars believe Quiroga read, which is currently housed at the Nettie Lee Benson Library in Austin, and that includes several passages that are underlined and briefly commented on in handwriting from the 16th century.[4] The markings and marginalia are particularly prevalent in Book Two, and, partly guided by these signposts, Zavala offers a point-by-point comparison between the fictional description of the island of Utopia and the list of forty-two prescriptive ordinances codified in Quiroga's *Ordenanzas*, which spell out every detail of the social, political, and economic organization of the hospital towns.

DOI: 10.4324/9781003145196-2

In addition to the Utopian connection, Quiroga's hospital towns continue to garner attention because of their unique history as semi-autonomous indigenous communities. Beginning in the 16th century, Quiroga managed to exempt the residents from paying tribute to the Spanish Crown, and he granted the towns almost complete autonomy.[5] Commenting on this aspect of his work, Ivonne del Valle suggests that, by doing this, Quiroga hoped to ensure that the order and administration of the communities fell to "none other than their own residents,"[6] to which she adds

> I know of no other similar document in the entire colonial corpus. It is not merely a matter of Quiroga having written the text with the indigenous' welfare in mind, but, beyond that, his taking it upon himself to bequeath to them a new dispensation, 'new tablets' which would guarantee them self-sufficiency and self-rule.[7]

It was not until 1872 that, despite considerable resistance from its residents, the hospital towns were gradually dismantled through legislation by the Liberal government that privatized communal landholdings.[8] In the case of Santa Fe de la Laguna, however, communal lands were restored in 1953 and, during the 1970s and 1980s, the town's residents fought again to protect communal landholdings from further incursions by cattle ranchers from the neighboring city, which, ironically, is named after Quiroga.[9] Since 2017, moreover, the town has been involved in a series of legal procedures over the town's right to self-determination. Inspired by the case of Cherán—which in 2011 was granted partial autonomy as a legal self-governing indigenous community—the town of Santa Fe de la Laguna is one of five towns seeking greater juridico-political autonomy.[10]

Vasco de Quiroga's enduring reputation is thus as much a product of his 16th-century Utopian experiments as it is of its postcolonial legacies. Not surprisingly, scholarship on Quiroga tends to be laudatory. Recent, more critical interventions, however, are helping reframe how we think about his project. To begin with, it is important to stress that Quiroga's hospital towns were established during a critical turning point in colonial policy as the Crown gradually shifted toward the segregationist dual republic model. The two-republic system was based on the creation of two separate commonwealths, one Spanish and one Indian, and it implied physically segregating indigenous groups from the rest of colonial society. María Elena Martínez points this out in her work, and she argues that Quiroga's hospital towns represent the very first attempt to create separate towns exclusively for the natives.[11] For her, rethinking these early socio-spatial experiments is critical because they offer insight into a policy that, even as it failed to create an apartheid-like social order, led to a greater regimentation of space and heightened anxieties about the liminal status of *mestizos* and other mixed-ancestry groups.[12] Martínez's work also foregrounds some of the contradictions inherent in the dualistic system, most notably, the fact that it developed in a context mestizaje that complicated how segregation was envisioned and codified. She also calls attention to the ways in which the management of reproductive sex became a key feature of the segregationist model.[13] Though Martínez does not develop these broader arguments specifically in relation to Quiroga, her insights are nevertheless highly productive for rethinking his project.

Daniel Nemser's work, on the other hand, has decisively shifted how we think about Quiroga's project by situating it within a much broader genealogy of spatial concentration that, as he persuasively argues, played a major role in shaping early processes of colonial racialization. Nemser characterizes Quiroga's project as "one of the earliest attempts to put the spatial logic of concentration into practice in New Spain" and, more specifically, he argues that his hospital towns are "the foundational moment of the program of congregation."[14] The policy of *congregación*—also known as *reducción*—was based on the resettlement of diverse indigenous communities into centralized, carefully organized towns, and it was meant to facilitate Christianization and rationalize the extraction of tribute and labor.[15] It also contributed to the dispossession of indigenous lands, and, as Carlos Paredes Martínez suggests, it marked the transition toward the consolidation of "Indian republics" or *repúblicas de indios*.[16] On a conceptual level, the policy of *congregación* is also critical to understand the emergence and consolidation of colonial systems of racialization. As Nemser contends, "congregation laid material foundations that brought heterogeneous indigenous groups into spatial proximity, weakened prior regimes of identification, and enabled the emergence of a new subjectivity based on the idea of the Indian as a single, homogenous type."[17] Nemser's argument destabilizes the idea of the Indian as a meaningful category of identity prior to the conquest, and he compels us, instead, to consider the material practices that facilitated the composition of differently racialized groups. Within this framework, Quiroga's project becomes a crucial site for theorizing the inextricable link between processes of racialization and the spatial reorganization of social relations.

Drawing from Martínez's and Nemser's interpretative insights, this chapter examines how Quiroga's Utopian communities helped shape the segregationist dual republic model. I begin by analyzing how segregation was first envisioned and justified by Quiroga, and I consider how his writing helped change prevailing assumptions about socio-spatial organization. I further contend that Quiroga's discourse allows us to identify some of the ways in which reproductive sex between Spaniards and indigenous groups is problematized as part of his appeal for segregation, and I trace how he develops this issue while largely disavowing the context of mestizaje in which his project is inscribed. In the second section, I offer a reflection on the ways in which indigenous life is politicized in Quiroga's discourse and I consider what this means for thinking about the changing ways in which the power over life was reconfigured in early modernity. Specifically, I show that Quiroga strengthened his plea for segregation by referencing the demographic collapse of indigenous groups ushered in by colonization, and I contextualize his views and their implications by reconsidering More's influence from a historically grounded interpretation of *Utopia* that foregrounds the crisis of depopulation at the core of the narrative. In the final section, I turn to consider Quiroga's views on boundaries and their transgression. I argue that Quiroga conceptualizes the boundaries of the hospital towns both in terms of territory and jurisdiction, and I consider what extant sources tell us about the racial ascription of individuals who resided in the communities and could contribute to their perpetuation in space and time.

The Justification for Segregation

> *Porque el que no es posible ni practicable no es remedio.*
> Vasco de Quiroga[18]

Vasco de Quiroga's writing offers crucial insight to understand how the segregationist dual republic model was first envisioned and justified. One of the first letters Quiroga ever wrote to the Council of the Indies in his capacity as a judge for New Spain's Second Audiencia was precisely to advocate for the creation of separate indigenous communities. As he refined and expanded this argument in his better-known *Información en derecho* (1535), he had already founded two experimental communities that provided the model for future projects of spatial reorganization based on the idea of two segregated republics. The texts allow us to trace the perceived problems that Quiroga believed could be redressed through interventions in the production of colonial space, and they help foreshadow some of the unintended effects and unforeseen contradictions of his project, particularly, as it moved from discursive articulation to material implementation. A critical analysis of Quiroga's writing also reveals some of the guiding assumptions that inform his thinking and is suggestive of the broader structuring logic that underpins the two-republic system as it later became official policy throughout Spanish America.

For Quiroga, there are three key problems that he suggests colonial authorities can address by creating separate indigenous communities. The first is an issue that he identifies shortly after arriving in Mexico-Tenochtitlan in January of 1531 and that can be broadly characterized as a problem of socio-spatial disorder. His views at the time were informed by the dramatic transformations taking place in the city, which had been under Spanish domination for about a decade, and was still undergoing profound social, architectural, and infrastructural changes. Not only was the European-style city of Mexico being materially superimposed over the ruins of the Aztec capital—an architectural feat that resulted in the death of so many indigenous laborers that the Franciscan friar Motolinía described it as "the seventh great plague"— the changes also displaced most the city's native residents into surrounding areas, where indigenous authorities managed to reconfigure their authority and establish a limited jurisdiction.[19] Quiroga's understanding of the problem later morphed in relation to different types of socio-spatial dynamics that he witnessed in the province of Michoacán, but his proposed solution remained consistent. As he moved forward with his plan to create separate indigenous communities, he believed the measure was fundamental to the consolidation of the incipient colonial order, and he presented it as advantageous both for the Spaniards and the natives. As the epigraph suggests, Quiroga was a practical colonial official who acted based on his belief in feasible objectives, even when he tried to actualize the key organizational principles of More's fictional *Utopia*.

After only a few months of living in Mexico-Tenochtitlan, Quiroga wrote the above-mentioned letter to the Council of the Indies in which he offers his first account of the city's socio-spatial disorder. Dated August 14, 1531, the letter emotively describes how the city is being overwhelmed by large numbers of destitute and needy orphans. Quiroga is unambiguous in stating that their presence is the result of colonizing violence and ongoing exploitation, and he suggests that action must be taken to relieve Spaniards' guilty consciousness:

> que será una grande obra pía y muy provechosa y satisfactoria para el descargo de las conciencias de los españoles que acá an pasado, que se cree que mataron e fueron causa de ser muertos en las guerras y minas los padres y madres de los tales huerfanos y de aver quedado así pobres, que andan por los tianguez e calles a buscar de comer lo que dexan los puercos y los perros, cosa de gran piedad de ver y estos guerfanos y pobres son tantos, que no es cosa de se poder creer si no se ve.[20]

The passage is striking in that it registers a unique concern: namely, how to deal with a large group of destitute individuals who are the aftermath of war and that are now a problem that colonial officials must tend to. As vagrants rummaging for food in the public markets and streets, the orphans are depicted as placeless and likened to undomesticated animals. The scale of the problem is further emphasized by Quiroga by referencing the biblical expression "ver para creer" as a way to dispel any skepticism about the seemingly incredulous situation. By exhorting authorities to act, moreover, Quiroga suggests that the orphans' presence in the city cannot be simply disavowed. Rather, he includes them as members of the polity, even as registered as a problem. The crucial question for Quiroga is how to integrate them, and, in this case, his proposed solution is to gather them in orphanages. In other words, he suggests bringing them into the fold of colonial society by spatially confining them in discrete, separate institutions under Spanish jurisdiction.

A second issue concerning socio-spatial disorder that Quiroga presents as an even more pressing challenge for colonial officials is what he describes as the chaotic dispersion of the natives. Speaking about this, he writes "no hay quien entienda el caos," and, as if to help visualize the magnitude of their dispersion, he adds "son tantos como las estrellas."[21] It is in relation to this issue that he first articulates his proposal for the creation of new, separate, communities where the indigenous can be taught to live in order: "en toda buena horden de policía y con santas y buenas y católicas hordenanzas."[22] Although in the letter Quiroga does not give a reason for the indigenous' scattered living arrangements, he does in *Información en derecho*. Like with the vagrant orphans, he stresses that the perceived dispersion problem is a direct result of colonization. He asserts that the natives have fled to the mountains and fields in "natural defense" because of the violence they have been subjected to, and he states that large groups of them are scattered in the countryside because Spaniards choose to treat them not as men but as beasts.[23] By then, Quiroga's views were more closely influenced by what he had witnessed in Michoacán—where abuses by *encomenderos* had left the land in turmoil— and they are informed by his active involvement in the spatial politics of the province, where he helped launch the policy of *congregación*.[24] The trope of disorder that frames Quiroga's argument is thus consistently tied to his denunciation of abusive colonial practices, but it is at the same time deployed as a means to justify an ambitious nucleation project premised on what Nemser describes as a "spatial logic of concentration."[25]

Quiroga's argument for spatially concentrating diverse indigenous groups is presented as a precondition for order, and it is meant to appeal to both the economic and evangelizing interests of colonial authorities. In the letter from 1531, he argues that by relocating the natives to what he describes as barren, uncultivated, plots, they can be put to work to make the land more productive.[26] He also asserts that the creation of separate indigenous communities will facilitate the conversion efforts and, more specifically, will help prevent young natives from "reverting" to their parents' idolatrous practices.[27] The statements evince Quiroga's perception of American space as open for occupation and transformable through indigenous labor, and they suggest that Quiroga attributed spatial reorganization a distinctive instrumentality in shaping social subjects. Similarly, in *Información*, he uses verbs like "juntar" and "recoger" to argue that it is only by gathering the natives that they can be taught to live in order, and he stresses that their conversion depends on being relocated to properly ordered communities.[28] The spatial logic that underpins Quiroga's project is aptly summarized by a passage in which he writes: "para juntarlos, ordenarlos, encaminarlos y enderezarlos, y darles leyes y reglas y ordenanzas en que vivan en buena y católica policía."[29] Here, the progression from spatial concentration to disciplinary subjection is rendered explicit, and it speaks to the social engineering project that is at the heart of Quiroga's call for separate indigenous communities.

The viability of Quiroga's project hinges, of course, on the possibility of spatially concentrating different indigenous groups, and the author pre-empts possible objections by insisting from the beginning that the natives will pose no resistance to their relocation. In the letter, he asserts that the indigenous are innately docile, and he compares them to malleable soft wax: "como tabla rasa y cera muy blanda."[30] He reiterates this homogenizing description throughout his *Información*,[31] and he routinely suggests that, because of their alleged docile nature, their lives can be transformed in accordance with the civilizing and Christianizing principles of the consolidating colonial order. Notably, the trope of soft wax also discloses one of the key conceptual presuppositions of Quiroga's project. As Orlando Bentancor argues, the expression is used by Quiroga to establish an analogy between the indigenous' dispersed and shapeless living arrangements and the amorphous matter of soft wax. Like soft wax, Quiroga suggests that, if properly contained, the lives of indigenous subjects can be shaped by imperial spatial designs. This position, Bentancor argues, synthesizes the ontological presuppositions of humanism and scholasticism based on the principle of subordination of imperfect matter to perfect form, which presumed the plasticity of nature and was used to justify the transformation of the physical environment and its inhabitants.[32] Betancor's argument thus helps elucidate the epistemological grounds that inform Quiroga's instrumental views on space. It also clarifies the fact that, for Quiroga, rearranging the lives of human subjects is justified on a conceptual level by the same logic that sanctions the transformation of nature and the environment.[33]

The second major problem that Quiroga suggests can be addressed by founding separate indigenous communities is tied to his representation of Spaniards as a bad example. He makes this claim explicitly in *Información en derecho*, and the argument played a decisive role in changing prevailing assumptions.[34] From the earliest phases of colonization in the Caribbean, the Spanish Crown rehearsed different approaches to civilize and Christianize the indigenous. All approaches assumed that Spaniards were a good example that could provide an imitable model for the natives, and most of the early experiments required that both groups live in close physical proximity, including the *encomienda* system.[35] Quiroga, however, helped change this paradigm. Referencing repeatedly the Papal Bulls of donation, he asserts that the Christianizing mission is Spain's legal obligation, and he insists that Spaniards' bad example is detrimental to the cause: "Y nosotros, viniendo a edificarla [la iglesia], con nuestros malos ejemplos y obras, peores que de infieles, así la destruimos."[36] Here, his daring comparison of Spaniards to infidels helps destabilize the idea that social mimicry is an effective approach to conversion. It also suggests that, as part of his larger plan to spatially gather indigenous groups to constitute a congregation, it is first necessary to set apart and isolate them from the Christian colonizers and their bad examples. His writing, in other words, begins to disclose a differentiating logic that assumes the existence of at least two discrete groups of people whose very sense of groupness is facilitated and made legible through his plan to physically segregate them.[37]

The segregationist logic that underpins Quiroga's project is expressed more clearly in another passage where he elaborates on his theory of Spaniards' as a bad example. Notably, his development of this point also reveals the way in which his understanding of segregation gets intertwined with considerations about reproductive sex. He writes in his *Información*:

> temo que piensan [los indígenas], y aún no sé si algunas veces lo han dicho y dicen, que jugar y lujuria y alcahuetar es oficio propio de cristianos, y cosa en que ellos piensan mucho, los sirven y procuran contentar, no pensando que yerran sino que aciertan, por ver, como ven los que con españoles conversan, la disolución que anda en esto, de pedirles indias hermosas a docenas y medias docenas, y tenerlas en sus casas paridas y preñadas, y traerlos a muchos dellos por alcahuetes dellas, y otras muchas cosas de aqueste jaez y de otros malos ejemplos que les damos, que sería largo de contar, que ven hacer a malos cristianos, en que mucho les daña y nada les aprovecha nuestra conversación.[38]

At the center of what Quiroga identifies as the colonizers' bad example is an indictment of their moral behavior, and, specifically, of their sexual relations with indigenous women. For him, the problem is twofold. First, he suggests that said relationships give the natives the false impression that lustfulness is a characteristically Christian trait. Second, he presents the relations as informal polygamous unions, and he uses hyperbole to emphasize their reproductive consequences—since all women are represented as pregnant or puerperal. Quiroga, however, obfuscates the question of sexual violence by asserting that indigenous women were exchanged rather than forcefully appropriated by Spanish men, and he forecloses the possibility of kinship by depicting the relations as informal and polygamous. At stake for Quiroga is the development of long-term Christian marriages and legitimate reproductive practices, and, within this framework, Spaniards' involvement with indigenous women is presented as an objectionable model. It is again this framework that justifies his call for separation, but here we begin to see an important inconsistency: that is, the fact that, although he acknowledges the reproductive consequences of indigenous–Spanish relations, he also leaves unaddressed the potential problem this poses for the creation of two segregated republics.

The final issue that Quiroga contends can be redressed by creating separate indigenous communities is the problem of depopulation. In addition to his claims about the socio-spatial disorder and the Spaniards' bad example, Quiroga stresses the devastating impact that colonization has had on the native population and he urges colonial authorities to act. Here, it is important to note that, unlike what I pointed out earlier about the passage in the 1531 letter when Quiroga is trying to convey the problem of Amerindian dispersion and, in so doing, says about them "son tantos como las estrellas," in *Información* he never refers to the indigenous population as abundant. Instead, he stresses the demographic collapse of indigenous groups and uses this to highlight the urgency of his request for separate indigenous communities. This aspect of Quiroga's *Información* represents a significant shift in his thinking and is a critical argumentative thread that offers insight into the biopolitical implications of his project. To fully contextualize this point, though, it is necessary to consider Quiroga's discourse in relation to broader discourses that inform and are reflected in his writing.

The Politicization of Indigenous Life

> La principal población que ha de permanecer en estas partes para la sustentación dellas, ha de ser la mesma natural.
>
> Vasco de Quiroga[39]

During the initial decades of Spanish colonization in the Americas, the drastic demographic decline of indigenous groups generated a range of reflections on what to do about the crisis.[40] Some colonial officials, like the royal historian Gonzalo Fernandez de Oviedo and the friar Domingo de Betanzos, argued that the disappearance of the native population was inevitable—indeed, even sanctioned by divine providence— and they advocated for promulgating laws premised on their impending demise.[41] Others, like Quiroga and Bartolomé de las Casas, believed instead that protecting the indigenous was the Crown's duty, and they drew out paternalistic plans for spatial reorganization based on their shared goal of conserving and fostering indigenous demographic growth. These competing discourses are critical examples of the way in which indigenous life becomes an object of political reflection and, as such, they offer crucial insight into the changing ways in which the power over life was reconfigured in early modernity.

In Quiroga's case, there are a number of ways in which we can think about the politicization of indigenous life and its broader implications. First, it is important to situate his project as part of a much larger shift toward a novel form of power that Foucault theorizes as biopower. In Foucault's genealogy of the concept, he stresses that one of its key features is that it encompasses both disciplinary technologies centered on the individual body—what Foucault terms "an anatomo-politics of the human body"—and regulatory controls aimed at the population as a whole—or what he calls "a biopolitics of a population."[42] The disciplinary character of Quiroga's project is evident in his plans for spatial concentration discussed earlier, and it is further confirmed by his prescriptive *Ordenanzas*, where he includes stipulations restricting residents' movements and even specifies how they should dress. As Quiroga envisions ways to solve the demographic collapse of indigenous groups, moreover, we can recognize that the very question of how to regulate life at the level of collectivities enters his discourse and makes the topic of population *as such* intelligible as a political and economic problem.

On the topic of population, Quiroga's discourse is best contextualized in dialogue with two key sources that he drew inspiration from, and that allows us to better understand the biopolitical stakes of his project. On the one hand, it is important to recognize that Quiroga's understanding of the population crisis and how to address it is informed by Bartolomé de las Casas *Memorial de remedios para las indias*. Las Casas prepared his *Memorial* for king Ferdinand, but it was ultimately presented to the Franciscan cardinal Ximénez de Cisneros given the king's death in January of 1516.[43] The text consists of a list of fourteen "remedies" designed to address what Las Casas presents as a population crisis, and it is followed by a specific series of denunciations about what is happening in the islands of Española, Cuba, Jamaica, and San Juan. The document represents Las Casas' first written denunciation of what was happening in the American colonies, but it is also intended as a pragmatic plan to move forward and address the unfolding demographic crisis.

The textual similarities between Las Casas' *Memorial* and Quiroga's *Información* become apparent when we consider how both authors frame their views on the depopulation crisis. To begin with, it is important to note that both texts present plans for spatial reorganization premised on the relocation of indigenous groups, and both highlight the importance of their respective proposals by referencing the high number of native deaths they have witnessed.[44] In the case of Las Casas, he mentions the unquantifiable number of deaths as a way to strengthen his plea for the creation of new communities: "para que tanto número de ánimas no perezcan, porque son casi innumerables los indios que allí han pasado."[45] As Las Casas develops his argument, he constantly returns to the high mortality rate, but his proposal is explicitly aimed at helping stabilize and foster the reproduction of what he presents as a homogenous population group. For his part, Quiroga begins by setting up a dichotomy between the real inhabitants of the land ("los verdaderos pobladores") who recognize the destruction of the land and the depopulation of the towns, and Spaniards who, acting against equity and justice, care only about "populating" the mines with indigenous laborers.[46] He later condenses this argument by simply repeating that while the mines are populated, towns are being depopulated.[47] Quiroga also stresses that if something is not done everything will be lost: "esto de esta tierra temo se ha de acabar todo."[48] Like Las Casas, though, he counterbalances the emphasis on death and depopulation by speaking overtly about the necessity to "conserve" the indigenous population.[49] It is particularly significant that the Caribbean islands are the constant referent that he goes back to strengthen his proposal and further emphasize the sense of urgency.[50] Indeed, the devastation of the indigenous population in the Caribbean serves as a type of cautionary tale to which he consistently goes back to, frequently only to add that, in the case of Mexico, "aún no es tarde."[51]

A second area of correspondence between both texts is noticeable when we examine the reasons given by Las Casas and Quiroga to explain the high mortality rate. For one, it is noteworthy that neither of them focuses on disease as a primary cause. Las Casas does discuss the importance of creating hospitals in the new communities, and he specifies that one of their immediate uses would be to help cure "indios enfermos" so that "por falta de medicina no perezcan, como hasta aquí han perecido."[52] Beyond this, though, he does not elaborate on this point aside from stating that hospitals should be well stocked and have a surgeon. He also considers the question of mass suicide, but he only mentions this issue once, and he frames it within a paternalistic discourse in which he assumes the need to protect the indigenous from themselves, for, as he puts it, "ellos son débiles de corazón."[53] Quiroga, on the other hand, rarely refers to actual sickness, and, more often, talks about diseases in non-literal terms. He argues that the root cause of their illness is improper living arrangements—which, as mentioned earlier he links to colonizing violence—and he likens Spaniards to the plague when he suggests that the indigenous flee to the mountains to escape their deadly influence "huyendo y escondiendose ... de toda gente española como de la misma muerte y pestilencia."[54] Thus, while neither disease nor suicide is presented as a primary cause to understand the demographic crisis, what is notable is the way in which life begins to be politicized in Las Casas's and Quiroga's discourse.

Both Las Casas and Quiroga identify abusive labor conditions as one of the key reasons why the indigenous are dying. Notably, though, neither of them makes exploitation the central object of their critiques. Rather, their criticism is presented as a biopolitical concern in which life—specifically indigenous life, that is, racially qualified life—is transformed into an object of political reflection. In Las Casas's first "remedy" he calls for the temporary suspension of indigenous labor so that the population may recover. The very literal emphasis on "making live" is typified by his rationale. He suggests that by suspending their work *indios* will fatten up and grow stronger: "engordarán, o a lo menos arreciarán algo."[55] He further stresses that during this period, the indigenous should be provided with enough food and, in cases where their own supply is not enough, they should be given food from what they have produced for the Spaniards since, as he points out, "todo lo trabajaron ellos."[56] Here, Las Casas's statement appears to open up toward a broader critique of accumulation by dispossession and the effects this has on food production and access, but he quickly forecloses the possibility of a more radical critique by suggesting that the suspension of indigenous labor would only be a temporary measure. Thus, despite these momentary critical openings, ultimately, as Daniel Castro argues, Las Casas's first remedy "constituted a detailed plan for the exploitation of the islands with the full cooperation and utilization of the Indians."[57]

Similarly, in *Información* Quiroga unambiguously identifies Spaniard's abusive laboring conditions as the central reason why the indigenous are dying *en masse*.[58] In fact, the text was specifically written to argue against new legislation that encouraged the propagation of indigenous slavery.[59] Yet, as Ivonne del Valle points out in her analysis of Quiroga's project, it is important to recognize that his proposal was never intended to do away with exploitation but rather to moderate it. Del Valle argues that his condemnation of indigenous slavery was based not only on his rejection of it as immoral but also as ultimately unprofitable and unsustainable in the long run.[60] She further contends that Quiroga's homogenizing depiction of the indigenous—a characterization based partly on their common docility—was based on a particular understanding of them as commoners or peasants. That is why he often uses the Nahuatl term *macehual* to describe them.[61] Indeed, del Valle suggests that in Quiroga's discourse—as well as in the organization of his hospital towns—we can trace a critical transformation in the view of the indigenous, one that moves from their depiction as barbarians (in contradistinction to the Spaniards as civilized) to an economic category based on their association with poverty.[62] Much like what we see in Las Casas's case, then, the indigenous population is homogenized around a conceptualization of them as laborers. Both Las Casas and Quiroga agree on the need to preserve and foster the growth of that population, but their calculated management of life is not devoid of economic interests that are perfectly compatible with imperial reason.

Recognizing the ways in which indigenous life becomes increasingly politicized in Las Casas' and Quiroga's discourse allows us, in turn, to reframe how we think about the profound influence that More's *Utopia* had on Quiroga. In Zavala's well-known study on the subject, he focuses almost exclusively on the close correspondence that exists between Quiroga's *Ordenazas* and the fictional description of Utopia that we find in Book Two. By doing so, he overlooks a crucial aspect of Quiroga's project. That is, the fact that the historical context that informs Book One is fundamental to Quiroga's vision of socio-spatial reform. It is in Book One that we find More's political reflections on enclosures and the criminalization of vagrancy in England, in other words, on processes that Karl Marx would later associate with Primitive Accumulation.[63] Quiroga's project is both informed by and inscribed in these broader dynamics. As Fredric Jameson argues, we cannot dissociate the historical circumstances that inform the "political commentary and motivation of Book One" from the Utopian vision of Book Two, and, in Quiroga's case, this textual interconnection is all the more relevant.[64]

On one level, reconsidering More's influence from a historically grounded interpretation of *Utopia* is productive in that it allows us to recognize that the topic of population crisis is central to the narrative. As Antonis Balasopoulos' argues, More's vision of reform is intricately intertwined with the experience of social disintegration that was the result of critical socio-economic and political transformations. Not only was the period preceding the writing of *Utopia* marked by a series of depopulating disasters in Europe (including the "Black Death" and large-scale famines), but it also corresponds with the dissolution of feudal economic and social structures in the transition to early capitalism. As Balasopoulos explains,

> particularly after 1500, a combination of factors—which included population growth, the extensive monetization of agrarian relations, and enclosure and privatization of the commons—brought down the price of labor, made food prices unsustainable for most of the poor, and increased the number of the unemployed, homeless, and destitute.[65]

Utopia, he argues, bears witness to these processes and can be read as a "fiction of population," in the sense that the question of forcibly displaced, and economically "surplus" populations is the central problem that the narrative attempts to imaginatively solve.[66]

For Balasopoulos, the importance of thinking about *Utopia* from this perspective is that, on the one hand, it allows us to trace a key historical moment when the question of population emerges as an object of political and economic reflection. According to him, the very intelligibility of the topic of population is a direct result of the historical crisis outlined above, and he suggests that More's narrative registers it as a problem even before the bureaucratic apparatuses of the modern state.[67] In dialogue with Foucault, but productively reworking his periodization, Balasopoulos elevates the conceptual stakes of More's narrative as an inaugural site for thinking about changing conceptions of power's hold over life, both at the level of individual bodies and in the general sense of the population.

On the other hand, Balasopoulos contends that one of the key limitations of More's text is that it circumvents the very crisis of population that it identifies. As a thought experiment, he suggests, *Utopia* seeks to respond to the historical problem of a population having nowhere to live but does so in a way that, rather than address the issue, it imaginatively displaces it, since, in Book Two, More offers a different view of society where all things are held in common and where private property is abolished. For Balasopoulos, this ends up neutralizing the critique of the processes of accumulation by dispossession that made the population intelligible in the first place—as both "surplus" and "dangerously mobile"—and he reads this gesture as More's attempts to deal with the question of surplus population through the "spatial fix" of colonization.[68] In other words, he argues that More's text tries to solve the tendency of capital accumulation to "liberate" more and more people from the land and hence from subsistence through access to the means of agrarian production, by exporting supernumerary labor forces to an imaginary colonial territory.[69]

As a working conceptual framework, Balasopoulos' insights are productive in that they allow us to broaden our understanding of how the problem of population begins to be registered in early modern discourses. The key limitation of his argument, though, is that it is narrowly focused on the historical transformations in Europe that made the problem intelligible there. He ignores concurrent discourses on the depopulation crisis in the Americas, and he leaves unchallenged prevailing assumptions about the colonies as "empty spaces" that can be used to solve European crises.[70] This oversight is particularly problematic considering that, as scholars Victor Baptiste and Daniel Castro argue, More had read Las Casas' *Memorial*, and the text may have been an important source of influence for *Utopia*.[71] This indicates that, at least on some level, More himself must have been aware of the devastating population crisis in the Americas, and it suggests that the colonial context is a crucial counterpart to his understanding of the burgeoning population problem. The connection between More and Las Casas' *Memorial* also confirms the fact that, in thinking about More's influence over Quiroga's project, it is necessary to consider the triangulated mediation of the Lascacian text.

One of the benefits of thinking about how the problem of population becomes simultaneously intelligible in Europe and the Americas is that it brings into focus the fact that power's hold over life functions differentially on the basis of class, race, and sex. In More's text, the problem of population is broadly conceived in relation to the twin problems of land concentration and the privatization of the commons. In the Latin copy of *Utopia* that Quiroga read, for instance, we find a marked passage in which the fictional character Raphael Hythloday is talking to his interlocutors (Tomas More and Peter Giles) about a conversation he recently had regarding the death penalty for thieves in England.[72] Hythloday's position is that said punishment is too harsh and ultimately ineffective for it does not get at the root cause of what is compelling people to steal. The cause, he says, has to do in part with the creation of large-scale land enclosures for sheep pastures and wool production. As a result, tenants and farmers are being evicted and have no place to go, which, in turn, forces them to steal or be jailed as idle vagrants.[73] The passage speaks to the link that the narrative establishes between land concentration and poverty, and, notably, it questions the effectiveness of resorting to capital punishment—premised on the sovereign power's right to take life—to deal with the growing number of poor and vagrant individuals. We can thus recognize that the problem of population is framed as inextricably linked to the socio-economic processes that produced a differentiated group vulnerability based on class.

In the writings of Las Casas and Quiroga, by contrast, the politicization of life at the level of collectivities is tied to a process of differentiation that contributed to the composition of differently racialized groups. Their common depiction of diverse indigenous groups as poor laborers is still a fundamental part of their discourse, but their views speak to the way in which class considerations intersect with other racializing assumptions. In Las Casas' *Memorial*, we see this in some of the regulatory immigration policies he recommends as part of his overall plan to stabilize the indigenous population. In his 11th "remedy," for example, he openly calls for the importation of enslaved Africans to replace what he presents as the vulnerable population of indigenous workers. As Castro explains, this is perhaps the best-known part of Las Casas's *Memorial*, but it is also his most controversial.[74] In articulating this issue, Las Casas justifies his petition by arguing that black slaves will be able to collect more gold than double the number of Indians.[75] Here, Las Casas assumes the existence of two discrete categories of people with supposedly different laboring capabilities, and he attempts to quantify, in human terms, the benefits of replacing one labor pool with another. Indeed, if the indigenous are dying because of abusive labor conditions, and if this is the problem that his *Memorial* sets out to solve, then, his logic implies, exposing one enslaved African to the same laboring conditions that he objects to is better than doing the same for two indigenous subjects. Paradoxically, the apparent valuation of African's labor power depends on the devaluation of their lives as it exposes them to the same laboring conditions that he insists are decimating the indigenous.

Las Casas also proposes that families of farmers from Spain be sent to the Antilles as part of his larger plan to stabilize the indigenous population. As he develops this argument, he begins by simply asserting that there are excessive numbers of poor and needy farmers in the kingdom that can be used in the colonies: "[manden] de cuantos en estos reinos hay sobrados y por ventura necesitados, para que siempre allá permanezcan."[76] Implicit in his statement is an acknowledgment of the momentous socio-economic transformations happening in Europe and the effects this had on the poor. Not only does he recognize the presence of large numbers of destitute farmers in Spain, but he also represents this segment of the population as "surplus," and he devises a plan to help deal with the problem while simultaneously addressing other issues in the colonies. In this sense, Las Casas' suggestion anticipates what Balasopoulous reads as More's gesture to deal with the question of "surplus population" through the "spatial fix" of colonization, but it also prefigures later policies designed to deal with the poor in Spain, including the Poor Laws of 1523–1558. The Poor Laws provided a general guideline to address the growing problem of vagrancy and the increasing number of paupers in the kingdom, and they were partly issued in response to social unrest caused by large-scale famines—many of which were tied to problems with grain supply produced by price speculation. They also helped institute significant disciplinary measures like requiring licenses to beg, rounding-up paupers, and spatially confining the poor in hospices.[77]

Las Casas' request for Spanish farmers also brings into focus a different set of racializing assumptions that inform his writing. For one, it is imperative to note that, as María Elena Martínez explains, colonial officials tended to favor the immigration of peasant farmers with their families because farmers were considered among the "purest" groups in the kingdom since they were seen as having less contact with "impure" groups like Jews, *conversos,* and *moriscos.*[78] Though Las Casas does not make this point explicitly, he does caution against the presence of heretics in the colonies, and he calls for establishing the Inquisition to root out "impure" elements among the colonizers:

> Y asimismo suplico a vuestra reverendísima señoría por Dios, en todo lo expuesto por su señalado ministro, que mande enviar a aquellas islas e Indias la Santa Inquisición, de la cual creo yo que hay muy gran necesidad....pues ya se han hallado y han quemado dos herejes.... Porque puede ser que muchos herejes se hayan huido destos reinos y pensando de salvarse se hobiesen pasado allá.[79]

Las Casas' views reflect the type of internal racializing distinctions that the notion of purity of blood had already generated within Spain, where not only Jews and Muslims but also *conversos, moriscos,* and their descendants were seen by many as irredeemably other. They also point to a generalized fear of an "enemy within" whose infiltration of society was a key driving force for the Inquisition.

An additional reason why Las Casas' request for Spanish farmers is significant is that it is tied to one of the only comments in which he overtly addresses the subject of reproduction. Speaking about the benefits of sending farmers to the colonies, he asserts that they will help establish new communities where Spaniards and the indigenous can live and work together, and he suggests that the latter will benefit and learn through emulation.[80] Strikingly, he also adds "y asimismo se mezclarán casándose los hijos de los unos con las hijas de los otros, etc. Y así multiplicarse ha la tierra de gente y de fruto."[81] Las Casas not only endorses the then-dominant view about how Spaniards would provide a good example for the indigenous, but he also sanctions a model of social organization based on their close spatial proximity, and he proposes a reproductive scheme based on "racial mixture" or mestizaje. Concerning the latter point, his assertion is noteworthy because it both illustrates the way in which explicit calculations about the procreative effects of sex factor into his project, and because it helps disclose some of the racializing exclusions on which it is premised. Indeed, whereas Spanish farmers are presented as ideal agents to help repopulate the land by "mixing" with the natives, the procreative effects of sex are never even considered in relation to his request for enslaved Africans. African bodies are strictly presented as a labor pool whose presence will help stabilize the indigenous population by relieving the latter from exploitative practices, but the very possibility of sexual intercourse between Africans and other groups is entirely elided. This speaks to the type of exclusionary qualifications that underpin Las Casas' views, and they help foreground some of the racializing assumptions that are at the core of his biopolitical project.

In Quiroga's case, we can likewise trace a series of critical specifications and conspicuous omissions that evince the way in which his politicization of indigenous life functions in relation to consolidating ideas about racial difference. To begin with, it is important to point out that ideas about purity of blood are consistently evoked in his writing. As mentioned earlier, in his letter from 1531, Quiroga partly justifies his call for separate indigenous communities by asserting that the measure will help deter young natives from reverting to their parents' idolatrous practices.[82] He cautions that, if things are left as they are, young men and women who have already been indoctrinated by the missionaries will return to their old religious beliefs for, as he puts it, "como sea cosa natural toda cosa volverse fácil a su naturaleza."[83] The passage illustrates Quiroga's conceptual conflation between a person's religious beliefs and human nature, and it is suggestive of the ways in which notions of purity of blood inform his early views on the indigenous. It also points to a tension between, on the one hand, the idea that blood and genealogy exert a deterministic influence over a person's religious beliefs, and, on the other, Quiroga's confidence that spatial reorganization could help offset supposedly hereditary inclinations. In *Información,* Quiroga appears to address this tension when he specifies that, in addition to being malleable and docile, the natives are also barely tainted: "[son] gente libre y tan mansa y doméstica como aquesta, *y tan poco infesta.*"[84] Here, Quiroga's ambivalence is noteworthy. He suggests that the indigenous are not pure, but their impurity is presented as a matter of degree rather than a clear-cut formulation of either/or. In other words, he does not present their impurity as an irredeemable quality and is thus able to avoid the implications this would have for his project.[85] Significantly, when Quiroga wrote this, the purity status of the indigenous was still being debated, since it was not until the second half of the 16th century that indigenous groups who had successfully been brought under Spanish colonial rule were regarded as "gentiles no infectados" and officially granted purity of blood status.[86]

On the subject of African slavery, Quiroga is noticeably silent. This is particularly significant considering that Michoacán had a significant African population already in the 16th century, and that, over the years, the number of afro-mestizos consistently increased.[87] One of the only documents in which Quiroga mentions the topic is in his testament, where he frees all of his personal slaves: "declaro y es mi voluntad que todos los esclavos que tengo, hombres y mujeres, sean libres sin adición alguna, porque esta es mi voluntad."[88] He also references a *mulato* servant but says nothing other than how he should be rewarded for his services. His project is clearly inscribed in a context of changing demographics and proliferating discourses about mixed-raced categories, but this setting is mostly left unacknowledged in his call for separate indigenous towns. Aside from his comments about how Spanish men are providing a bad example by being sexually involved with indigenous women, he largely circumvents the question of mestizaje and ignores the potential challenges this poses for the creation of two segregated republics. At a discursive level, his politicization of indigenous life is suggestive of the ways in which new modes of power became invested in the regulation of racialized collectivities, but, unlike Las Casas, his discourse is more narrowly focused on one form of racially qualified life.

Quiroga's reflections on the depopulation crisis offer a first-hand account of an unparallel situation that generated a range of competing discourses and ushered in a series of regulatory measures that decisively shaped the contours of Spanish colonialism. By contextualizing his views in relation to Las Casas' *Memorial* we can recognize how the problem of population begins to come into focus for colonial officials, and we can discern some of the ways in which political calculations about the management and regulation of life gain increasing centrality in their discourse. This confirms Stoler's insistence that Foucault's theory of biopower needs to be reconfigured in relation to the colonies, and it calls attention to some of the ramifications this has for thinking about how the politicization of life operates in relation to racialization. Both Las Casas and Quiroga racially qualify the life that they seek to "protect" and foster, and both propose reproductive measures that evince profoundly different approaches to long-term population growth. While Las Casas's endorsement of mestizaje is premised on its own set of racializing implications, Quiroga's problematization of reproductive sex between Spanish men and indigenous women is suggestive of the ways in which his ideas about spatial reorganization are premised on the creation of boundaries that are, at once, territorial and racial. By turning now to this aspect of his work, we can see some of the contradictions that surface through the material implementation of his segregationist project.

On Boundaries and Their Transgression

> Que los padres y las madres naturales, y de cada familia, procuréis de casar vuestros hijos, en siendo de edad legítima: ellos de catorce años arriba, y ellas de doce; con las hijas de las otras familias del dicho Hospital, y en defecto de ellas, con hijas de los comarcanos, pobres; y todo siempre según odern de la Sta. Madre Iglesia de Roma, y no clandestinamente.
>
> Vasco de Quiroga[89]

An analysis of how the notion of boundaries operates in Quiroga's work allows us to probe into the ways in which the author envisioned and sought to secure the territorial limits of his experimental hospital towns. It also suggests that his conceptualization of space was intricately tied to ideas about jurisdiction that prefigure the legal pluralism that characterizes the dual republic model, and it offers additional insight into the racializing implications of his project. As spaces intended to help foster the demographic growth of the indigenous, Quiroga's hospital towns were premised, at least theoretically, on the exclusion of differently racialized individuals.[90]

Their sustainability over time, moreover, was understood by Quiroga to depend on the physical reproduction of the community, and, as the epigraph suggests, to ensure this, he explicitly stipulates that procreative sexual relations should be managed internally and circumscribed within the communities' limits. Only in exceptional cases does he sanction marriage with "outsiders," but even in this case, he specifies that non-internal marriages should be arranged with the neighboring poor; in other words, with people from an economic category that he routinely associated with the indigenous.[91] This discloses a different articulation of boundaries that operates through embodiment and delimits the border between those who belong in the hospital towns—and can contribute to their perpetuation in space and time— and those whose constitutive exclusion serves to demarcate the socio-racial and sexual boundaries of the communities.[92] Each of these different conceptualizations are critical to understand Quiroga's project and its inherent contradictions, and they shed light on how ideas about boundaries and their transgression helped shape the segregationist dual republic model.

As the material basis for his Utopian experiments, the plots of land on which Quiroga founded the communities of Santa Fe are important sites to begin inquiring into the power dynamics involved in the process of fixing the communities' territorial boundaries. Beginning in August of 1532— roughly a year after writing the letter in which he first advocated for the creation of separate indigenous towns— Quiroga purchased the first plot of land on which he established Santa Fe de los Altos. That same year, he bought a second plot in an adjacent locality, and again in 1534, 1535, and 1536.[93] In all, Quiroga obtained seven bills of sale and he managed to considerably expand the communities' physical territory. Quiroga used his own salary and savings to purchase the land, and, according to Benedict Warren's estimate, he paid around 6,000 or 7,000 pesos for his first hospital town, a considerable cost given that his annual salary was 1,700 pesos.[94] As his friend Juan de Zumárraga put it at the time:

> siendo oidor, gasta cuanto S.M. le manda dar de salario a no tener un real y vender sus vestidos para proveer a las congregaciones cristianas que tiene en sus hospitales...haciéndoles casas repartidas en familias a su costa y comprándoles tierras y ovejas con que se puedan sustentar.[95]

The process of acquiring land is also suggestive of the broader context and power relations in which Quiroga's project is inscribed. For one, Quiroga purchased most plots of land from Spaniards, which speaks to the context of accumulation by dispossession in which he was operating. He was also involved in a land dispute with an indigenous community who claimed that Quiroga appropriated an island that was theirs. In 1536, the indigenous *cacique* representing the community of Ocoyoacac presented the case to Audiencia. The *cacique*, Don Pedro, stated that the island of Tultepec was part of their community and was being plowed and cultivated by them. He claimed that Quiroga had seized the island against their will, and he affirmed that, although the community had initially hesitated to complain because of Quiroga's powerful standing as a judge, they now demanded its restitution. Quiroga dismissed the lawsuit as groundless and ineptly presented, and states that he had just titles to prove that he had purchased and donated it to the residents of Santa Fe "para el mantenimiento de los indios."[96] He also claimed that the land was empty ("era tierra vacía") and that the indigenous from Ocoyoacac were not using it as they claimed but rather that it was being plowed and cultivated by a different community whom he says he compensated for their labor.[97] To all this, he added:

> también se compró para hacer allí un oratorio donde han de haber personas de indios bien doctrinados, e que doctrinen y enseñen la doctrina cristiana a los del dicho pueblo de Ocoyoacac y los otros de la comarca, e les digan misas, e porque no vivan como viven como bestiales.[98]

The passage confirms Quiroga's ongoing justification of his project as the only effective way to civilize and Christianize the indigenous, and it evinces his biting sense of authority in the face of opposition. The fact that Quiroga won the dispute later that year also attests to the asymmetrical colonial power relations in which he sought to forge his Utopian project.

In the case of Santa Fe de la Laguna, the land was initially informally donated by the indigenous governor of Michoacán, Don Pedro Cuinierángari.[99] Fearing that the informal deal would put the community at risk because of its legally vulnerable claim to the land, in 1538, Quiroga asked the governor and his wife to prepare a formal bill of sale and paid them 150 pesos. He also pressured them to increase the size of the property by referencing a royal decree mandating that "unused lands" be allocated to the hospital towns for the benefit of their residents.[100] That same year, Quiroga moved the civil capital and episcopal see from the former P'urhépecha capital Tzintzuntzan to Pátzcuaro—a move that implied significant changes in the delimitation of the dioceses and its jurisdiction—and tensions were high.[101] Specifically, the status of various towns known as "los pueblos y barrios de la Laguna"—which included Santa Fe—were being disputed by the powerful *encomendero* Juan Infante. Infante had traveled to Spain to secure his legal titles over the towns, and by the summer of 1539, he was preparing to take possession. In anticipation, however, Quiroga rallied indigenous leaders to take action against Infante and to prevent him from annexing the towns as part of his *encomienda*.

According to extant sources, when Infante sent his men to Santa Fe de la Laguna to take possession, he found the community on the brink of war, and he accused Quiroga and Cuinierángari of coordinating the resistance. After months of legal disputes, the conflict again escalated in October of 1539. As Infante and his men were on their way to Santa Fe, Quiroga and other armed Spaniards attempted to dissuade them, but, as they continued to advance, they were warned that 6,000 indigenous men were ready to attack.[102] The tactic deterred Infante temporarily, but he presented a criminal accusation against Quiroga, claiming that the bishop attempted to murder him.[103] Eventually, this and other related disputes compelled Quiroga to return to Spain between 1547 and 1554 to try to obtain better protections for his hospital towns. The New Laws of 1542—which were meant to impose real limits on the encomienda system and on the use of indigenous slave labor—helped support Quiroga's claims. Infante himself is mentioned in one of the paragraphs from the New Laws for possessing an excessive number of natives, and Quiroga cunningly pointed this out in his appeal. Two royal decrees were granted in Madrid in 1553 favoring Quiroga, but they were unsuccessfully challenged by Infante and the dispute was finally settled in 1575.[104]

A second way in which we can think about how notions of boundaries operate in Quiroga's project is by analyzing how his prescriptive *Ordenanzas* set the contours of the communities through the legal interpellation of its residents. Like in More's *Utopia*, Quiroga stipulates in his *Ordenanzas* that the indigenous living in the hospital towns can travel both within and outside of the community's boundaries, but only with prior permission. Internally, he specifies that individuals can travel to some of the less urban areas, but he emphasizes that they must have the authorization to do so, and that said individual can only travel on the condition that s/he will live and work with the *familias* in rural areas so as to avoid idleness.[105] This allows us to better envision how space was internally organized into rural and urban enclaves—which were in turn ordered into multi-family units of up to fifteen houses (what Quiroga refers to as *familias*)— and it makes clear the type of disciplinary regulations that impinged on the residents' mobility.[106]

Quiroga's *Ordenanzas* also stipulate that residents wanting to travel outside the hospital towns must have authorities' legal consent. In his words,

> cuando del dicho hospital saliéredes, y queráis salir; con licencia empero del Rector y Regidores de él, y no de otra manera, llevéis sabido la doctrina, policía, sanas y católicas cristianas, y oficios que así despediéredes y hayas desprendido, que enseñéis y podáis enseñar.[107]

Here, it is important to begin by clarifying how the administration of justice functioned within the hospital towns. Internally, the juridico-political system was based on two main elected positions: that of *principales* and *regidores*. Families were distributed equally within the quadripartite territorial division of the towns (that is, the four *barrios*), and the eldest male within each household agreed on one or two candidates whom they proposed for the position of *principales*. *Principales* constituted the maximum authority within the hospital towns and they governed for three to six years.[108] *Regidores*, on the other hand, were also elected by the male representatives of each household, and they served for one year. This position constituted the government, and they elected other necessary officials. *Regidores* were also in charge of administering justice as evinced in the passage above. The only external authority that Quiroga recognizes in his *Ordenanzas* come from two different sets of actors. The first is the *rector*, who was a Spanish priest that oversaw the functioning of the hospital towns, and the second was the Cabildo Catedralicio de Michoacán, an ecclesiastical body in charge of appointing the rector.[109] As Paz Serrano Gassent explains, all of this created an exceptional juridico-political situation. The communities recognized no other authority besides the rector and the ecclesiastical Cabildo, and, as mentioned earlier, they were exempt from paying tributes and tithes.[110]

In light of this context, it is easier to understand the significance of Quiroga's ordinances restricting the indigenous' mobility. To begin with, the gesture points to the fact that the regimentation and policing of space is a necessary counterpart to the effort to spatially concentrate a racially qualified population. Indeed, it is suggestive of the ways in which the enforcement of concentration was envisioned by Quiroga after the initial moment of "gathering" different indigenous groups. Moreover, the fact that the figure of the Spanish rector is endowed with the power to restrict the residents' movement and decide who may or may not leave, is indicative of the significance this issue had for Quiroga since on most other matters he grants the communities' internal authorities a greater level of autonomy. It is also notable that the possibility of wanting to leave the hospital towns is not only accounted for by Quiroga, it is presented in the passage above as a means to disseminate the catholic doctrine and orderly living that informs the author's very justification for concentrating the indigenous in the first place. In other words, it speaks to the ways in which power operates within these communities to produce subjects and mold their very conduct so that if and when they do decide to leave, they have already internalized the civilizing and Christianizing ideals of its founder. This foregrounds the subjectifying element of Quiroga's *Ordenanzas* and it calls attention to some of the insidious operations through which the law functions to target individuals through discipline in space.

In addition to the question of restricted mobility, Quiroga also stipulates the cases in which a resident may be banished from the hospital towns:

> que si alguno de vosotros o de vuestros sucesores en este dicho Hospital, hiciere cosa fea y de mal ejemplo, por do no merezca ni convenga estar en él, y de ello se recibiese escándalo y desasosiego, por ser revoltoso, o escandaloso, o mal cristiano, o se emborrachar, o demasiado perezoso, o que no quisiere guardar estas Ordenanzas, o fuere o viniere contra ellas, y fuere en ello incorregible, o fuere o viniere contra el pro y bien común de este dicho Hospital, sea luego lanzado de él, y restituya

lo que de él se aprovechó, como ingrato del bien en él recibido, y así el Principal y Regidores del dicho Hospital, lo ejecuten, con parecer del Rector del dicho Hospital.[111]

Notably, Quiroga frames the issue of banishment by appealing to the same trope that he uses in *Información* to justify segregation: namely, the notion of the bad example. In this case, though, the source of possible corruption is internal to the communities, and the trope of the bad example is deployed in order to discern said corrupting elements. For Quiroga, it is not simply a matter of listing transgressive actions that warrant expulsion—including being rebellious, being a bad Christian, and not following his *Ordenanzas*—it is also about who is worthy of inclusion. This is why he uses words like "merecer" to talk about residents who deserve to live in the communities and benefit from their inclusion, and it explains why he specifies that individuals who are banished are also liable to pay restitution for their ingratitude. The passage also raises important questions about the legal standing of a banned individual. Aside from the issue of being physically removed (or "lanzados") from the communities—which suggests a sense of territorial boundaries—the banned individual is put in a vulnerable legal position, no longer exempt from tribute and other legal obligations but rather at the threshold between distinct juridical orders. What we see here, then, is the way in which space and jurisdiction begin to overlap in Quiroga's conceptualization of boundaries.

On a conceptual level, Quiroga's *Ordenanzas* offer crucial insight into how the movement of people was envisioned as part of the long-term viability of the project. They also allow us to consider some of the implications that these ordinances have for thinking about the hospital towns' relative autonomy, and about the relation between space and jurisdiction. They tell us very little, however, about the actual circulation of people both within and outside the communities' boundaries. The fragments of information that we have about this come from tangential references in archival sources that offer mere glimpses into this aspect of Quiroga's project. We know, for instance, that in 1536 Quiroga obtained a royal decree offering protection to Santa Fe de los Altos against "unwelcomed outsiders." The document begins by stating that, since the hospital town is located near the main road to the mines in Michoacán, Matalcingo, Colima, and Jalisco, its residents are frequently harassed by Spanish travelers who steal their means of self-subsistence and try to forcefully take them as "tamemes" (a Nahuatl word used to describe men who carried large loads on their backs). Against what is described as "[estos] malos tratamientos de los españoles" the document specifies that the purpose of the decree is to offer "nuestra guardia e seguro e amaparo e defendimiento real a todos los susodichos vecinos e moradores de el dicho pueblo y hospital de Santa Fe e a sus mujeres e hijos e criados."[112] It also references the different jurisdictions in the area—stating that civil and criminal charges should be brought to the corresponding authorities— and it specifies a fine of 200 pesos for anyone contravening these orders.[113] The decree effectively barred Spaniards from residing in the hospital town, and, significantly, it was issued the same year as one of the earliest laws codifying the segregationist dual republic model.[114]

Additionally, we know of two cases involving enslaved Africans that allow us to better understand how the incursion of "outsiders" was handled by Quiroga and the residents of the hospital towns. First, there is a dispute that the Spaniard Gonzalo Ruiz brought against the community beginning in 1556. According to Ruiz, sometime in July of that year, a large group of indigenous from the hospital town, accompanied by two secular priests and some of Quiroga's servants, forced two enslaved Africans out of a plot they were plowing. They then brought their own plows and ox and proceeded to cultivate the land. Since Gonzalo was ill, he sent his son Francisco to forcefully expel the group, and a violent confrontation ensued. When the residents of Santa Fe took the case to Audiencia, they complained they had been physically mistreated, and Francisco Ruiz and his slaves were arrested. In the course of the dispute, Gonzalo Ruiz stressed that the community of Santa Fe was too large, that it was not being used for self-sustainability, and that its residents did not pay tribute and were all rich. He also complained that runaway slaves were finding refuge there.[115] Though we do not know the ultimate outcome of this dispute, the case nevertheless allows us to understand how the ongoing problem of land encroachment by Spaniards was actively contested by the community. It also calls attention to the ambiguous place of the enslaved Africans who, on the one hand, were violently confronted by the community for following their master's orders. On the other hand, the claim that runaway slaves were finding refuge in the community destabilizes the idea of the community as a racially exclusive "Indian town."

The claim that runaway slaves were finding refuge in Santa Fe de los Altos was also voiced in the high-profile dispute between Quiroga and the *encomendero* Juan Infante. As part of the drawn-out process from the 1540s, the Spaniard Pedro de Solís was called as a witness against Quiroga and his first hospital town. In his testimony, Solís declared that Quiroga had forcefully taken an enslaved girl that belonged to him. He stated that Quiroga had only given him thirty pesos for the girl when she was in fact worth 200. In response, Quiroga declared that the girl had arrived, half dead, in the nearby town of Tacubaya, where she recovered and had lived for 7 years as a free person, without any suspicion that she was enslaved. Her old masters, according to Quiroga, did not express any interest in getting her back during that period. Later, she married a man from Santa Fe and was living there when several black slaves broke into the town at midnight and forcefully took her back to Solís. A group of indigenous from Santa Fe again took the case to the Audiencia, and the judge found that since it was impossible to prove that the woman had indeed been a slave, and in order to uphold her Christian marriage to the man from Santa Fe, she could continue to reside there on condition that Quiroga paid thirty pesos to Solís.[116] At the time, indigenous slavery was still being debated, and since the document does not specify how the woman was racially categorized, it does little to clarify whether or not non-indigenous people lived in the community. It does, however, give us a concrete example of an indigenous man from the town who married an outsider who then went to reside there with her husband. Yet, it is unclear if the couple was interracial. Moreover, the fact that it was again black slaves who were sent on behalf of their masters to forcefully remove the woman is illustrative of the complex power dynamics that pitted enslaved Africans against indigenous groups.

The cases above also call attention to the question of how embodiment, and perceived racial markers or their absence, are factored into ideas about who "belonged" in the hospital towns. In the case of incursions by enslaved Africans, evidence suggests that they were recognized as outsiders. Indeed, both cases show that there were violent confrontations with the slaves who entered the communities on behalf of their masters and were seen as threats by the residents. Yet, the repeated claims that runaway slaves were finding refuge in the communities, as well as the ambiguous case of the slave girl who married the man from Santa Fe, point to a potentially more varied socio-racial makeup in the hospital towns. While extant records do little to clarify the matter fully, the questions raised are symptomatic of some of the broader conceptual problems at the heart of segregationist projects in Spanish America. For one, the cases call into question the effectiveness of Quiroga's *Ordenanzas* to actually restrict people's movement in and out of the hospital towns. In this sense, his case seems to validate Kathryn Burns' argument about how the idea of the two republics was in large part a "juridical fiction" that, in practice, failed to restrict the movement of groups of people and to segregate "Indians from non-Indians."[117] Nevertheless, dismissing the idea of the dual republic model as a mere "juridical fiction" fails to account for the material practices that did develop, and that decisively shaped the reconfiguration of colonial space and social relations. Quiroga's project, as Nemser shows, was one of the earliest attempts to spatially concentrate the indigenous, and his experimental communities served as the prototypical model for the policy of *congregación* that forcibly resettled countless natives and deeply influenced the production of colonial space.[118] These material transformations cannot be ignored, and, in fact, they compel us to think further about how the regimentation of space increased after the initial drive to spatially gather the indigenous. His case also offers incisive insight into what the material foundation of "Indian towns" implied for shifting conceptualizations of boundaries and their perceived transgression, not only in terms of territory but also in relation to racial markers and embodiment.

Conclusion

Vasco de Quiroga's experimental hospital towns in colonial Mexico occupy a unique place in the history of segregation in Spanish America. As early models of concentrated "Indian towns," they signal a critical turning point in colonial policy as the Spanish Crown gradually shifted toward the dual republic. This later model of governance was based on the idea of separate republics—the *república de españoles* and the *república de indios*—and as part of the Crown's efforts to materially forge this dualistic order, colonial authorities were granted the power to experiment with different forms of republics—what Martínez calls "ensayos de repúblicas."[119] Quiroga's Utopian hospital towns not only epitomize the experimental character of these early republics but also provided a model for a more systematic attempt to spatially concentrate diverse indigenous groups that gained track during the second half of the 16th century through the policy of *congregación* or *reducción*.

An analysis of Quiroga's project offers crucial insight into how the segregationist dual republic model was first envisioned and justified. His writings allow us to identify three key issues that Quiroga believed could be redressed by founding separate indigenous towns: namely, socio-spatial disorder, Spaniard's detrimental "bad example," and indigenous depopulation. They also provide a written record of Quiroga's denunciation of colonizing violence, but they disclose the way in which he articulated the need for indigenous segregation as perfectly compatible with the economic and evangelizing interests of the Spanish Crown. Quiroga's actions, moreover, point to some of the inherent contradictions of the dualistic system. For one, as Quiroga moved to found his two hospital towns, he acknowledged the reproductive consequences of indigenous-Spanish relations—indeed, he sought to morally police these interactions through his rhetoric of the bad example—but he disavowed the fact that changing demographics associated with mestizaje complicated the idea of two segregated republics. Additionally, he experienced first-hand the challenges of implementing strict segregation. In 1536, Quiroga asked for royal protection to dissuade non-indigenous outsiders from entering Santa Fe de los Altos, and, though he obtained a royal decree that effectively barred Spaniards from residing in the community, extant records suggest that incursions from Spaniards and enslaved Africans working for their masters did not seize. His *Ordenanzas* further suggest that establishing indigenous jurisdiction over a specific territory was a critical component of segregation, one that actually gave the community certain levels of autonomy but also interpellated its residents and compelled them to stay in a circumscribed space.

In terms of the broader conceptual implications of Quiroga's project, it is also important to highlight two key points. On the one hand, it is essential to stress that the politicization of indigenous life that as the core of Quiroga's project reflects a much larger shift in terms of the ways in which the power over life was reconfigured in early modernity. Quiroga's views on the demographic decline of the natives point to a critical historical moment in which the question of population, at the level of collectivities, begins to emerge as an object of political and economic reflection. This shift corresponds to similar trends happening in Europe—it is reflected, for instance, in More's *Utopia*—and it underscores the importance of supplementing Foucault's account of biopower by considering the American colonies. On the other hand, it is imperative to consider the racializing implications of Quiroga's project. Not only did Quiroga's project aim to stabilize and foster the demographic growth of a specifically qualified form of life—which, in turn, implied the politicization of indigenous women's reproductive capacity—his intervention in the production of colonial space helped consolidate the idea of the Indian as a single homogeneous type. Quiroga's project compels us to think about the interrelations between race, sex, and segregation, and the following chapters foreground a series of additional cases that evince the productivity of tracing these dynamics by examining the development of segregationist policies in Spanish and Portuguese America.

Notes

1 Benedict Warren, *Vasco de Quiroga en África* (Fimax Publicistas, 1998), 15; Rodrigo Martínez Baracs, *Convivencia y utopía. El gobierno indio y español de la 'ciudad de Mechuacan,' 1521–1580* (Instituto Nacional de Antropología e Historia, 2005), 167–168.

2 Benedict Warren, *Vasco de Quiroga y sus Hospitales-Pueblo de Santa Fe* (Ediciones de la Universidad Michoacana, 1977), 112–120.

3 Silvio Zavala, "La 'utopia' de Tomás Moro en la Nueva España," in *La utopia mexicana del siglo XVI. Lo bello, lo verdadero y lo bueno*, ed. Tovar de Teresa (Grupo Azabache, 1992), 76–93.

4 Silvio Zavala, *Recuerdo de Vasco de Quiroga* (Editorial Porrua, 1965), 79, 81, 102.

5 Felipe Tena Ramírez, *Vasco de Quiroga y sus pueblos de Santa Fe en los siglos XVIII y XIX* (Editorial Porrúa, 1977), 104–111; Paz Serrano Gassent, *Vasco de Quiroga. Utopía y derecho en la conquista de América* (FCE Política y Derecho, 2002), 226.

6 Ivonne del Valle, "A New Moses: Vasco de Quiroga's Hospitals and the Transformation of Indians from 'Bárbaros' to 'Pobres'," in *Iberian Empires and the Roots of Globalization*, edited by Ivonne del Valle, Anna Moore, Rachel Sarah O'Toole (Vanderbilt University Press, 2020), 56.

7 Ibid.

8 Felipe Tena Ramírez, *Vasco de Quiroga y sus pueblos de Santa Fe en los siglos XVIII y XIX*, 162; James Krippner Martínez, "Invoking 'Tata Vasco': Vasco de Quiroga Eighteenth Twentieth Centuries," *The Americas* 56, no. 3 (2000): 17–18.

9 Gerardo Alberto Hernández Cendejas, "El liderazgo y la ideologia comunal de Elpidio Dominguez Castro en Santa Fe de la Laguna, Michocan, 1979–1988," *Tzintzun. Revista de Estudios Históricos* 39 (2004): 116–117, 122–123.

10 See *Colectivo Emancipaciones*: https://colectivoemancipaciones.org. For more on Cherán, see *Juchari eratsikua, Cherán K'eri: retrospective histórica, territorio e identidad étnica*, edited by Casimiro Leco Tomás, Alicia Lemus Jimenez, Ulrike Keyser Ohrt (Consejo Mayor delGobierno Comunal de Cherán, 2018).

11 María Elena Martínez, *Genealogical Fictions: Limpieza de Sangre, Religion, and Gender in Colonial Mexico* (Stanford University Press, 2008), 99.

12 María Elena Martínez, "Space, Order, and Group Identities in a Spanish Colonial Town: Puebla de Los Angeles," in *The Collective and the Public in Latin America: Cultural Identities and Political Order*, edited by Luis Roniger and Tamar Herzog (Sussex Academic Press, 2000), 13, 25.

13 María Elena Martínez, "Space, Order, and Group Identities," 13–14, 31.

14 Daniel Nemser, *Infrastructures of Race: Concentration and Biopolitics in Colonial Mexico* (University of Texas Press, 2017), 35, 49.

15 Daniel Nemser, *Infrastructures of Race*, 20–21, 49; Daniel Nemser, "Primitive Accumulation, Geometric Space, and the Construction of the Indian," *Journal of Latin American Cultural Studies* 24, no. 3 (2015): 341, 345, 347.

16 Carlos Paredes Martínez, *Historia de los pueblos indígenas de México* (Centro de Investigaciones y Estudios Superiores en Antropología Social, 2017), 177–178.

17 Daniel Nemser, *Infrastructures of Race*, 4–5, 59.

18 Vasco de Quiroga, *Información en Derecho del licenciado Quiroga sobre algunas provisiones del real consejo de Indias* [1535], edited by Carlos Herrejón Peredo (Secretaría de Educación Pública, 1985), 52.

19 Barbara Mundy, *The Death of Aztec Tenochtitlan, the Life of Mexico City* (University of Texas Press, 2015), 72–73.

20 Vasco de Quiroga, "Carta al Consejo de Indias," in *Don Vasco de Quiroga. Taumaturgo de la organización social*, edited by Rafael Aguayo Spencer (Ediciones Oasis, 1970), 80.

21 Vasco de Quiroga, "Carta al Consejo de Indias," 78.

22 Ibid.

23 Vasco de Quiroga, *Información en Derecho*, 62, 64, 68.

24 Daniel Nemser, *Infrastructures of Race*, 49; Rodrigo Martínez Baracs, *Convivencia y utopía*, 135, 138, 156, 214, 233.

25 Daniel Nemser, *Infrastructures of Race*, 35.

26 Vasco de Quiroga, "Carta al Consejo de Indias," 78.

27 Vasco de Quiroga, "Carta al Consejo de Indias," 79.

28 Vasco de Quiroga, *Información en Derecho*, 64, 82.

29 Vasco de Quiroga, *Información en Derecho*, 91–92.

30 Vasco de Quiroga, *Información en Derecho*, 79.

31 Vasco de Quiroga, *Información en Derecho*, 68–69, 168, 175–176, 195, 198.

32 Orlando Bentancor, "La disposición de la materia en la *Información en derecho* de Vasco de Quiroga," in *Estudios transatlánticos postcoloniales II: Mito, archivo, disciplina: Cartografías culturales*, edited by Ileana Rodríguez, Josebe Martínez (Anthropos Editorial, 2011), 192–195.

33 For more on imperial metaphysics, see Orlando Bentancor, *The Matter of Empire. Metaphysics and Mining in Colonial Peru* (University of Pittsburg Press, 2017). For more on the implications of the conflation between nature and indigenous people, see Jason Moore, *Capitalism and the Web of Life* (Verso, 2015).

34 Magnus Mörner, *La corona Española y los foráneos en los pueblos de indios de América* (Almqvist & Wiksell, 1970), 27.

35 Magnus Mörner, *La corona Española*, 22–27; Lewis Hanke, *The Spanish Struggle for Justice in the Conquest of America* (Little, Brown and Company, 1965), 19.

36 Vasco de Quiroga, *Información en Derecho*, 52, 82, 167.

37 The etymology of the word segregation can be traced to the 1540s. From the Latin *se,* meaning "apart from" and *grege,* ablative of *grex,* meaning "herd or flock." *Segregare* literally meant to "separate from the flock," and was later used to describe the process to "set apart, lay aside; isolate; divide." See https://www.etymonline.com/word/segregation.

38 Vasco de Quiroga, *Información en Derecho*, 164–165.

39 Vasco de Quiroga, *Información en Derecho*, 172.

40 For estimates on the pre-Hispanic population in central Mexico, see Nicolás Sánchez-Albornoz, "The Population of Colonial Spanish America," in *The Cambridge History of Latin America. Volume II*, edited by Leslie Bethell (Cambridge University Press, 1984), 3–34.

41 Gonzálo Fernández de Oviedo y Valdes Oviedo, *Historia General y Natural de las Indias. Tomo I* (Editorial Guarania, 1535), 253; Lewis Hanke, *All Mankind is One. A Study in the Disputation Between Bartolomé de las Casas and Juan Ginés de Sepúlveda in 1550 on the Intellectual and Religious Capacity of the American Indians* (Northern Illinois University Press, 1974), 27; Lewis Hanke, *The Spanish Struggle for Justice*, 91.

42 Michel Foucault, *The History of Sexuality: An Introduction, Volume I*, trans. Robert Hurley (Vintage Books, 1990 [1976]), 139.

43 Daniel Castro, *Another Face of Empire. Bartolome de las Casas, Indigenous Rights, and Ecclesiastical Imperialism* (Duke University Press, 2007), 69.

44 See Daniel Castro, *Another Face of Empire*, 72.

45 Bartolomé de Las Casas, "Memorial de remedios para las Indias," in *Biblioteca de autores españoles. Obras Escogidas de Bartolomé de las Casas. Opúsculos, Cartas y Memoriales*, Tomo 110, edited by Juan Perez de Tuleda Bueso (Real Academia Española, 1958), 6. Also see Bartomolé de las Casas "Memorial de denuncias," in *Biblioteca de autores españoles. Obras Escogidas de Bartolomé de las Casas. Opúsculos, Cartas y Memoriales.* Tomo 110, edited by Juan Perez de Tuleda Bueso (Real Academia Española, 1958). For more on population decline in the Caribbean, see Massimo Livi Bacci, *Conquest and the Destruction of the American Indios* (Polity Press, 2008); Noble David Cook, *Born to Die. Disease and New World Conquest, 1492–1650* (Cambridge University Press, 1998).

46 Vasco de Quiroga, *Información en Derecho*, 48–49.

47 Vasco de Quiroga, *Información en Derecho*, 157, 187.

48 Vasco de Quiroga, *Información en Derecho*, 62, 85.

49 Vasco de Quiroga, *Información en Derecho*, 82, 91–92.

50 Vasco de Quiroga, *Información en Derecho*, 57, 82–83, 86, 172.

51 Vasco de Quiroga, *Información en Derecho*, 86.

52 Bartolomé de Las Casas, "Memorial de remedios para las Indias," 13, 16, 19.

53 Bartolomé de Las Casas, "Memorial de remedios para las Indias," 8.

54 Vasco de Quiroga, *Información en Derecho*, 85, 154.

55 Bartolomé de Las Casas, "Memorial de remedios para las Indias," 6.

56 Ibid.

57 Daniel Castro, *Another Face of Empire*, 71.

58 Vasco de Quiroga, *Información en Derecho*, 62, 81–82.

59 In Spanish America, indigenous slavery was abolished in 1542 by the New Laws. For more on indigenous slavery in Spanish America, see Nancy Van Deusen, *Global Indios: The Indigenous Struggle for Justice in Sixteenth-Century Spain* (Duke University Press, 2015); Lewis Hanke, *The Spanish Struggle for Justice*; Kathleen Myers, *Fernández de Oviedo's Chronicle of America: A New History for a New World* (University of Texas Press, 2007), 116.

60 Ivonne del Valle, "A New Moses," 50, 59.

61 Ivonne Del Valle, "A New Moses," 58.

62 Ibid.

63 See Karl Marx, *Capital Volume I* (Penguin Classics, 1990), 896–904. Marx's theory of Primitive Accumulation has been developed by Marxist critic David Harvey, who describes the process as Accumulation by Dispossession. See, among others, chapter 4 of David Harvey's *The New Imperialism* (Oxford University Press, 2003), 137–182.

64 Fredric Jameson, *Archaeologies of the Future: The Desire Called Utopia and Other Science Fictions* (Verso, 2007), 34–35.

65 Antonis Balasopoulos, "Dark Light: Utopia and the Question of Relative Surplus Population," *Utopian Studies* 27, no. 3 (2016): 617.

66 Antonis Balasopoulos, "Dark Light," 618, 624.

67 Antonis Balasopoulos, "Dark Light," 619.

68 Antonis Balasopoulos, "Dark Light," 619–620.

69 Antonis Balasopoulos, "Dark Light," 622.

70 For more on the implications of representing the Americas as "empty spaces" see Daniel Nemser, "Primitive Accumulation, Geometric Space, and the Construction of the Indian," *Journal of Latin American Cultural Studies* 24, no. 3 (2015): 335, 336, 339.

71 Victor N. Baptiste, *Bartolomé de las Casas and Thomas More's Utopia* (Labyrinthos, 1990), vii–viii; Daniel Castro, *Another Face of Empire*, 72.

72 See Thomas More, *Utopia*. [1516] 1518 Latin Copy. At Nettie Lee Benson Library in Austin. The annotated copy of *Utopia* that Quiroga read originally belonged to the bishop of Mexico Juan de Zumárraga. Though Zavala initially believed that the annotations could have been made by Quiroga himself—given his initially close friendship with Zumárraga—, later investigations led him to conclude that the markings are more likely the latter's. See Silvio Zavala, *Recuerdo de Vasco de Quiroga* (Editorial Porrua, 1965), 79, 81, 102. For more on the relation between Zumárraga and Quiroga, see also Rafael Aguayo Spencer, *Don Vasco de Quiroga, taumaturgo de la organización social seguido de apéndide documental* (Editorial Polis, 1939), 192–193.

73 See English translation of *Utopia* by Robert Adams (Norton & Company, 1991), 57–63.

74 Daniel Castro, *Another Face of Empire*, 74.

75 Bartolomé de Las Casas, "Memorial de remedios para las Indias," 9.

76 Bartolomé de Las Casas, "Memorial de remedios para las Indias," 7.

77 James Casey, *Early Modern Spain: A Social History* (Routledge, 1999), 125–130; Linda Martz, *Poverty and Welfare in Habsburg Spain* (Cambridge University Press, 1983), 12.

78 María Elena Martínez, "Space, Order, and Group Identities," 22.

79 Bartolomé de Las Casas, "Memorial de remedios para las Indias," 15.

80 Bartolomé de Las Casas, "Memorial de remedios para las Indias," 7.

81 Ibid.

82 Vasco de Quiroga, "Carta al Consejo de Indias," 79.

83 Ibid.

84 Vasco de Quiroga, *Información en Derecho*, 68–69.

85 For other instances in which Quiroga refences notions of purity of blood, see "Testamento," in *Don Vasco de Quiroga. Taumaturgo de la organización social*, edited by Rafael Aguayo Spencer (Ediciones Oasis, 1970), 278.

86 María Elena Martínez, *Genealogical Fictions: Limpieza de Sangre, Religion, and Gender in Colonial Mexico* (Stanford University Press, 2008), 96.

87 Herman L. Bennett, *Colonial Blackness: A History of Afro-Mexico* (Indiana University Press, 2010), 56; Maria Guadalupe Chavez Carvajal, *Propietarios y esclavos negros en Valladolid de Michoacán, 1600–1650* (Universidad Michoacana de San Nicolás de Hidalgo, 1994), 14–16.

88 Vasco de Quiroga, "Testamento," in *Don Vasco de Quiroga. Taumaturgo de la organización social*, edited by Rafael Aguayo Spencer (Ediciones Oasis, 1970), 290.

89 Vasco de Quiroga, *Ordenanzas* 253.

90 For other arguments about the racial exclusivity of the hospital towns, see Felipe Tena Ramírez, *Vasco de Quiroga y sus pueblos de Santa Fe en los siglos XVIII y XIX*, 14, 106.

91 Ivonne del Valle, "A New Moses," 58.

92 For more on the construction of social boundaries and how this intersects with sex and gender, see Doreen Massey, *Space, Place and Gender* (University of Minnesota Press, 2009).

93 Benedict Warren, *Vasco de Quiroga y sus Hospitales-Pueblo*, 58–61.

94 Benedict Warren, *Vasco de Quiroga y sus Hospitales-Pueblo*, 67.

95 Quoted in Benedict Warren, *Vasco de Quiroga y sus Hospitales-Pueblo*, 68.

96 See Rafael Aguayo Spencer, *Don Vasco de Quiroga, taumaturgo de la organización social seguido de apéndide documental* (Editorial Polis, 1939), 457.

97 Aguayo Spencer, *Don Vasco de Quiroga*, 459.

98 Ibid.

99 Rodrigo Martínez Baracs, *Convivencia y utopía*, 221.

100 Benedict Warren, *Vasco de Quiroga y sus Hospitales-Pueblo*, 122–123.

101 Aida Castilleja, "La configuración del espacio local en tres pueblos de la laguna de Pátzcuaro. El componente político-administrativo de la diferenciación del espacio: articulación e integración," in *Del territorio a la Arquitectura en el Obispado de Michoacán*, edited by Carlos Paredes Martínez, Catherine Ross Ettinger (Consejo Nacional Para la Ciencia y Tecnología, 2008), 283.

102 Benedict Warren, *Vasco de Quiroga y sus Hospitales-Pueblo*, 124, 129–139.

103 Benedict Warren, *Vasco de Quiroga y sus Hospitales-Pueblo*, 138.

104 Paz Serrano Gassent, *Vasco de Quiroga*, 224; Benedict Warren, *Vasco de Quiroga y sus Hospitales-Pueblo*, 143.

105 Vasco de Quiroga, "Reglas y Ordenanzas para el Gobierno de los Hospitales de Santa Fe de México y de Michoacán," in *Don Vasco de Quiroga. Taumaturgo de la organización social*, edited by Rafael Aguayo Spencer (Editorial Polis, 1940), 259.

106 For more on the meaning of *familias* and the architectural organization of the towns, see Miguel Covarrubias Reyna, "Santa Fé. Utópico pueblo absorbido por la ciudad de México," *Arqueología Mexicana* no. 134 (2015): 74–79.

107 Vasco de Quiroga, "Reglas y Ordenanzas," 253.

108 Paz Serrano Gassent, *Vasco de Quiroga*, 215.

109 Paz Serrano Gassent, *Vasco de Quiroga*, 215, 216, 218.

110 Paz Serrano Gassent, *Vasco de Quiroga*, 226. It is also important to note that Quiroga modeled his hospital towns on the Castilian comuneros. For more on that, see Aurelio Espinosa, *The Empire of the Cities. Emperor Charles V, the Comunero Revolt, and the Transformation of the Spanish System* (Koninklijke Brill NV, 2009); Stephen Haliczer, *The Comuneros of Castile. The Forging of a Revolution, 1475–1521* (The University of Wisconsin Press, 1981).

111 Vasco de Quiroga, "Reglas y Ordenanzas," 263.

112 See Nicolás León, *Documentos inéditos referentes al ilustrísimo señor Don Vasco de Quiroga. Existentes en el Archivo General de Indias* (José Porrúa e Hijos, 1940), 6.

113 León, *Documentos inéditos*, 5–6.

114 See Law 23, Title 3, of Book 6, of the *Recopilación de Leyes para las Indias, 1681*. Content downloaded from https://home.heinonline.org

115 Benedict Warren *Vasco de Quiroga y sus Hospitales-Pueblo*, 88–92. For other cases citing the presence of runaway slaves in the hospital towns, see Benedict Warren, *Vasco de Quiroga y sus Hospitales-Pueblo*, 81, 87, 89, 98.

116 Benedict Warren, *Vasco de Quiroga y sus Hospitales-Pueblo*, 86–87.
117 Kathryn Burns, "Unfixing Race," in *Rereading the Black Legend: The Discourses of Religious and Racial Difference in the Renaissance Empires*, edited by Margaret R. Greer, Walter D. Mignolo, Maureen Quilligan (University of Chicago Press, 2007), 191.
118 Daniel Nemser, *Infrastructures of Race*, 26, 35, 36, 49.
119 María Elena Martínez, "Space, Order, and Group Identities," 23.

2 The Codification of Segregation in a Context of Mestizaje

By the second half of the 16th century, efforts to segregate indigenous groups into separate communities were well underway in places like colonial Mexico and Peru. In Mexico, Vasco de Quiroga's experimental hospital towns were superseded by a more systematic form of spatial concentration that was institutionalized in the 1550s as part of the policy known as *congregación* or *reducción*.[1] Hundreds of towns were built following European models of urbanization designed to visually inscribe the new colonial order, and countless indigenous groups were relocated there to be Christianized and civilized.[2] By then, indigenous slavery had been officially prohibited, but "Indian towns" (or *pueblos de indios*) were intentionally designed to help extract indigenous labor power and tribute more efficiently, including, by being located in strategic areas near mines and global trade routes.[3] As the policy extended to colonial Perú, it reached a new zenith in 1569 when more than a million indigenous subjects were forcibly resettled as part of a relocation campaign that Jeremy Mumford describes as marking the beginning of a new era in the history of European colonialism, one that foreshadowed the modern state.[4]

In urban settings, the project of indigenous segregation also influenced city planning. Cities were laid out according to an orthogonal grid that divided the Spanish center (known as *traza*) from surrounding indigenous neighborhoods or barrios.[5] In Mexico City, there was also a canal that physically separated the two zones.[6] In Lima, colonial authorities even built a walled indigenous neighborhood known as Santiago del Cercado, which was officially inaugurated by viceroy Francisco de Toledo in 1571.[7] Some of the Cercados' residents had been forcefully resettled there, and, some scholars have suggested that the walls of this urban *reducción* were "intended to keep its coerced residents from fleeing at night."[8]

The creation of Indian towns and barrios also implied a profound restructuring of the juridico-political system. The dual republic model was based on the creation of two separate republics, and, as part of this, indigenous communities were granted limited autonomy. These communities were still subject to the authority of the Spanish Crown, but they were allowed to maintain their own customary law (or *uso y costumbre*), so long as this

DOI: 10.4324/9781003145196-3

did not contradict the Catholic faith.[9] Indian towns also had their own Spanish-style elected government, known as *cabildos*, and each republic had separate courts.[10] All of this profoundly reshaped native power structures, and it led to the consolidation of two primary administrative units and jurisdictions: the Republic of Spaniards and the Republic of Indians.[11] The dual republic model was thus both a spatial project with concrete material effects and a juridico-political framework that operated—even when unevenly—on the basis of bounded notions of territory that tied geography to law.[12]

Another salient feature of the segregationist dual republic model is that it developed in a context of major demographic changes that were the result of expanding global economic networks that brought diverse populations into contact.[13] Enslaved Africans were imported into the Caribbean as early as 1502, and between 1580 and 1640, the Atlantic slave trade expanded dramatically throughout the Americas, with Mexico and Peru receiving some of the largest numbers of slaves during that period.[14] Descendants of enslaved Africans who had been born and raised in Iberia also made it to the New World in large numbers, many of them with their masters, but also as free men and women.[15] Moreover, as trade with Asia intensified during the second half of the 16th century following the inauguration of the Manila-Acapulco Galleon, countless individuals from the Indian subcontinent and Southeast Asia traveled to the Americas, primarily as slaves, but also as free migrants, where they were all categorized as *chinos*.[16]

These different waves of immigration complicated the binary structure on which the dual republic model was premised, but segregationist laws were adapted accordingly. In the case of enslaved Africans and their descendants, colonial authorities neglected to allot a distinctive social space for them, but rather included them de facto into the Republic of Spaniards by explicitly prohibiting that they reside in Indian towns or barrios.[17] Jane Landers also argues that the colonial government considered and partly authorized the creation of a "third republic" as a result of different forms of African resistance, including the formation of maroon communities which, in some cases, were able to achieve limited autonomy as free-colored townships.[18] In the case of enslaved Asians (or "chino slaves"), they were mostly absorbed into urban centers that were part of the Republic of Spaniards. Notably, though, free natives from the Philippines—who were sometimes called *indios chinos* to distinguish them from Asian slaves—were technically allowed to become members of the Republic of Indians since the term *indio* applied to all indigenous peoples in Spanish colonies, including natives from Asia.[19]

The demographic makeup of colonial society further grew in complexity as people from different origins and backgrounds engaged in reproductive sexual relations. This complexity is reflected by the myriad labels that began to be used by colonial officials to characterize people from mixed-ancestry backgrounds, including terms like *mestizo, mulato, zambaigo, lobo, coyote, gíbaro, salta atrás,* and a host of other demeaning names that abound in the archival record and that point to an ever-exacting system of socio-racial classification that was instituted by the Spanish Crown to manage its vast empire.[20] In segregationist legislation, *mestizos, mulatos,* and *zambaigos* figure prominently, and though their presence in Indian towns was generally proscribed, some important exceptions were granted for *mestizos* and *zambaigos.*[21] The consolidation of the socio-racial label *mestizo* can also be traced by considering how segregation was codified since the term only appears gradually as the Spanish Crown and nascent colonial state began to regulate the spatial mobility of this growing segment of the population.

Scholars have long described these different changes by appealing to concepts like mestizaje, racial mixture, and miscegenation, and, this history has long been considered, as Ben Vinson puts it, as "a hallmark feature of the region's demography."[22] This context is also critically tied to the history of segregation in the region since mestizaje is regularly invoked to dismiss the effectiveness of segregationist efforts and to argue that the dual republic model failed from its inception. One of the most common arguments that are made by scholars who adopt this position is that colonial authorities failed to truly separate indigenous groups from the rest of colonial society. On the one hand, this failure is attributed to the fact that reproductive sex between differently racialized people took place from the earliest years of colonization and continued unabated despite segregationist efforts.[23] On the other hand, scholars also point out that colonial authorities were never able to effectively control the movement of people despite existing laws that sought to prevent both indigenous subjects from residing outside of Indian towns and non-indigenous people from residing in those same communities.[24] The narrative about the dual republic's failure thus articulates two interrelated claims. The first is about sex, and it is premised on the assumption that the regulation of reproductive sexual unions between differently racialized groups was necessary in order for segregation to work but untenable from the beginning. The second is about space, and it posits that the regulation of spatial boundaries between republics was ineffective, partly because, as some scholars acknowledge, the Crown's economic system structured the two republics as interdependent and often required that indigenous and African laborers continue to work together in close physical proximity, particularly in urban Spanish households and in rural industries like mining and ranching.[25]

The problem with dismissing the dual republic model as either ineffective or untenable from the beginning is that it leaves a series of critical conceptual questions unanswered. In particular, it fails to account for the way in which processes of racialization developed in Spanish America. Indeed, mestizaje is generally considered an exception to fixed notions of race and racial purity, and, often, when scholars invoke the concept, little attention is paid to the way in which notions of racial mixture actually work to reify social constructs of race. Ben Vinson, for instance, argues that: "Perhaps the main problem with the republic system was that it was predicated on the persistent and vigilant exercise of maintaining racial purity. But almost from the outset of the colonial period, miscegenation occurred."[26] Similarly, Karen Vieira Powers describes the dual republic model as "a construct intended to facilitate colonial exploitation and to preserve cultural and racial 'purity'" and she contends that, as mestizaje accelerated—partly due to the lack of Spanish women in the early years of colonization— the division that the two-republic system sought to institute slowly crumbled.[27] Both of these arguments assume that the separation between the Spanish and Indian republics was based on essentialized notions of racial difference between these groups—or what they describe as "racial purity"—but neither author considers the fact that, as Joshua Lund argues, *"mestizaje as the exception to racial purity ultimately makes possible, legitimates, and reconfirms that purity."*[28] If we reframe how we think about processes of racialization from this perspective, we can better trace the system of socio-racial classification that developed in Spanish America.

In this chapter, I offer a reevaluation of the dual republic model's presumed failure by considering how the project of indigenous segregation was codified in the context of mestizaje. Rather than assume that mestizaje undermined segregationist efforts, I show that segregationist laws actually account directly for processes of racial mixture, including by becoming progressively focused on regulating the movement of *mestizos* and other mixed-ancestry groups. I further argue that the sense of spatial and sexual boundaries between the Indian and Spanish Republics that was instituted through the dual republic framework was not initially based on fixed or essentialized notions of racial difference. Instead, the boundaries between republics were acknowledged as breached from the beginning because of mestizaje, but, not only did this not deter segregationist efforts, it actually contributed to the gradual consolidation of distinct socio-racial categories as colonial authorities were compelled to make ever-exacting distinctions between different groups of people in order to regulate their circulation within the dualistic system. As Robert Bernasconi argues, although it is sometimes claimed that racial mixture works to undermine fixed notions of race by blurring the sense of boundaries between differently construed groups of people, it is actually hard to find any historical support for this view. For Bernasconi, race is better theorized as a border concept that is premised on the demarcation of both spatial and sexual boundaries between differently racialized groups, but that is never actually reliant on the fixed essentialisms that it seeks to establish through those borders.[29] For him, it is precisely the fluidity of racial categories that allows us to trace the way in which racial constructs are historically produced, and the history of mestizaje in Spanish America offers crucial insight in this regard.[30]

In the first part of the chapter, I begin by analyzing a series of royal edicts and instructions that evince the fact that the Spanish Crown sought to regulate reproductive relations between differently racialized groups. I argue that these juridical discourses demonstrate that reproductive sex was politicized by the Spanish monarchy and nascent colonial state, and I show that this politicization was articulated specifically in relation to consolidating ideas about racial difference. In the second and third sections, I move to analyze the codification of indigenous segregation. In the Section "The Justification and Regulation of Indigenous Segregation," I show that the project of indigenous segregation was justified by pointing out that the measure was necessary for the demographic growth of a homogeneously construed population group, I consider the biopolitical implications of this formulation, and I analyze the way in which the regulation of peoples' movement based on the racial ascription *indio/a* contributed to the consolidation of that socio-racial category. In the final section, I focus on the way in which *mestizos* and other mixed-ancestry groups are referenced in segregationist laws. I trace the gradual emergence of the term *mestizo/a* in said legislation, I show that *mestizos, mulatos,* and *zambaigos* are one of the main targets of segregationist laws, and I discuss a series of archival cases from colonial Mexico that illustrate the way in which the enforcement of segregation was supported and enforced by indigenous agents who demanded the removal of mixed-ancestry groups from their communities.

The Racializing Effects of Juridical Discourses and Prohibitions about Reproductive Sex

Beginning in the early 16th century, there are a number of royal edicts and instructions that evince the fact that the Spanish Crown sought to regulate reproductive relations between differently racialized groups. The earliest juridical discourses that address the topic focus on marriages between Spaniards and Indians, and they provide key insight to understand how these unions were instrumentalized by the Spanish Crown for a number of political and economic reasons, including populating the land and establishing kinship alliances with *caciques* (or indigenous chiefs). As the African slave trade expanded throughout the American colonies, we also begin to see a consistently articulated Crown policy that sought to promote marriages among enslaved Africans, while at the same time forcefully discouraging reproductive unions between indigenous groups and the enslaved African population. In the latter case, this was viewed as particularly important given that Spanish laws on slavery were based on the principle of free womb (or *vientre libre*), which meant that the offspring of enslaved men and free indigenous women were legally considered free because of their mother's status.[31] These different juridical discourses thus call attention not only to the fact that reproductive sex was politicized by the Spanish monarchy and nascent colonial state but also to the fact that this politicization was articulated specifically in relation to consolidating ideas about racial difference.

The juridical discourses that address the topic of marriages between Spaniards and Indians are first of all noteworthy because they suggest that the regularization of reproductive unions between these groups was narrowly circumscribed from the beginning. Scholars have long pointed out that, from the outset of colonization, countless indigenous women were raped, exchanged, and forcefully appropriated by Spanish conquistadors and their allies,[32] but rather than address these forms of colonizing violence, early juridical discourses focus instead on the tactical importance of promoting *some* marital unions between these groups. These discourses offer only a partial account of how the Crown viewed and began to legislate reproductive relations between these groups, but they nevertheless offer key insight into the process of differentiation that helped solidify a legal and socio-racial distinction between *españoles/as* and *indios/as*.

One of the earliest edicts that comments on Spanish-indigenous marriages is from 1503, and, in it, King Ferdinand and Queen Isabel emphasize the importance of Christian marriages, presenting them as compulsory for indigenous subjects. They also instruct colonial authorities to favor some marital unions between Spaniards and indigenous groups:

> y asimismo procure que algunos cristianos se casen con algunas mujeres indias, y las mujeres cristianas con algunos indios, porque los unos y los otros se comuniquen y enseñen, para ser doctrinados en las cosas de nuestra Santa Fe Católica.[33]

Here, Spanish men and women are specifically referred to as *cristianos* and *cristianas*, respectively, and the terms *indio* and *india* are used in contradistinction to establish a difference based on religion. Intermarriage between these groups is presented as a means to disseminate Catholic mores, and the working assumption is that Spaniards will serve as good examples for indigenous Christianization. It is also notable that the document explicitly sanctions marriages between Christian women and Indian men, since, at the time, very few Spanish women were actually present in the colonies.[34] The open acceptance of these unions is thus more of a rhetorical gesture than a reflection of a common practice.

In a subsequent decree from 1514, King Ferdinand begins by highlighting the tactical importance of promoting marriages between Spanish men and indigenous women. He states that he has been informed that such unions are advantageous, a service to God and himself, and a convenient way of populating the island of Hispaniola:

> Sabed que a mí es fecha relación que si los naturales destos Reinos de Castilla que residen en la isla Española se casan con mujeres naturales desa isla, sería muy útil y provechoso al servicio de Dios y nuestro y conveniente a la población desa dicha isla.[35]

As the passage indicates—and as the rest of the document confirms—the sovereign is precise in describing these unions in terms of gender, advocating specifically for marriages between indigenous women and Spanish men. In this case, the presumed distinction between these groups is articulated in terms of place of origin rather than religion, and it is notable that Spaniards are specifically referred to as "naturales destos Reinos de Castilla." This calls attention to the fact that the Spanish monarchy was organized into politically autonomous kingdoms—of which Castile was but one—and it suggests that the term Spaniard was not yet commonly used to express a sense of common identity. The King's qualification also represents a tacit acknowledgment that, as Antonio Feros points out, although all Christian inhabitants of the peninsular kingdoms were granted the right to migrate to the colonies and obtain lands and offices, it was nevertheless Castilians who represented the vast majority of the colonizers and royal officials during most of the colonial period.[36]

In the 1514 edict, King Ferdinand goes on to say that, having taken into consideration the information he has received, he now grants explicit permission so that Castilian men can marry native women without thereby incurring any penalty: "por la presente doy licencia y facultad a qualsquier personas naturales destos dichos Reinos para que libremente se puedan casar con mujeres naturales desa dicha isla sin caer ni incurrir pro ello en pena alguna."[37] In this case, the topic of marriage—and therefore heterosexual reproductive sex—between Castilians and natives is framed as a legal issue since the monarch himself declares these unions as lawful. The legality of these unions, moreover, is linked to a specific political goal: namely, fostering population growth as a means to ensure long-term colonial settlements.[38] The King also emphasizes the importance of this issue when he instructs colonial authorities to publicly display his edict in plazas, marketplaces, and other crowded areas.[39] Marriages between these differently construed groups are thus explicitly instrumentalized, and they are presented as a critical matter for the administrative colonial apparatus.

In the third edict from 1515, which is the last issued by King Ferdinand, the monarch reaffirms that colonial authorities should not place any impediment on Spanish–indigenous marriages. He begins by appealing directly to the governor, judges, and other high-ranking officials, and he declares that, although many continue to impede these marriages, it is his will that *indias* and *indios* be granted complete "liberty" to marry whomever they choose.[40] The order is framed by paternalistic rhetoric that highlights the King's interest in protecting the natives, and, as part of this, their right to freely marry is affirmed. In this case, the instrumentality of Spanish–indigenous marriages is not overtly discussed—in contrast to the edict from the year before— but what is notable is the sovereign's emphasis on the Indians' "liberty" to choose their own partners, which illustrates that the Spanish Crown consistently upheld the canon law principle of free marriage choice.[41]

The formation of kinship ties through marriages is also addressed in two additional documents from the early 16th century that offer further insight into the instrumentalization of Spanish-indigenous unions. In official instructions from 1516, the interim government of Cardinal Francisco Jimenez de Cisneros begins to shift away from the broader acceptance of Spanish-indigenous marriages that we see in the earlier edicts, to focus more narrowly on the advantages of kinship alliances with native elites.[42] Notably, though, the document begins by instructing religious authorities to establish indigenous towns. The instructions specify that authorities should build these communities, particularly in areas near gold mines, they stipulate the towns' size and architectural design, they discuss the process of relocating Indians to form these communities, and they even outline the type of jurisdiction that indigenous *caquices* should have over the town's residents.[43] Both in terms of space and jurisdiction, the document thus presages the eventual formation of dual republics, but what is remarkable is that, even as it emphasizes the need the create separate indigenous communities, it nevertheless goes on to sanction marriages between Spanish men and elite indigenous women.

After the initial discussion about the need to found separate indigenous communities, the instructions from 1516 go on to state:

> Y si algún castellano o español de los que allá están o fueren a poblar se quisieren casarcon alguna caciqua o hija de cacique a quien pertenece la sucesión por falta de varones, este casamiento se haga con acuerdo y consentimiento del religioso o clérigo o de la persona que fuere nombrada para la administración de aquel pueblo, y casándose desta manera éste sea cacique y sea tenido y obedecido y servido como cacique a quien sucedió según y como abajo se dirá a los otros caciques, porque desta manera muy presto podrán ser todos los caciques españoles y se excusarán muchos gastos.[44]

The first thing to note here is that the term *español* is used for the first time in relation to the question of marriages with indigenous women. Initially, a nominal distinction is made between Castilians and Spaniards, but, by the end of the passage, the sole focus is on ensuring that *españoles* secure high positions of political power by marrying either female indigenous leaders or the daughters of *caciques*. The passage thus evinces the way in which the term *español* was gradually consolidating into a meaningful category of socio-racial identity, and it calls attention to the way in which this sense of common Spanish identity was articulated specifically in relation to reproductive unions with indigenous women.[45] What we find in these instructions, then, is a clear instrumentalization of Spanish–indigenous marriages for political and economic reasons, as well as an early indication of how the project of indigenous segregation was envisioned as compatible with a policy of intermarriage.

In a royal decree from 1525, King Charles V similarly endorses marital alliances between Spaniards and Indians. He begins by stating that he has been informed that many male indigenous leaders and *caciques* wish to marry their sons and daughters to "cristianos y cristianas españoles," and he says that Spaniards are likewise interested in establishing kinship alliances with Indians.[46] In this case, the King sanctions these marriages by arguing that they are instrumental for the pacification of the land and the stabilization of colonial governance: "sería muy servido y vernía mucho provecho y paz a la dicha tierra y sosiego y gobernación entre los dichos cristianos e indios della."[47] He also urges authorities to favor and facilitate these unions. Throughout the document, the monarch uses almost exclusively the term *españoles,* though he does regularly qualify the word by adding Christian to that designation. This confirms that a common sense of "Spanishness" was gradually consolidating in the context of the Americas in contradistinction to the indigenous precisely as reproductive sex between these groups was being legislated. It is also significant that, in terms of gender, the King equally endorses marriages between men and women from both groups. Yet, much like the 1503 decree, the monarch's apparent openness to having Spanish women marry indigenous men is again largely a rhetorical gesture since, at the time, Spanish women in the Americas represented only about 5–6 % of the Spanish population.[48]

By the 17th century, many of the decrees and instructions discussed thus far were codified into laws that were intended to apply uniformly across Spanish America. The edicts from 1514 and 1515, for instance, are acknowledged as key sources for Law 2, Title 1, Book 6 of the *Recopilación de Leyes para las Indias* (1680). The law states the following:

> Es nuestra voluntad, que los Indios, e Indias tengan, como deben, entera libertad para casarse con quien quisieren, así con Indios, como con naturales de estos Reynos, o Españoles, nacidos en las Indias, y que en esto no se les ponga impedimento. Y mandamos que ninguna orden nuestra, que se hubiere dado, o por nos fuere dada, pueda impedir, ni impida, el matrimonio entre los Indios, e Indias con Españoles, o Españolas, y que todos tengan entera libertad de casarse con quien quisieren, y nuestras Audiencias procure que así se guarde, y cumpla.[49]

Here, the right of Indians to marry whomever they choose is stressed from the beginning, and this issue frames the entire legal narrative in ways that closely emulate what we find in the 1515 edict. Notably, the law also specifies that the indigenous are free to marry both Spaniards and "Españoles, nacidos en las Indias," which points to a further classificatory distinction between peninsular Spaniards and descendants of Spaniards who were born in the Americas (also known as *criollos*).[50] The law, however, fails to mention the reasons why these marriages were viewed as politically expedient, including by avoiding any mention of the way in which they are instrumentalized in the 1514 decree to ensure population growth and the stability of long-term colonial settlements. The law also conveys the sense that marriages between indigenous men and Spanish women, as well as between Spanish men and indigenous women, were widely accepted.[51] The law's central narrative thus disseminates an ideological claim that presents the nascent Spanish colonial state as openly encouraging Spanish-indigenous unions. Yet, in addition to failing to accurately reflect the original edicts from which the law was compiled, the law also conceals the fact that, as part of the gradual transition toward the two-republic model, Spanish-indigenous unions were actively discouraged by other means, even if they were never officially prohibited.[52]

Another important issue to consider is that royal legislation consistently sought to promote marriages among enslaved Africans and to regulate and deter reproductive unions with other groups. One of the main laws from the *Recopilación* that comments on the topic of marriage between black slaves is Law 5, Title 5, of Book 7, which begins by stating the following: "Procurese en lo posible, que habiendo de casarse los Negros, sea el matrimonio con Negras."[53] Here, the enslaved status of the people in question is not explicitly mentioned, but, as the following clause clarifies, the racial ascription *negro/a* is associated with slavery: "Y declaramos que estos, y los demas que fueren esclavos, no quedan libres por haberse casado, aunque intervenga para esto la voluntad de sus amos."[54] The main purpose of the law is to emphasize that black slaves who marry are not therefore free, but, notably, as included in the *Recopilación,* Law 5 actually leaves out an important aspect that is mentioned in one of the decrees on which the law is based and which provides important context.

In the edict from 1541 on which Law 5 is based, King Charles V begins by noting that black slaves in the province of Peru have many indigenous women. He also states that this is causing harm to the natives, and he stipulates that the situation should be remedied by requiring black men to marry black women:

> A nos se nos ha hecho relación que los negros esclavos que en esa provincia residen, tienen diversidad de mujeres indias, algunas de su voluntad y otras contra ella, lo cual diz que ha resultado y resulta mucho daño y prejuicio a los naturales desa tierra, y que para lo remediar, convernía que se mandase que los negros esclavos que en esa provincia hubiese, se casasen con negras.[55]

As the passage indicates, the prescription for black slaves to marry among themselves is presented as a potential deterrence for the perceived problem of black men engaging in reproductive relations with Indian women. In this sense, we see that the endorsement of endogamous marriages among blacks is at least partly correlated with the increasing problematization of Afro–indigenous reproductive relations. This again calls attention to the way in which ongoing processes of socio-racial differentiation were being articulated in legislation that aimed to regulate procreative sex between differently construed groups of people.

In terms of relations between enslaved Africans and Spaniards, there are limited legal discourses that comment on the topic. Law 6, Title 5, of Book 7 from the *Recopilación* is among the few that comment on this issue, and, as the heading for the law suggests, it specifically focuses on what to do with the children of Spanish men and enslaved black women (or "hijos de españoles y negras"). The brief document is based on a single decree from 1563, and it simply states that some Spanish men have fathered children with slave women and wish to buy them in order to free them: "Algunos españoles tienen hijos en esclavas, y voluntad de comprarlos, para darles libertad: Mandamos que habiéndose de venderse prefieran los padres, que los quisieren comprar, para este efecto."[56] Notably, the law openly acknowledges that reproductive unions between Spanish men and enslaved black women were taking place, but it offers no indication of how the Crown viewed these relations other than the fact that this did not affect the status of the children given the Roman legal principle of *partus sequitur ventrem,* which established that the legal status of enslaved children followed that of their mothers.[57] Indeed, in contrast to the 1541 decree analyzed above, there is no overt problematization of these relations precisely because it did not affect the reproduction of the enslaved population other than by giving priority to Spanish men who chose to free their own children. The law again foregrounds the way in which Spanish legislation began to account for reproductive relations between differently racialized people, and it brings into focus the way in which socio-racial classification influenced the way in which these relations were regulated.

In contrast to the paucity of sources that comment on unions between *españoles/as* and *negras/os*, the legislation that aimed to regulate reproductive relations between *negros/as* and *indios/as* is ample, and tends to focus on two key themes: forcefully discouraging these unions, and addressing the implications these relations had for the payment of tribute. These issues can be illustrated by considering three laws from the *Recopilación* that comment on these topics. First, the forceful discouragement of these relations is clearly evinced in Law 7, Title 5, Book 7. The law begins by prohibiting black men and women, both free and enslaved, from "using" Indian men and women. The wording of the law is highly ambiguous, and there is little explanation of what this idea of "using" *indios/as* means since the law simply prohibits "que se sirvan los Negros, y Negras... de Indios o Indias." The only elaboration on this point is framed in relation to perceived sexual transgressions. Specifically, the law states that many black men "use" indigenous women as their concubines (or *mancebas*), and it states that they oppress these women and treat them badly. The law goes on to specify that enslaved blacks who "use" Indian women should be punished by one hundred public lashes for the first offense, and by cutting off their ears for the second offense. It also stipulates that free blacks who go against this prohibition should be punished by one hundred lashes the first time, and by banishment the second time. The entire law is framed by a paternalistic rhetoric that purports to act in the interest of protecting the indigenous population in general and Indian women in particular, and it explicitly represents black men and women as delinquents in discourses that are largely about sexuality.[58]

It is also important to note that, although Law 7 acknowledges only two edicts as its sources—one from November 14, 1551, and one June 14, 1589— it is also remarkably similar in content to a third decree November 19, 1551 that goes unmentioned. In the latter decree, King Philip II begins by stating that there are many black slaves in the city of Lima ("mucha copia de ellos"), and he overtly bans them from carrying arms, whether they are enslaved or not.[59] He also goes on to declare that:

> vista la desorden que en esta ciudad y sus términos ha habido y hay en los negros y negras, así libres como esclavos de servirse de indios e indias muy sueltamente, y aun muchos dellos las tienen de mancebas y las tratan mal y tienen opresas. Y para remediar lo susodicho, ordenaron y mandaron que de aquí adelante, ningún negro ni negra, de cualquier calidad y condición que sea, sea osado de tener ni servirse de indio ni de india en esta ciudad ni sus términos, so pena al negro que fuere hallado tener india y servirse della, le sea cortada su natura, y si se sirviera de indio, le sean dados cien azotes públicamente, y si fuere negro esclavo, por primera vez le sean dados cien azotes, y por la segunda cortada las orejas, y si fuere libre, por la primera vez le sean dados cien azotes y por la segunda, destierro perpetuo de estos reinos.[60]

As evinced by the passage, the similarity in content between what is stated here and what we find in Law 7 is striking. In this case, though, the prescribed punishment for black men who "use" Indian women as concubines is castration. This foregrounds the way in which state-sanctioned brutalization of black men's bodies was ideologically justified in the name of "protecting" indigenous women, and it shows the extent to which violence was condoned in order to forcefully deter reproductive unions between black men and indigenous women. Though none of these juridical discourses directly address the fact that reproductive relations between black men and indigenous women led to the freedom of enslavement for the children born of these unions because of free womb laws, this issue seems to be at the core of these forceful prohibitions. Indeed, as Herman Bennet explains, in colonial Mexico, there was already a sizable free population of Afro–indigenous descendants by the end of the 17th century.[61] The increasing violence justified by these laws seems to reflect a growing awareness and concern about this fact.

Regarding the question of tribute, Law 8, Title 5, of Book 6 and Law 2, Title 5, of Book 7 stipulate that the children of black men and indigenous women should pay tribute as *indios*. Law 8 declares: "Que los hijos de Negros, e Indias habidos en matrimonio, tributen como Indios." Similarly, Law 2 states: "Hase dudado si los hijos de Negros libres, o esclavos, habidos en matrimonio con Indias, son exentos de pagar el tributo personal, sin embargo de que alegan, que no son Indios, y ha parecido, que estos son obligados a tributar como los Indios, y que las Audiencias provean, que asi se haga." Both laws are based on different edicts from 1572 and 1573, and, in each case, the emphasis is on the children born of marriages between blacks and Indians. This suggests that these marriages were not uncommon since Spanish legislation was casuist, meaning that it was issued to address particular issues, not abstract problems.[62] It is also noteworthy that the mixed-ancestry children that are born of these marriages are not given a different socio-racial label, but rather instructed to pay tribute as if they were *indios*. This is significant considering that, by the second half of the 16th century, terms like *zambiago* and *mulato* were already commonly used to describe people of Afro–indigenous descent,[63] but, by avoiding making a nominal distinction, both laws further confirm the sense that these individuals were to be legally considered *indios*. This points to the fluidity and inconsistent use of socio-racial categories, and it evinces the tactical use of these labels in some contexts but not in others depending on what was most beneficial for the colonial state. In this case, since the children of indigenous women and black men were legally free, their payment of tribute as *indios* was economically advantageous.

As this initial analysis shows, the regulation of marriage and reproductive relations between differently construed groups of people is a prevalent topic in Spanish legislation about its American colonies. Not only is sex politicized by the Spanish monarchy and nascent colonial state, but it was also precisely through the act of legislating reproductive relations between different groups that we see the emergence and consolidation of distinct socio-racial categories. While labels like *español*, *indio*, and *negro* begin to be consistently used in this legislation—marking a distinction between these emerging socio-racial categories in terms of sexual relations that were deemed lawful or unlawful— mixed-ancestry labels were still used inconsistently. It is only in legislation about indigenous segregation that we begin to see a more consistent use of mixed-ancestry labels as colonial authorities were forced to deal with the reproductive effects of sexual relations between differently racialized groups. Indeed, as Robert Schwaller argues, the issue of intermarriage—and, I would add reproductive sex more broadly—cannot be separated from the rise of the two-republic system. To fully understand how processes of racialization developed in Spanish America it is necessary to turn now to a consideration of how the codification of segregation influenced this process.[64]

The Justification and Regulation of Indigenous Segregation

The codification of segregation in Spanish America can be traced by considering a series of laws that are compiled in Books Six and Seven of the *Recopilación de Leyes para las Indias* (1680). The *Recopilación* summarizes almost two centuries of legislation in 6,400 laws—which are a compilation of some 400,000 royal provisions and decrees— and it provides key insight into the rationalization of Spanish imperial ideology.[65] The project was first approved by the Consejo de Indias in 1624, and it was completed by historian Antonio de León Pinedo with the contribution of jurist Juan de Solórzano y Pereira. [66] Although the *Recopilación* does not include a section specifically devoted to the topic of segregation, there are 42 laws dispersed across five titles from Book Six and one title from Book Seven that can be thematically grouped and analyzed as a means to better understand the gradual transition toward the segregationist dual republic model and its multiple implications.[67] Here, I focus specifically on laws that comment on two key sets of themes: the justification for indigenous segregation and the regulation of people's movement based on racial ascription. In this section, I discuss the way in which indigenous life is politicized through segregationist laws, I argue that this contributed to the consolidation of the socio-racial label *indio/a* as a meaningful category of identity, and I show that the ascription of this label had concrete implications for how *indios/as* could circulate within the dual republic system.

One of the most striking aspects of the way in which the project of indigenous segregation is justified in juridical discourses is that it evinces a clear biopolitical aim to foster the growth of a homogeneously construed population group. This justification is overtly expressed in two laws from the *Recopilación* that reference a number of decrees ranging from 1538 to 1578, and it again calls attention to the importance of this period for tracing critical transformations in the power over life or what Foucault theorizes as biopower. Chronologically, Law 19, Title 1, of Book 6, is the earliest law that offers an explicit justification for segregation since it is based on a single royal decree from 1538. The law, as included in the *Recopilación*, states the following:

> Para que los indios aprovechen más en Christiandad, y policía, se debe ordenar, que vivan juntos, y concertadamente, pues de esta forma los conocerán sus Prelados y atenderán mejor a su bien y doctrina. Y porque así convienen mandamos que los Virreyes y Gobernadores lo procuren por todos los medios posibles, sin hacerles opresión y dándoles a entender quan útil, y provechoso será para su aumento, y buen gobierno, como está ordenado.[68]

As in the original decree on which the law is based, the justification for spatially gathering *indios* is premised on the claim that spatial concentration will help facilitate the Crown's twin goals of Christianizing and civilizing this group of people, which is homogeneously represented as an identifiable population. The exhortation to carry out the measure by any means possible further conveys a sense of urgency—which is also present in the 1538 decree— and the clause stating that authorities should not oppress the indigenous in the process discloses the ideological and paternalistic character of the law. As noted in the previous chapter, Vasco de Quiroga insisted that the indigenous would not object to their relocation given their "docile nature" and, in this case, the law likewise assumes that the natives will be persuaded to relocate, or coerced if need be.

It is also notable that Law 19 instructs colonial authorities to persuade the natives to relocate voluntarily by pointing out that the policy will be beneficial to the latter's demographic growth: "provechoso será para su aumento."[69] Here, population growth is made the object of juridico-political reflection and intervention, and, more specifically, indigenous lives are politicized as a distinct population group. The law also appeals to the indigenous directly to quite literally help "save" themselves through a policy that is presented as critical for their self-preservation. The entire formulation is based on a series of unstated assumptions about how spatial concentration will help foster reproductive sexual relations among indigenous groups, but, again, these various groups are depicted as a single, homogeneous population. Another noteworthy aspect of this law is this emphasis on indigenous demographic growth is not actually present in the original decree from 1538. In fact, the issue is not even mentioned in that document.[70] The inclusion of this topic in the law calls attention to important alterations that happened in the process of compilation, and it is indicative of the fact that the *Recopilación'* compilers had an important role in shaping legislative narrative.

A second law that calls for indigenous segregation is Law 1, Title 3, of Book 6, which is based on a series of royal edicts and instructions from 1551, 1560, 1565, 1568, 1573, and 1578. The law begins by explaining that in 1546 members of the Council of the Indies and other religious authorities met to discuss how to best Christianize and civilize the indigenous. It also specifies that said authorities determined that the natives should be systematically concentrated in communities in order to achieve that objective: "resolvieron que los Indios fueses reducidos a Pueblos, y no viviesen divididos, y separados por las sierras, y montes, privándose de todo beneficio espiritual, y temporal."[71] Both Vasco de Quiroga and Bartolomé de las Casas were part of the junta that reached this conclusion, and, in the following decade, the policy of indigenous *reducción* became officially institutionalized throughout Spanish America.[72] Like Law 19, Law 1 also instructs authorities to carry out relocation campaigns in a gentle and kind way so as to avoid inconveniences. Authorities are also instructed to persuade the natives to relocate voluntarily in order to persuade others to willingly follow.[73] In contrast to Law 19, Law 1 says nothing about how the efforts to spatially concentrate the indigenous were viewed by authorities as a means to foster indigenous population growth—including by figures like Quiroga—but, in this case, this is actually a conspicuous omission that becomes clear when we examine two of the main sources on which the law is based.

Out of the six royal edicts and instructions that are acknowledged as sources for Law 1, both the royal provision from 1551 and the royal decree from 1565 explicitly state that indigenous relocation campaigns are necessary to promote the demographic growth of a homogeneously construed population group. In the royal provision from 1551, King Charles V highlights the convenience of gathering the natives in separate, well-ordered towns, and he explicitly states that one of the benefits of doing so is that it will contribute to indigenous population growth: "mandamos ...[se] hiciesen juntar en uno o más pueblos donde pudiesen vivir y multiplicar, y ser industriados en las cosas de nuestra santa Fe Católica."[74] In this case, the King's emphasis on promoting "indigenous multiplication" discloses the euphemistic and religiously-based way in which the sovereign endorses reproductive sex among indigenous groups.[75] The phrasing also calls attention to the quantifying logic that informs the way in which life is politicized by the King, and this logic is reiterated when he again stresses the need to foster the demographic multiplication of the natives: "para que mejor puedan multiplicar."[76] As these passages indicate, the management of sex is presented as a legitimate area of intervention on the basis that its procreative effects are of concern to the colonial state apparatus. We thus that the administration of life at the level of collectivities becomes progressively tied to the project of indigenous relocation, and that, as part of this, reproductive sex becomes increasingly politicized.

The royal decree from 1565 likewise emphasizes the need to promote indigenous population growth by having the natives gathered in towns, but again, this issue is omitted in Law 1. By then, King Phillip II was in power, but the fact that his decree reiterates this point evinces the continuation of a consistently articulated policy. The text begins by stating that the monarch was informed that in the provinces of Peru colonial authorities were not following royal orders to spatially gather the natives in separate towns:

> A nos se ha hecho relación que en esa tierra no hay el cuidado que conviene en mandar guardar lo que nos está ordenado y mandado sobre que los indios naturales desa tierra se recojan a vivir en pueblos y han buena policía y orden.[77]

At the time, Francisco de Toledo was not yet viceroy of Peru, and the situation that the King is asking authorities to address foreshadows some of the dramatic changes that would happen under Toledo's leadership. Indeed, once Toledo was in power, his sweeping reforms included a massive relocation campaign in 1569 that resettled more than a million indigenous subjects into *reducciones* and the inauguration of a walled indigenous neighborhood in Lima in 1571.[78]

In the 1565 decree, the monarch goes on to state that the lack of efforts to spatially concentrate the indigenous is causing many inconveniences. He also affirms that, as his audience should know, the measure is necessary for indigenous demographic growth: "es cosa muy conveniente y necesaria para el aumento de los dichos indios."[79] The passage allows us to trace how indigenous life continued to be politicized through spatial politics, and it again foregrounds the way in which implicit and euphemistic references to sex were a consistent feature of early segregationist efforts. The fact that Law 1 does not even mention the topic of indigenous population growth in relation to concentration efforts is thus not representative of what we actually find in two of the sources from which the law was compiled. Moreover, the fact that this issue *is* mentioned in Law 19—even though the decree on which that law is based does not reference the topic—is highly suggestive of the type of narrative license afforded to the compilers in the process of creating the *Recopilación*.

These different juridical discourses allow us to recognize that the politicization of indigenous lives as a homogeneously construed population group is one of the key features to understand the justification for segregation in Spanish America. The explicit will to conserve and foster the demographic growth of the indigenous population that is evident in these discourses is also illustrative of what Daniel Nemser describes as biopolitics of care—which, for him, typifies a crucial aspect of Spanish colonial governance—and which again calls attention to the ways in which the power over life was being reconfigured in the colonies.[80] This analysis, however, would be incomplete if we did not also consider the progressive emphasis that we see in segregationist laws regulating the spatial mobility of *indios/as*, particularly after the initial phase of resettlement.

One of the earliest laws that addresses the topic of indigenous movement is Law 12, Title 1, of Book 6, which is based on a single decree from 1536. Notably, the law begins by affirming that *indios* should be allowed to move from one place to another based on their own free will. This affirmation, however, is immediately undermined by a qualifying clause that states: "excepto donde por las Reducciones, que por nuestro mandato estuvieren hechas, se hay dispuesto lo contrario, y no fueren perjudicados los Encomenderos."[81] Here, the law explicitly impinges upon the ability of indigenous subjects to move after being resettled into *reducciones*, but the restriction of their mobility is still presented as an exception. This foregrounds the fact that the project of indigenous segregation was still in the early phases of implementation, but it nevertheless calls attention to the way in which the regulation of movement based on racial ascription was beginning to be legislated. The reference to both *reducciones* and *encomenderos*, moreover, reflects the overlap of these systems, which characterized the transition toward the two-republic model.

Over the next few decades, we find a legislative gap on the topic of indigenous mobility, but by the late 16th century, this issue again begins to
be addressed and becomes particularly prominent in laws based on sources
from the early 17th century. Two laws based on sources from the late 16th
century that comment on the topic focus specifically on the perceived
problem of *indios* "becoming separated" from their caciques. Both laws
emphasize that indigenous subjects should remain in their initial places of
resettlement, under the jurisdiction of their respective caciques, and they
specify that indigenous authorities should work to re-incorporate individuals who have moved away without aggravating them. As Law 7, Title 7, of
Book 6 states:

> En algunas partes de las Indias se han separado muchos Indios de sus
> Caciques, y no conviene permitirlo: Ordenamos que todas las veces que
> vacaren, se vuelvan a incorporar al gobierno y jurisdicción del Cazi-
> cazgo natural, cuyos eran, y que a sus caciques y principales no se las
> haga agravio con estas separaciones como está ordenando respeto a las
> reducciones.[82]

These instructions are again reiterated by Law 28, Title 8, of Book 6.[83]
Each of these laws thus calls attention to the way in which the circulation
of indigenous subjects continued to be monitored in order to ensure that
they remained in their places of resettlement, and it brings into focus the
fact that the control of racialized bodies in space was viewed as a critical
component of segregationist projects.[84]

In the early 17th century, the emphasis on preventing *indios* from leaving
their *reducciones* is again stressed in two additional laws. Law 19, Title 3,
of Book 6, begins by underscoring the importance of preventing indigenous
subjects from leaving the towns where they had been resettled:

> Considerando quanto importa que los Indios reducidos no se vayan a
> vivir fuera de los Lugares de su Reducción: Ordenamos y mandamos
> a los Gobernadores, Jueces y Justicias de cada provincia, que no den
> estas licencias si no fuere en algún caso raro, como a Indio huérfano.[85]

The law is based on a single decree from 1604, and, as the expression
"indios reducidos" suggests, it addresses the aftermath of indigenous resettlement campaigns. Indeed, the law assumes that indigenous groups have
already been resettled, but the regulation of their spatial mobility is presented as an ongoing concern. As a corrective to the perceived problem,
the law commands colonial authorities to prevent indigenous subjects from
living outside of their segregated communities, and it goes on to specify
a series of penalties for anyone found contravening the law. Additionally,
Law 18, Title 3, of Book 6, stipulates that *indios* should not be allowed to
move from one *reducción* or *pueblo de indio* to another: "Mandamos que

en ningún Pueblo de Indios haya alguno que sea de otra Reduccion, pena de veine azotes, y el Cacique de quatro pesos para la Iglesia, cada vez que lo consintiere."[86] Here, corporal punishment is sanctioned as a way to deter individuals from moving even from one Indian community to another. The role of indigenous caciques in monitoring the movement of their subjects is also stressed by the law, which calls attention to the way in which indigenous authorities were directly compelled to help enforce segregation. What we find in both laws, then, is a consistent policy that aimed to prevent the free circulation of indigenous subjects after the initial period of resettlement. This evinces a growing regimentation of space, and it suggests that the regulation of peoples' movement based on racial ascription only increased as a result of the institutionalization of the dual republic model in the mid-16th century.

Another noteworthy aspect of this legislation is that it becomes progressively focused on trying to prevent indigenous women from residing outside of Indian towns. There are three laws in the *Recopilación* that address this issue—all based on a single source from 1618—and they help bring into focus the fact that gender considerations were a crucial component in the conceptualization and enforcement of segregation. Law 6, Title 17, of Book 6, begins by stating that the greatest harm to *reducciones* comes from people who remove natives from these communities to serve as laborers in commercial activities linked to the circulation of goods. In this case, the reason why "indios reducidos" are leaving their communities is explicitly addressed, and it is tied to the ongoing reliance on their labor. What is particularly notable, though, is that the law shifts from a general condemnation of this action to a specific stipulation about how indigenous women should not be removed unless they are accompanied by their husbands: "Mandamos que ninguna persona, de qualquier estado, y condición que sea, en ningún caso pueda sacar India, si no fuese con su marido, y que ningún indio salga de su Provincia, por urgente causa que se ofrezca."[87] As the passage indicates, the legal prohibition concerns single indigenous women specifically, since the "removal" of married women is presented as a permissible exemption. The law itself does not provide any context to understand the reason for this specific prohibition—aside from the initial assertion that the removal of indigenous subjects from their *reducciones* is the greatest harm to the continuation of the segregationist system—but the single source on which the law is based provides important insight in this regard.

The acknowledged source for Law 6 is a document from October 10, 1618, in which King Philip III formally approved a series of ordinances proposed by the judge Francisco de Alfaro. As Magnus Mörner explains in his analysis of the policy of indigenous residential segregation, the so-called Ordenanzas de Alfaro were meant to extend this policy to more peripheral areas, and, as such, they represent a critical moment to understand the development of the two-republic system.[88] Though much of the 1618 document is primarily a reiteration of points made by Alfaro, in the opening lines the King offers some additional commentary that helps contextualize the explicit emphasis that we see in Law 6 on the regulation of indigenous women's mobility in particular. Specifically, the sovereign states that he has been informed that indigenous subjects are being abused—including by men who "use" indigenous women and prevent them from marrying—and he declares that this has led to their demographic decline: "por lo cual han venido en notable disminución."[89] The explicit prohibition against removing single indigenous women from *reducciones* that we find in Law 6 can thus be read as an extension of earlier arguments that justified segregation by pointing out that the policy was necessary to ensure the demographic growth of the indigenous population. In this case, though, the law also calls attention to the way in which women's reproductive capacity was implicitly politicized to ensure that future child bearers remained in segregated communities, and could thus contribute to the reproduction of a racially qualified population. In other words, the law brings into focus the fact that the politicization of indigenous life at the level of collectivities affected women differently than men, partly because, as Silvia Federici argues, once population growth became an area of intervention for state power, women's reproductive capacity was more closely regulated.[90]

Law 14, Title 13, of Book 6 likewise prohibits indigenous women from residing outside of Indian towns. In this case, married indigenous women are proscribed from serving as laborers in Spanish households unless their husbands serve in the same house: "Ninguna India casada pueda concertarse para servir en casa de Español, ni a esto sea apremiada, si no sirviere su marido en la misma casa, ni tampoco las solteras, queriéndose estar, y residir en sus Pueblos."[91] Like Law 6, Law 14 tacitly acknowledges the ongoing reliance on indigenous labor power, which points to the economic system that structured the two republics as interdependent. Both laws, moreover, reiterate the importance of physically segregating indigenous groups in their *reducciones*, while at the same time sanctioning exceptions for married women. The exceptions for married women in turn call attention to the underlying patriarchal assumptions of the laws, including the fact that married women were assumed to be better "protected" under the tutelage of their husbands. This issue suggests that the project of indigenous segregation was not merely about spatial separation but also about trying to regulate reproductive sex between differently racialized people. Indeed, the exemption to allow married indigenous women to work outside of their *reducciones* is consistent with the policy of trying to promote indigenous demographic growth through endogamous sex. The working assumption is that indigenous women would be, at least in principle, less likely to reproduce with someone other than their indigenous husbands. In this sense, both laws can be interpreted as trying to discourage sex between differently racialized people by, on the one hand, emphasizing the ongoing need to maintain single indigenous women in their *reducciones*, and, on the other, by only allowing married ones to temporarily leave or reside outside of those communities when accompanied by their husbands.

The final law that comments on indigenous women's mobility is Law 13, from Title 17, of Book 6. It states:

> Habiéndose reconocido por experiencia graves inconvenientes de sacar Indias de los Pueblos, para que sean amas de leche: Mandamos que ninguna India, que tenga su hijo vivo, pueda salir a criar hijo de Español, especialmente de su Encomendero, pena de perdimiento de la encomienda.[92]

Here, the prohibition is specifically against removing indigenous women to serve as wetnurses for the children of Spaniards. The reliance on this embodied female form of labor is again tacitly acknowledged, but in this case, the law proscribes this action without exception. The document also singles-out *encomenderos* as potential violators of the law, and it specifies no less than the loss of their *encomienda* for going against the order. Like other laws, Law 13 was intended to address a concrete problem that had already been denounced in the late 16th century by two *mestizo* activists from the New Kingdom Granada who complained that *encomenderos* used indigenous women as wetnurses and forced them to leave their own infants without maternal care.[93] The law, however, can also be read as reflecting much broader discourses about breastmilk that are critical to understand how consolidating notions of racial difference were articulated in relation to women.

In 15th-century Spain, breastmilk was regularly invoked in discussions over purity of blood because both fluids were considered one and the same substance.[94] Like blood, maternal milk was thought to transmit the behavioral and moral characteristics of the lactating woman, and, in the context of heightened anxieties about blood purity, there were growing concerns about how "impure" wetnurses—typically associated with women of Jewish, Muslim, or *converso* backgrounds—could contaminate Old Christian children.[95] In the context of the Americas, influential figures like the Spanish missionary José de Acosta also argued that indigenous breastmilk could lead to corporeal corruption and heresy.[96] Similarly, Fray Reginaldo de Lizárraga emphasized the perceived "dangers" of having indigenous and black women as wetnurses for *criollo* children. Writing in the early 17th century, Lizárraga's comments:

> When the poor child is born, he is handed over to a dirty, lying Indian or a black woman, who nurses him.... How will this boy turn out? He will get his inclinations from the milk he drank...He who drinks a liar's milk is a liar, he who drinks a drunkard's milk is a drunkard, he who drinks a thief's milk is a thief, etc.[97]

The passage not only discloses a series of highly negative stereotypes about Indian and black women that illustrate the way that they were racially differentiated from Spaniards and their *criollo* descendants. It also emotively decries using them as wetnurses by explicitly stating that their breastmilk can transmit their perceived moral failings. The emphasis on proscribing the removal of indigenous women to serve as wetnurses that we see in Law 13 can thus be seen as reflecting these broader discourses that linked racial impurity specifically to women. All of this points to additional gender dimensions that are critical to understand the development of segregationist policies, and it calls attention to the way in which gender considerations intersect with consolidating ideas about racial difference.

The justification and regulation of indigenous segregation that we find in the series of laws analyzed above offer incisive insight into the process of racialization that led to the consolidation of the term *indio/a* as a distinct marker of socio-racial identity. Not only were indigenous lives politicized through a biopolitics of care that was quite literally aimed at "making live" a segment of the population that was racialized as different, but, in the process, Indian women's reproductive capacities became more closely regulated. All of this had profound implications for the way in which spatial mobility was legislated based on racial ascription and gender considerations, and it helps illustrate how, in the process of trying to demarcate the spatial boundaries between the Indian and Spanish Republics, reproductive sexuality became critical to that demarcation. As Abdul JanMohamed argues, "the racial border...is in fact always a sexual border,"[98] and the laws analyzed in this section help illustrate this point. What remains to be seen is how processes of mestizaje are accounted for in segregationist laws, and what this suggests about the way in which the boundaries between the Spanish and Indian republics were instituted and enforced even as they were paradoxically marked as already breached.

The Account of Mestizaje in Segregationist Laws

> To map the racial borders, the borders must be crossed.
>
> Robert Bernasconi[99]

Another noteworthy aspect that characterizes the way in which the topic of indigenous segregation is codified is the emphasis that segregationist laws place on the growing number of *mestizos/as* and other mixed-ancestry groups. The progressive emphasis on regulating the movement of these groups allows us to trace the development and consolidation of mixed-ancestry categories in legal discourses, and it calls attention to the fact that processes of mestizaje were directly accounted for from the moment that segregationist measures were introduced. An analysis of this body of legislation also helps illustrates the fact that processes of mestizaje did little to undermine segregationist efforts, and it foregrounds the way in which emerging ideas about racial mixture helped shape processes of racialization in Spanish America. In this final section, I begin by analyzing the gradual way in which the term *mestizo* is used in segregationist laws, and I argue that, by the late 16th century, that label had consolidated as a distinct marker of socio-racial identity. I also consider the way in which segregationist legislation sought to regulate the movement of *mestizos, mulatos,* and *zambaigos,* and I argue that increasingly negative views about mestizaje shaped this trajectory. I conclude by offering a brief analysis of a series of archival cases from colonial Mexico that illustrate the way in which segregation was supported by indigenous agents, and I contend that is indicative of the way in which segregationist laws were actively invoked and used to enforce spatial separation based on racial ascription.

The use of the term *mestizo/a* in segregationist laws can be traced by considering a series of royal edicts that are acknowledged as sources for Law 4, Title 4, Book 7 of the *Recopilación.* Law 4 is particularly significant because it simultaneously calls for indigenous segregation and lays out a strategy for how to integrate, into the Republic of Spaniards, an ambiguously construed group of people who are variously represented as "hijos o hijas de españoles que anden perdidos," "huérfanos," "desamparados," and *mestizos/as.* In the first part of the law, authorities are urged to segregate *indios* into separate communities, but, unlike the laws analyzed in the previous section, in this case, the measure is justified by appealing to a discourse about the perceived problems of vagrancy. In the opening lines, vagrancy is presented as a widespread problem that affects Spaniards, mestizos, and Indians alike, and vagrants are associated with idleness and disorder while economic productivity is linked to spatial rootedness. In order to address the perceived problem, authorities are instructed to gather all vagrants in towns, but with the important stipulation that the indigenous should be gathered in separate towns: "De los Españoles, Mestizos, e Indios, que viven vagabundos, y, holgazanes sin asiento, oficio, ni otra buena ocupación, procuren los Virreyes, y Presidentes formar algunos Pueblos, y que los de Indios estén separados."[100] Here, the terminological distinction that is made between *españoles, mestizos,* and *indios* works to highlight a difference between these groups even though they are all likened on the basis of their common socio-economic condition as vagrants. This distinction, moreover, singles-out indigenous vagrants as a distinct and identifiable population group, and, on the basis of this differentiation, segregation is prescribed. Notably, moreover, this distinction is articulated not only in relation to Spaniards but also in relation to *mestizos,* which works to racially differentiate *indios* from both.

In the second part of Law 4, the focus shifts significantly, as the law moves to specify a series of prescriptive measures that can be described as a strategy for *mestizo/a* integration. The law states that authorities need to gather information about this broadly construed segment of the population—who, as noted above, are variously described as "Mestizos/as" "hijos o hijas de españoles que anden perdidos," "huérfanos," and "desamparados"— and it stipulates that these individuals should be "recogidos" and placed in Spanish institutions like "colegios de varones" and "casas recogidas."[101] In other words, the proposed solution is to gather them in Spanish institutions, according to their gender, and thus to integrate them into the Republic of Spaniards. The law, in this sense, reflects the policy of mestizo *recogimiento* that, as Daniel Nemser and Kathryn Burns show, can be traced by considering the foundation of institutions like the Colegio de San Juan Letrán and the Convento de Santa Clara in Mexico and Peru respectively.[102]

In the case of the Colegio, the institution was founded in 1547 in what is today Mexico City, and it was described as a school for "for boys of mixed blood," and, more specifically, as a school for "orphans born of Spanish men and Indian women."[103] As Nemser explains, the institution was intended to spatially concentrate *mestizos* in order to discipline and integrate them into the Republic of Spaniards. It also sought to turn these individuals into productive members of colonial society by training them as missionaries who could aid in the project of indigenous religious conversion.[104] The project was partly premised on the assumption that *mestizos'* knowledge of indigenous languages would be beneficial for the conversion efforts, but, by the end of the 16th century, it was largely abandoned. By then, as Nemser shows, *mestizos* were increasingly viewed with suspicion, and their ordination to the priesthood had been officially prohibited.[105] Nemser's detailed account of Colegio's history also establishes the way in which the term mestizo "emerges as a racial category in its own right,"[106] and it emphasizes the socially constructed nature of that identity through material spatial practices.

In the case of the Convento de Santa Clara, which was founded in 1551 in Cuzco Peru, Burns shows that the institution was initially created to help "collect" and "protect" the daughters of Spanish *encomenderos* and indigenous women.[107] She further argues that Santa Clara was indented to help "create culturally Spanish young women"[108] who had "the potential for reproducing Spanish dominance."[109] In this sense, Burns establishes that these women were not initially seen as different from Spaniards, but rather included in the Spanish Republic precisely to help ensure the reproduction of that population group. Burns also explains that some of the *mestizas* at Santa Clara had been forcefully taken away from their indigenous mothers because, as she puts it, some believed the *mestiza*'s indigenous mothers were "an impediment to instilling anything good in them."[110] Like Nemser's study, moreover, Burns shows that, by the 1560s, *mestizas* were hierarchically differentiated from Spanish women and increasingly differentiated from Spaniards in general.[111] Both studies thus offer an account of a spatial practice of concentration that was aimed at integrating *mestizos/as* into the Republic of Spaniards, but both also show that, while this group was initially closely associated with Spaniards, it was increasingly marked as racially different.

In light of this context, the representation of *mestizo/as* that we find in Law 4, Title 4, Book 7 becomes all the more meaningful. Indeed, the ambiguity with which *mestizos/as* are represented in the law is surprising given that the *Recopilación* was written after the category of *mestizo/as* had already solidified as a distinct marker of socio-racial identity. This representation, though, actually reflects what we find in the edicts on which the law is based, and, an analysis of these edicts helps further clarify the gradual process through which the term mestizo consolidated as a meaningful category of socio-racial identity. Law 4 is based on four royal edicts from 1533, 1555, 1558, and 1569, and, with the exception of the 1558 decree, all others focus exclusively on what to do about *mestizos/as,* even though that term is not consistently used. The fact that Law 4 articulates both the topic of indigenous segregation and the policy of mestizo *recogimiento* is thus a product of the process of compilation, which again calls attention to the need to scrutinize laws as included in the *Recopilación.* Nevertheless, what interests me here is the inconsistent way in which the term *mestizo/a* is used in three out of the four edits in which Law 4 is based.

In the earliest of these decrees, from 1533, King Charles V begins by stating that he has been informed of a growing number of individuals who he describes as "hijos de españoles que han habido en indias" and "hijos de españoles que hubieren habido en indias."[112] In both cases, the King foregrounds the children's Spanish ancestry, and, in each case, as Robert Schwaller suggests, the indigenous mothers are represented as mere vessels for bearing said children.[113] The monarch also tacitly acknowledges the prevalence of reproductive relations between Spanish men and indigenous women when he states that many children have been born of such unions ("hay mucha cantidad"). It is also noteworthy that the King emphasizes that these children are "lost among the Indians" and "outside of Spaniard's power," an action which he decries by adding that many of them die or a sacrificed as a result.[114] After describing this growing segment of the population, the sovereign goes on to stipulate what authorities should do, instructing them to gather and house them in specifically designated institutions within Christian towns under Spanish jurisdiction:

> Por ende yo vos mando que ésta recibáis, proveáis cómo los hijos de españoles que hubieren habido en indias y anduviesen fuera de su poder en esa tierra entre los indios della, se recojan y alberguen en esa dicha ciudad y en los otros pueblos de cristianos que os pareciere.[115]

The King's instructions thus evince the way in which the group of people who would later be distinguished as *mestizos/as* was initially targeted for integration into the Republic of Spaniards as the children of Spanish men whose connection to their indigenous mothers was, at best, minimized.

Similarly, in the 1555 decree, King Charles V again urges authorities to integrate *mestizos/as* into the Republic of Spaniards. The sovereign begins by noting that Spanish men have fathered many children, and he again describes these children as lost:

> A nos se ha hecho relación que en esas provincias hay muchos hijos
> e hijas de españoles que son muertos sus padres y ellos y ellas andan
> perdidos, idolatrando y cometiendo otros delitos y pecados, fornicios y
> adulterios, robos y muertes....[116]

Remarkably, in this case, the King does not even acknowledge the indigenous ancestry of these individuals when he refers to them exclusively as "hijos e hijas de españoles." He also elides the possibility that the children's fathers might have abandoned them by stating instead that the Spanish men who fathered them are dead. Here, then, in addition to the trope of how *mestizos* are "lost" among the Indians, the King also appeals to a trope about orphanhood based on the patriarchal notion that any child without a father—even if the mother was alive—was legally considered an orphan. These "lost" and arguably orphaned individuals are then presented as more susceptible to religious, moral, and legal transgressions—including idolatry, sexual permissiveness, and crime— and this in turn is used to justify the process of collecting them and integrating them into the Republic of Spaniards:

> convernía que se mandase que vosotros hiciesedes regoger a los tales
> hijos e hijas de españoles en pueblos, apartándolos de la mala vida que
> traen y poniendo...en algún recogimiento o colegio a los varones en
> una parte y a las hembras en otra, donde fuesen enseñados en la doct-
> rina cristiana y ley evagelica.[117]

As earlier, the King continues to represent these individuals as the children of Spaniards, with no indication of who the mothers are. Toward the end of the edict, however, he does use the term *mestizos* when he reiterates what should be done with this group of people:

> vos mando que veáis lo suso dicho y con mucha diligencia y cuidado
> os informéis y sepáis qué hijos e hijas de españoles y mestizos hay en
> esa tierra que ansi andan perdidos y los recojáis y proveais de tutores.

In this case, the terms "hijos e hijas de españoles" and *mestizos* are essentially equated and presented as interchangeable, which undermines his earlier attempt to depict these individuals simply as the children of Spaniards. In both the 1533 and 1555 decrees, we thus see an ambiguous and inconsistent representation of *mestizos/as* that suggests that the category itself was not yet stable, but rather undergoing the gradual process of transformation that would gradually lead to its consolidation as a meaningful category of socio-racial identity. The use of the term in these documents, moreover, is not meant to differentiate *mestizos/as* from Spaniards, but rather to associate them with this group precisely to justify their integration into the Republic of Spaniards.

In the third decree that is also acknowledged as a source of Law 4, we find a remarkably different characterization of *mestizos/as*. The edict, from 1569, was issued by Phillip II, and never in the text does the King use phrases like "children of Spaniards" to describe this group of people; instead, he exclusively uses the term *mestizos*. Unlike the two previous edicts analyzed above, moreover, the monarch no longer attempts to present *mestizos* as unambiguously linked to their Spanish ancestry, but rather he depicts them as a distinct socio-racial identity. He begins by noting that *mestizos* represent a large segment of the population who live loosely and idly: "Nos somos informados que en esa tierra ay muchos mestizos que viven muy sueltamente y no tienen oficios en que se ocupar."[118] The King also instructs authorities to collect more information about this group, and he stipulates that *mestizos* should be compelled to work by serving lords or learning useful trades.[119] The prior emphasis on gathering and housing *mestizos/as* in Spanish institutions is entirely absent in this edict, but, while there is a tacit assumption that this group has already been integrated into the Republic of Spaniards, there is also a clear emphasis on differentiating them from Spaniards. What the document reflects, then, is a much broader shift in the representation of *mestizos/as* that, as Nemser, Burns, and other scholars have pointed out, began to happen in the latter part of the 16th century as increasingly negative views about *mestizos* in particular, and mestizaje in general became more prevalent.[120]

The changing attitudes about *mestizos/as* and other mixed-ancestry groups can also be illustrated by considering how segregationist laws sought to regulate the circulation of these groups within the dual republic model. There are several laws in the *Recopilación* that address the issue, but, as Magnus Mörner suggests, Law 21, Title 3, Book 6, is a cornerstone to understand the codification of segregation in Spanish America.[121] The law is based on a series of decrees and instructions from 1563, 1578, 1581, 1589, 1600, and 1646, and it states the following:

> Prohibimos y defendemos, que en las Reducciones, y Pueblos de Indios puedan vivir, o vivan Españoles, Negros, Mulatos, o Mestizos, porque se ha experimentado, que algunos Españoles, que tratan, traginan, viven, y andan entre los Indios, son hombres inquietos, de mal vivir, ladrones, jugadores, viciosos, y por huir los Indios de ser agraviados, dexan sus Pueblos, y Provincias, y los Negros, Mestizos, y Mulatos, demás de tratarlos mal, se sirven de ellos, enseñan sus malas costumbres, y ociosidad, y también algunos errores, y vicios, que podrán estragar, y pervertir el fruto, que deseamos en orden a su salvación, aumento y quietud; y mandamos, que sean castigados con graves penas, y no consentidos en los Pueblos; y los Virreyes, Presidentes, Gobernadores, y Justicias tengan mucho cuidado de hacerlo executar donde por

> sus personas pudieren, o valiéndose de Ministros de toda integridad; y en quanto a los Mestizos, y Zambaygos, que son hijos de Indias, nacidos entre ellos, y han de heredar sus casas, y haciendas, porque parece cosa dura separarlos de sus padres, se podrá dispensar.[122]

Here, the law begins by categorically banning four main socio-racial groups from residing in "Indian towns." The distinction between these groups is terminological in the beginning, but as the document goes on it also provides different reasons for banning *españoles,* on the one hand, and *negros, mulatos*, and *mestizos* on the other. Remarkably, moreover, some *mestizos* and *zambaigos* are exempted from the general ban; specifically, those who were born in "Indian towns" and who are described here as "hijos de Indias." These different qualifications call attention to the way in which indigenous segregation was codified in relation to the demographic changes that we associate with mestizaje, and they foreground the fact that this legislation was adapted precisely to help address the growing number of mixed-ancestry groups whose ambivalent place between republics was viewed as warranting additional regulation.

To fully contextualize Law 21 and its implications it is also important to consider how it differs from its original sources, which span more than 80 years of legislation. The first thing to note in this regard is that the law does not entirely reflect the reasons why Spaniards are barred from residing in "Indian towns." In the law, Spaniards who continue to reside with and have contact and labor relations with the indigenous are disparagingly represented as "inquietos, de mal vivir, ladrones, jugadores, viciosos."[123] The law also states that the reason why *indios* are leaving their *reducciones* and *pueblos de indios* is to avoid being aggravated by this particular group of Spaniards. This justification reflects almost verbatim what we find in the edict from 1600 on which the law is based,[124] but it entirely elides other critical reasons that are included in two of the other sources that are also acknowledged in the law and that focus exclusively on the presence of Spaniards in Indian towns.

In the decree from 1563 that is listed as one of the sources for Law 21, King Philip II begins by stating that non-married vagrant Spaniards who live among the Indians are harming them in many ways, including by "taking" indigenous women by force ("tomándoles por fuerza sus mujeres e hijas").[125] In order to avoid this and other abuses—which the King describes as "molestias intolerables"—he goes on to stipulate that said Spaniards should be prevented from living in Indian towns: "que ninguno de los dichos vagamundos españoles no casados, no vivan ni estén entre los dichos indios ni en sus pueblos por ninguna manera, so graves penas."[126] As the passage indicates, the law focuses narrowly on single vagrant Spaniards, whose unregulated mobility is linked directly to ongoing forms of sexual violence against indigenous women. The insistence on spatial separation is thus justified as a form of paternalistic protection, but it also discloses the way in which the regulation of sexual relations between differently racialized people was factored in through the project of indigenous segregation. This topic, however, is entirely avoided in Law 21, again calling attention to the role of the *Recopilación*'s compilers in shaping legislative narrative. In the law, the reproductive effects of mestizaje are acknowledged and addressed through the particular provisions about mixed-ancestry groups, but what is remarkable about the 1563 decree is that it also offers a reflection on the causes of ongoing racial mixture: namely, the Spaniard's forceful relations with indigenous women.

There is also a third decree from 1581 mentioned in Law 21 that likewise addresses the need to bar Spaniards from living in "Indian towns." In this case, Spaniards who live among the Indians are described as causing unspecified damages that aggravate indigenous subjects, and they are portrayed as negative influences whose vices are then mimicked by the natives. The prohibition that we find in the edict, however, is not against all Spaniards, but rather, against Spaniards who provide a bad example: "se debría mandar que ningún español viviese entre los dichos indios, sino fuese de muy buen ejemplo."[127] Here, the rhetoric about Spaniard's bad example harkens back to Vasco de Quiroga's initial justification for indigenous segregation. It is also used to exempt some Spaniards "of a very good example" to reside in Indian towns. This stance—premised on the distinction between Spaniards of good and bad examples—points to an important inconsistency in terms of how segregation was envisioned and sought to be enforced through the regulation of Spaniard's mobility. Indeed, not all Spaniards are represented as negative influences, which partly helped justify the ongoing presence of Spanish priests in Indian towns, but those who are become key targets of segregationist legislation, including those described in Law 21 as "inquietos, de mal vivir, ladrones, jugadores, viciosos." What the 1581 decree helps clarify then is the qualification that is made in Law 21 to target specifically the movement of Spaniards deemed as negative influences meant precisely to allow for some flexibility in terms of enforcing segregation. This points to the fluidity and malleability of these socio-racial categories in relation to the codification of segregation, but again, it also suggests that this malleability was deployed tactically in order to solve contradictions and maximize the benefits for the colonial state.

In the case of *negros* and mixed-ancestry groups, it is also important to note that Law 21 fails to reflect what is stated in some of its sources. As included in the *Recopilación*, the law begins by making a distinction between the need to ban *españoles*, on the one hand, and the need to exclude *negros, mulatos*, and *mestizos* on the other. In the latter case, all three groups are described as mistreating the natives, and, notably, the law represents them all as negative examples: "enseñan sus malas costumbres, y ociosidad, y también algunos errores, y vicios, que podrán estragar, y pervertir el fruto, que deseamos en orden a su salvación, aumento y quietud."[128] Here, we see the reactivation of the rhetoric about the bad example, but this phrasing is now adapted to justify segregating the indigenous from blacks and mixed-ancestry groups, rather than from Spaniards, as was initially intended by Vasco de Quiroga in his formulation of the theory of the bad example. The notion that these groups could "pervert the fruit" if allowed to reside among the Indians is also presented explicitly as counterproductive to the project of indigenous' religious salvation, demographic growth, and pacification. Now, while the law follows closely what is stated in the edict from 1578 on which it is based—where *mulatos, mestizos,* and *negros* are all described as "universalmente tan mal inclinados"[129] and are explicitly represented as bad examples for the indigenous—the are a number of points from the 1589 decree that are conspicuously left out.

In the 1589 decree on which Law 21 is based, it is notable that King Phillip II begins by noting specifically the perceived problem of having *negros* live in Indian communities. It is only after singling-out that group that the sovereign goes on to comment on other groups by stating "os envié a mandar lo procurásedes remediar y dar orden como tampoco viviesen entre ellos españoles, mulatos, mestizos, ni zambaigos, de cuya compañía asimismo se ha siempre presumido mucho daño de los dichos indios."[130] What is notable here is that *zambaigos* are listed among the excluded groups, in contrast to what we find in Law 21. It is also significant that the King goes on to further qualify the general ban against non-indigenous groups residing in Indian towns by restating that, while *negros* and *mulatos* should definitely be excluded, in the case of Spaniards, *mestizos,* and *zambaigos,* authorities should be particularly watchful of individuals from those groups that harm or mistreat the indigenous: los que "perjudicasen o maltratasen a los dichos indios." In other words, the King shifts from the general ban of the opening lines to a more narrow exclusion that allows authorities a greater level of flexibility in enforcing segregation. In the case of Spaniards, it is notable that the King even acknowledges that, for many of them, it is necessary to reside in Indian communities: "es mucho el número de los españoles a quien es forzoso vivir entre indios." Significantly, moreover, the King goes on to qualify his statement further by adding that *mestizos* and *zambaigos* can be exempted: "que son hijos de indios y nacidos entre ellos y han de heredar sus casas y haciendas, os parecía cosa dura sacarlos de con sus padres y que haciades desterrar entre los dichos indios a los negros y mulatos horros, porque son los esclavos."[131] The dispensation for *mestizos* and *zambaigos* that we find in Law 20 thus appears to come directly from this edict, but, as the passage indicates and the rest of the 1589 decree confirms, there are a number of additional considerations and outright inconsistencies that are not conveyed in the law as included in the *Recopilación*. In this case, we again see that the exclusion of mixed-ancestry groups from Indian towns allowed for important exceptions, but, nevertheless, we also see an increasing emphasis on marking a socio-racial differentiation between *indios* and mixed-ancestry categories.

The negative views about *mestizos* and other mixed-ancestry groups that we find in Law 21 also calls attention to the way in which processes of mestizaje were beginning to be thought about at the time. While in the juridical discourses about marriage and reproductive relations between differently racialized people that I analyzed in the first section—where the topic of racial mixture was not elaborated on—these later laws about the regulation of movement of mixed-ancestry groups do convey a greater awareness and problematization of mestizaje as such. The span of time that separates these legal discourses is one factor that can help explain this shift, but it can also be further clarified if we consider the views about mestizaje that are expressed by Juan de Solórzano y Pereira, who, as mentioned earlier, played a major role in compiling the *Recopilación*. By the time the *Recopilación* was finalized, Solórzano y Pereira had already published *Política Indiana* (1647), and in the latter text, he offers a series of reflections about mestizaje that help contextualize how the topic was viewed at the time. Antonio Feros and Orlando Bentancor describe *Política Indiana* respectively as "without doubt, the most influential contemporary text on the American reality,"[132] and "the most influential treatise on Spanish imperial law"[133] and, for this reason, the text's views about mestizaje can be seen as reflecting a dominant and widely disseminated position.

In *Política Indiana*, Solórzano y Pereira acknowledges that there are large numbers of *mestizos* and *mulatos* in the colonies, and he describes these groups as "tan malas castas, razas y condiciones."[134] He also attempt to explain the origins of term *mestizo* by stating that it refers to the "mixtura de sangre, y Naciones que se junto á engendrarlos"[135] and he describes *mestizos/as* in highly negative terms: "los más salen de viciosas, y depravadas costumbres, y son los que más daños, y vejaciones suelen hacer a los mismos Indios, como lo anota el mismo P. Fray Josef Acosta."[136] In the case of *mulatos*, he specifies that "son hijos de negra, y hombre blanco, ó al rebés," and he describes this mixture as "la más fea, y extraordinaria," which, he also uses to explain why its name evokes the nature of the mule: "e le comparan a la naturaleza del mulo."[137] In addition to his value-laden elaboration of what he sees as particularly "bad" forms of racial mixture, he also states that few honorable Spaniards would ever marry Indian or black women, and he contends that mixed-ancestry groups are the result of illicit and reprehensible unions: "Pero porque lo más ordinario es, que nacen de adulterio, ó de otros ilícitos, y punibles ayuntamientos."[138] Solórzano y Pereira's views thus offer a sustained reflection about mestizaje—even though he does not use that term specifically— and they help contextualize how developing ideas about racial difference were articulated specifically in relation to processes of racial mixture. As mentioned throughout this chapter, there are a number of significant narrative alterations that happened in the process of writing the *Recopilación*, and, while the topic still warrants further investigation, this brief account of Solórzano y Pereira's views about racial mixture help partly explain the type of conceptual framework that he brought to his work as a chief compilator for the *Recopilación*.

The final point that is important to consider about segregationist legislation is that, beyond the significance of its discursive articulation, it was also actively invoked in order to enforce segregation. Many of the decrees on which Law 21 is based, for instance, are referenced and actively used by indigenous agents trying to enforce segregation. There are three legal cases from Michoacán, Mexico, for instance, that can help illustrate the way in which the enforcement of segregationist laws was sought after by indigenous authorities. In the first, from 1575, the "indios de Tarecuato" decry the fact that Spaniards and *mestizos* are entering their communities, and staying more than three days "de por ordinario españoles e mestizos que se nos entran."[139] Here, the territorial boundaries of these communities are alluded to in the phrasing, but the maintenance of those boundaries is linked to monitoring the circulation of people in the communities based on racial ascription. They also state the King himself has prohibited this action, and they ask for justice since they state they receive "notorio agravio" from these incursions.

Similarly, there is a case from 1583 in which the *indios principales* from the town of Zinapécuaro appeal to authorities to help remove *españoles, mestizos, negros,* and *mulatos* from their community. They state that they are harassed and abused by these different groups, and they represent them as "gente vagabunda" with no set occupation.[140] The wording of the document evinces the way in which the petition was framed in relation to existing decrees about segregation like the sources for Law 21 analyzed above. There is also an additional case from 1590 in which authorities petitioned to enforce the royal decrees banning non-indigenous from living in the Indian town of Uruapan.[141] In this case, the focus is on the *españoles, mestizos y mulatos solteros* and it presents these single non-indigenous men as particularly pernicious. This again foregrounds the gender dimensions that are critical to understand the codification and enforcement of segregation, and it shows the way in which indigenous leaders sought to further restrict contact between indigenous women and non-indigenous men. The three groups cited in the 1590 case are also represented as "vagabundos y holgazanes" and the document states that "viven desordenadamente dando mal ejemplo a los naturales y maltratándolos y haciéndoles otras muchas vejaciones a que conviene poner remedio."[142] All of these cases evince the way in which indigenous segregation was enforced and sought after by indigenous agents, and the wording of these documents suggests that they were appealing directly to the type of legal language used in the decrees from the time, which shows an explicit awareness of legal discourses from the period.

Conclusion

My analysis of the different juridical discourses described in this chapter calls attention to a series of conceptual implications that are largely ignored by current scholarship on the segregationist dual republic model. To begin with, the way in which the Spanish monarchy and nascent colonial state politicized reproductive sex between differently racialized people is suggestive of the importance of considering how colonial dynamics shaped the genealogy of power relations that were consolidating in relation to the disciplining of bodies and the regulation of populations. What Foucault theorizes as biopower centers precisely on these two modalities of technologies of power,[143] and, even though Ann Stoler has rightly pointed out that his theory needs to be expanded and reconfigured in relation to the colonies, insufficient attention has been paid to how the history of colonization in Spanish America can contribute to this endeavor.[144] As my analysis of Spanish legislation about reproductive sex shows, these discourses are critical to understand the emergence and consolidation of distinct socioracial categories, and this issue cannot be disentangled from the history of segregation in Spanish America. Indeed, the politicization of reproductive sex only increased as segregationist efforts deepened, and, as I show in the Section "The Justification and Regulation of Indigenous Segregation," this politicization was explicitly articulated in relation to consolidating ideas about racial difference that had particular implications for how women's reproductive capacity came to be more closely regulated. Additionally, the increasing regulation of spatial mobility based on racial ascription that went hand in hand with the project of indigenous segregation further attests to the development of other forms of disciplinary control that were developing in the colonies in relation to consolidating ideas about racial difference. These different laws and juridical discourses offer incisive insight into the process of racialization that was developing in the region and they evince the fact that, even as processes of mestizaje were complicating the dualistic framework on which the dual republic model was premised, the sense of spatial and sexual boundaries between republics was further reified through this process. My analysis of how segregationist laws were used by indigenous agents further attests to the fact that this body of legislation shaped historical processes rather than just reflecting discursive practices. Admittedly, my project offers only a partial account of these laws, but, if we reframe how we think about the way in which these laws developed and were adapted in response to processes of mestizaje, we can better trace processes of racialization in the region.

Notes

1 Daniel Nemser, *Infrastructures of Race: Concentration and Biopolitics in Colonial Mexico* (University of Texas Press, 2017), 26, 37.
2 See Angel Rama, *La ciudad letrada* (Ediciones del Norte, 1984).
3 Daniel Nemser, "Primitive Accumulation, Geometric Space, and the Construction of the 'Indian,'" *Journal of Latin American Cultural Studies* 24, no. 3 (2015): 341, 345, 347. See also Law 10, Title 3, Book 6 of *The Recopilación de Leyes para las Indias*.

4 Jeremy Mumford, *Vertical Empire: The General Resettlement of Indians in the Colonial Andes* (Duke University Press, 2012), 1–2.

5 Daniel Nemser, *Infrastructures of Race*, 102; Ben Vinson, *Before Mestizaje: The Frontiers of Race and Caste in Colonial Mexico* (Cambridge University Press, 2018), 3.

6 Daniel Nemser, *Infrastructures of Race*, 102.

7 Karen Graubart, "Containing Law within Walls: The Protection of Customary Law in Santiago del Cercado, Peru" in *Protection and Empire: A Global History*, edited by Lauren Benton, Adam Clulow, Bain Attwood (Cambridge University Press, 2017), 34.

8 Quoted in Karen Graubart, "Containing Law within Walls," 29. See also Jeremy Mumford for more on the Cercado, *Vertical Empire*, 87–88.

9 Karen Graubart, "Learning from the Qadi: The Jurisdiction of Local Rule in the Early Colonial Andes," *Hispanic American Historical Review* 95, no. 2 (2015): 197; Yanna Yannakakis and Martina Schrader-Kniffki, "Between the 'Old Law' and the New: Christian Translation, Indian Jurisdiction, and Criminal Justice in Colonial Oaxaca," *Hispanic American Historical Review* 96, no. 3 (2016): 521.

10 Karen Graubart, "Competing Spanish and Indigenous Jurisdictions in Early Colonial Lima," *Latin American History: Oxford Research Encyclopedias* (published online 2016): 5, 16; Karen Graubart, "Learning from the Qadi," 212; Yanna Yannakakis and Martina Schrader-Kniffki, "Between the 'Old Law' and the New," 520.

11 Yanna Yannakakis and Martina Schrader-Kniffki, "Between the 'Old Law' and the New," 520. See also Ben Vinson, *Before Mestizaje: The Frontiers of Race and Caste in Colonial Mexico* (Cambridge: Cambridge University Press, 2018), 3.

12 For more on the associations between law and geography and its implications for thinking imperial sovereignty see Lauren Benton, *A Search for Sovereignty: Law and Geography in European Empires 1400–1900* (Cambridge: Cambridge University Press, 2014).

13 Ben Vinson describes this period as "one of the greatest eras of population contact in human history." See *Before Mestizaje*, 15.

14 Herman L. Bennet, *Colonial Blackness: A History of Afro-Mexico* (Bloomington: Indiana University Press, 2009): 4; Henry Louis Gates Jr., *Black in Latin America* (New York: NYU Press, 2012): 61, 92, 95, 120; Ben Vinson, *Before Mestizaje*, 6; Frank Trey Proctor, "African Diasporic Ethnicity in Mexico City to 1650," in *Africans to Spanish America: Expanding the Diaspora*, edited by Sherwin K. Bryant, Rachel Sarah O'Toole, Ben Vinson (Champaign: University of Illinois Press, 2012): 51.

15 Leo J. Garofalo "The Shape of a Diaspora: The Movement of Afro-Iberians to Colonial Spanish America," in *Africans to Spanish America: Expanding the Diaspora*, edited by Sherwin K. Bryant, Rachel Sarah O'Toole, Ben Vinson (Champaign: University of Illinois Press, 2012): 33–41. For more on the African slave trade to Iberia see also James H. Sweet, "The Iberian Roots of American Racist Thought," *The William and Mary Quarterly* 54, no. 1 (1997): 143–166.

16 Tatiana Seijas, *Asian Slaves in Colonial Mexico: From Chinos to Indians* (Cambridge: Cambridge University Press, 2014), 1, 3, 143–150; Tatiana Seijas, "Asian Migrations to Latin America in the Pacific World, 16th–19th Centuries," *History Compass* 14 (2016): 577; Christina H. Lee and Ricardo Padrón, "Introduction," in *The Spanish Pacific, 1521–1815: A Reader of Primary Sources* (Amsterdam: Amsterdam University Press, 2020): 13–14.

17 Herman L. Bennet, *Africans in Colonial Mexico: Absolutism, Christianity, and Afro-Creole Consciousness, 1570–1640* (Bloomington: Indiana University Press, 2005): 30–31.

18 Jane G. Landers "Cimarrón and Citizen: African Ethnicity, Corporate Identity, and the Evolution of Free Black Towns in the Spanish Circum-Caribbean," in *Slaves, Subjects, and Subservsives:Blacks in Colonial Latin America*, edited by Jane G. Landers, Barry M. Robinson (Albuquerque: University of New Mexico Press, 2006), 112, 130–132.

19 Tatiana Seijas, "Asian Migrations," 573, 577; Tatiana Seijas, *Asian Slaves*, 1, 3, 4, 143–150.

20 Ben Vinson, *Before Mestizaje*, 1.

21 The term *mestizo* was used in the Americas to describe people of mixed Spanish and indigenous descent, but the term can be traced to Iberia, see Ruth Hill "*Casta* as Culture and the *Sociedad de Castas* as Literature," in *Interpreting Colonialism*, edited by Byron Wells and Philip Stewart (Oxford: Oxford University Press, 2004): 231–259. See also Verena Stolcke for more on the term mestizo in "Los mestizos no nacen sino que se hacen," *Avá* 14 (2009). Also see Joanne Rappaport on the inconsistent use of the term mestizo in *The Disappearing Mestizo: Configuring Difference in the Colonial New Kingdom of Granada* (Duke University Press, 2014). The term *mulato* was typically used to describe people of mixed Spanish and African descent, though, Robert C. Schwaller shows that in colonial Mexico it was also used to describe people of mixed African and indigenous descent, see "Mulata, Hija de Negro y India: Afro-Indigenous Mulatos in Early Colonial Mexico," *Journal of Social History* 44, no. 3 (2011): 889–914. Ben Vinson also points out cases where the term *mulato* was used to describe the progeny of *negros* and *chinos*, see *Before Mestizaje: The Frontiers of Race and Caste in Colonial Mexico* (Cambridge: Cambridge University Press, 2018), 70. The term *zambaigo* was used to describe people of mixed African and indigenous descent, and Berta Ares Queija shows that it begun to be used in the Andes starting in the 1560s, see "Mestizos, mulatos y zambaigos (Virreinate del Perú, siglo XVI)," in *Negros, mulatos, zambaigos: derroteros africanos en los mundos ibéricos* (Escuela de Estudios Hispano-Americanos, 2000): 78.

22 Ben Vinson, *Before Mestizaje*, 15. Magnus Mörner makes a similar point in his classic study *Race Mixture in the History of Latin America* (Boston: Little Brown, 1967), 2, 4.

23 For arguments about the dual republic's failure because of mestizaje see Kathryn Burns, "Unfixing Race," in *Rereading the Black Legend: The Discourses of Religious and Racial Difference in the Renaissance Empires*, edited by Margaret R. Greer, Walter D. Mignolo, Maureen Quilligan (Chicago: University of Chicago Press, 2007): 191; Karen Vieira Powers, "Conquering Discourses of 'Sexual Conquest': Of Women, Language, and Mestizaje," *Colonial Latin American Review* 11, no. 1 (2002): 15; Vieira Powers, *Women in the Crucible of Conquest: The Gendered Genesis of Spanish American Society, 1500–1600* (Albuquerque: University of New Mexico Press, 2005), 72; Ben Vinson, *Before Mestizaje: The Frontiers of Race and Caste in Colonial Mexico* (Cambridge: Cambridge University Press, 2018), 6; Magnus Mörner, *La Corona Española y los foráneos en los pueblos de indios de América* (Madrid: Ediciones de Cultura Hispánica, 1999), 11.

24 See Rachel Sarah O'Toole, *Bound Lives: African, Indians, and the Making of Race in Colonial Peru* (Pittsburgh: University of Pittsburgh Press, 2012), 9; Karen Graubart, "Containing Law within Walls," 36.

25 See María Elena Martínez, "Space, Order, and Group Identities in a Spanish Colonial Town: Puebla de los Angeles," in *The Collective and the Public in*

Latin America: Cultural Identities and Political Order, edited by Luis Roniger and Tamar Herzog (Sussex: Sussex Academic Press, 2000): 25; Robert Schwaller, "Mulata, Hija de Negro y India: Afro-Indigenous Mulatos in Early Colonial Mexico," *Journal of Social History* 44, no. 3 (2011): 895–896; Rachel Sarah O'Toole, *Bound Lives: African, Indians, and the Making of Race in Colonial Peru* (Pittsburgh: University of Pittsburgh Press, 2012), 18.

26　Ben Vinson, *Before Mestizaje*, 6.

27　Vieira Powers, *Women in the Crucible*, 72.

28　Joshua Lund, *The Impure Imagination. Toward a Critical Hybridity in Latin American Writing* (Minneapolis: University of Minnesota Press, 2006), 15.

29　Robert Bernasconi, "Crossed Lines in the Racialization Process: Race as a Border Concept," *Research in Phenomenology* 42 (2012): 207–208, 211–213.

30　Bernasconi also draws from Ann Laura Stoler who argues that "racisms gain their strategic force, not from the fixity of essentialisms, but the internal malleability assigned to the changing features of racial essence." See Robert Bernasconi, "Crossed Lines," 208. More recently, Stoler argues that "Racial formations combine elements of fixity and fluidity in ways that make them both resilient and impervious to empirical, experimental counterclaims." See Ann Laura Stoler, *Duress: Imperial Durabilities in Our Times* (Durham: Duke University Press, 2016), 239.

31　See María Elena Martínez, "Space, Order, and Group Identities," 29. For more on slave marriages also see Michelle A. McKinley, "Such Unsightly Unions Could Never Result in Holy Matrimony: Mixed-Status Marriages in Seventeenth Century Colonial Lima," *Yale Journal of Law and the Humanities* 217 (2010).

32　See Kathryn Burns, "Unfixing Race," in *Rereading the Black Legend: The Discourses of Religious and Racial Difference in the Renaissance Empires*, edited by Margaret R. Greer, Walter D. Mignolo, Maureen Quilligan (University of Chicago Press, 2007): 191; Karen Vieira Powers, "Conquering Discourses"; Stuart B. Schwartz, "Pecar en colonias: Mentalidades populares, inquisición y actitudes hacia la fornicación simple en España, Portugal y las colonias americanas," *Cuadernos de Historia Moderna* no. 18 (1997): 62–63.

33　See "Instrucción para el gobernador y los oficiales sobre el gobierno de las Indias," in *Colección de Documentos para la Formación Social de Hispanoamérica 1493–1810*, edited by Richard Konetzke, Volumen I (1493–1592) (Consejo Superior de Investigaciones Científicas, 1953), 12.

34　See Susan Migden Socolow, *The Women of Colonial Latin America* (Cambridge: Cambridge University Press, 2000), 33; Ben Vinson, *Before Mestizaje: The Frontiers of Race and Caste in Colonial Mexico* (Cambridge University Press, 2018), 5; Vieira Powers, *Women in the Crucible*, 53–54.

35　See the decree from October 19, 1514, "R.C. Que las indias se puedan casar con españoles" in *Colección de Documentos para la Formación Social de Hispanoamérica 1493–1810*, edited by Richard Konetzke, Volumen I (1493–1592), 61.

36　Antonio Feros, *Speaking of Spain: The Evolution of Race and Nation in the Hispanic World* (Cambridge, MA: Harvard University Press, 2017), 27.

37　See decree from October 19, 1514 "R.C. Que las indias se puedan casar con españoles" in Richard Konetzke, Volumen I, 61.

38　In his analysis of this edict, Robert Schwaller suggests that "the prospect of augmenting the population through Spanish-*india* unions had become politically expedient." See *Géneros de Gente in Early Colonial Mexico: Defining Racial Difference* (Norman: University of Oklahoma Press, 2016), 66.

39　See decree from October 19, 1514 "R.C. Que las indias se puedan casar con españoles" in Richard Konetzke, Volumen I, 62.

40 Ibid.
41 María Elena Martínez, "Space, Order, and Group Identities," 29.
42 King Ferdinand died in January of 1516, and the Franciscan cardinal Ximénez de Cisneros was temporarily in power. See Daniel Castro, *Another Face of Empire. Bartolome de las Casas, Indigenous Rights, and Ecclesiastical Imperialism* (Durham: Duke University Press, 2007), 69. The fact that Cisneros was in power is also significant because, as discussed in the previous chapter, he had received Las Casas' *Memorial de remedio para las Indias.*
43 See "Instrucciones dada a los padres de la orden de Orden de San Jeronimo," in Richard Konetzke, Volumen I, 63, 64.
44 See "Instrucciones dada a los padres de la orden de Orden de San Jeronimo" in Richard Konetzke, Volumen I, 64.
45 For more on the gradual consolidation of a sense of common "Spanishness" see Antonio Feros, *Speaking of Spain*, 5, 26–27, 49.
46 See decree from March 19, 1525 "R.C. Sobre casamientos de españoles con indios" in Richard Konetzke, *Colección de Documentos para la Formación Social de Hispanoamérica 1493–1810,* Volumen I, 77.
47 Ibid.
48 Ben Vinson, *Before Mestizaje*, 5. For additional context on Spanish legislation on marriage, see Verena Stolke, "O enigma das interseções: classe, "raça", sexo, sexualidade. A formação dos impérios transatlânticos do século XVI ao XIX," *Estudos Feministas* 14, no. 1 (2006): 15–42; Daisy Rípodas Ardanaz, *El matrimonio en Indias: realidad social y reulación jurídica* (Fundación para la Educación, la Ciencia y la Cultura, 1977); and Robert Schwaller, *Géneros de Gente.*
49 See Law 2, Title 1, Book 6 of the *Recopilación de Leyes para las Indias, 1681.* Content downloaded from https://home.heinonline.org
50 It is significant that the law does not use the term criollo since, as Robert Schwaller explains, the term was used in the 1570s by the royal cosmographer López de Velasco. See *Géneros de Gente,* 42.
51 For his analysis of the 1514 decree, see Robert Schwaller, *Géneros de Gente,* 66.
52 It is also important to point out that, in a decree from January 25, 1586, marriages between Spanish *encomenderos* and indigenous women are overtly problematized, even if not officially prohibited. See "Consulta de la Junta de la contaduria mayor sobre la perpetuidad de las encomiendas" in Richard Konetzke, *Colección de Documentos para la Formación Social de Hispanoamérica 1493–1810,* Volumen I, 562.
53 See Law 5, Title 5, of Book 7, of the *Recopilación de Leyes para las Indias, 1681.* Content downloaded from https://home.heinonline.org
54 Ibid.
55 See decree from October 26, 1541"R.C. Que los negros se casen con negras" in Richard Konetzke, *Colección de Documentos para la Formación Social de Hispanoamérica 1493–1810,* Volumen I, 210.
56 See Law 6, Title 5, of Book 7 of the *Recopilación de Leyes para las Indias, 1681.* Content downloaded from https://home.heinonline.org
57 Jennifer Morgan, "Partus sequitur ventrem: Law, Race, and Reproduction in Colonial Slavery," *Small Axe* 22, no. 55 (2018): 1, 12.
58 See Law 7, Title 5, Book 7 of the *Recopilación de Leyes para las Indias, 1681.* Content downloaded from https://home.heinonline.org
59 See "R.C. Que no se puedan servir los negros de indio ni de india y no traigan armas" in Richard Konetzke, *Colección de Documentos para la Formación Social de Hispanoamérica 1493-1810,* Volumen I, 290.

60 See "R.C. Que no se puedan servir los negros de indio ni de india y no traigan armas" in Richard Konetzke, *Colección de Documentos para la Formación Social de Hispanoamérica 1493-1810,* Volumen I, 291.

61 Herman L. Bennett, *Colonial Blackness,* 5.

62 Robert Schwaller, *Géneros de Gente,* 53.

63 For more on the use of the terms *zambaigo* and *mulato* see Berta Ares Queija "Mestizos, mulatos y zambaigos," 78; Robert C. Schwaller "Mulata, Hija de Negro y India," 889–914.

64 See Robert Schwaller, *Géneros de Gente,* 68.

65 John Lynch, "The Institutional Framework of Colonial Spanish America," *Journal of Latin American Studies* 24 (1994), 69; Anna More, *Baroque Sovereignty: Carlos Sigüenza y Góngora and the Creole Archive of Colonial Mexico* (Philadelphia: University of Pennsylvania Press, 2013), 38.

66 Orlando Bentancor, *The Matter of Empire: Metaphysics and Mining in Colonial Peru* (Pittsburgh: University of Pittsburgh Press, 2017), 289.

67 This chapter only offers a partial analysis of these laws, but the list in its entirety is as follows: from Book 6, there are 3 laws from Title 1 that pertain to the policy of segregation: Law 10, Law 12, and Law 18; from Title 3 there are 29 laws: Law 1–29; from Title 9 there are 4 laws: Law 11, and Laws 13–15; from Title 13 there is one law: Law 14; and from Title 17 there are two laws: Law 6 and 17. From Book 7 there are three laws from Title 4: Laws 1, 2, and 4. In his analysis of segregationist laws, Magnus Mörner only considers ten laws. See Magnus Mörner, *La Corona Española y los foráneos en los pueblos de indios de América* (Madrid: Ediciones de Cultura Hispánica, 1999), 112–113. For more on laws that focus on indigenous land rights see Tamar Herzog, "Colonial Law and 'Native Customs': Indigenous Land Rights in Colonial Spanish America," *The Americas* 69, no. 3 (2013): 303–321.

68 See Law 19, Title 1, Book 6 of the *Recopilación de Leyes para las Indias, 1681.* Content downloaded from https://home.heinonline.org

69 Ibid.

70 For the decree from 1538 on which Law 19, Title 1, Book 6 is based see "R.C. Para que se pongan en policía los indios," in Richard Konetzke, *Colección de Documentos para la Formación Social de Hispanoamérica 1493-1810,* Volumen I, 186.

71 See Law 1, Title 3, of Book 6, of the *Recopilación de Leyes para las Indias, 1681.* Content downloaded from https://home.heinonline.org

72 Magnus Mörner, *La Corona Española y los foráneos en los pueblos de indios de América* (Madrid: Ediciones de Cultura Hispánica, 1999), 44.

73 See Law 1, Title 3, of Book 6, of the *Recopilación de Leyes para las Indias, 1681.* Content downloaded from https://home.heinonline.org

74 See "R. Provision que trata de la libertad de los indios y a que se reduzcan y recojan a prublos congregados" in Richard Konetzke, *Colección de Documentos para la Formación Social de Hispanoamérica 1493-1810,* Volumen I, 284.

75 As Jennifer Morgan argues "The long-standing consensus that God had created Adam and Eve to 'be fruitful and multiply" gave way in the course of the 16th and 17th centuries to "secular concerns about the extent to which the size of a given population drove economic successes and failures." See *Reckoning with Slavery: Gender, Kinship, and Capitalism in the Early Black Atlantic* (Duke University Press 2021), 94.

76 Ibid.

77 See "R.C. Para que los indios se recojan a vivir en pueblos" in Richard Konetzke, *Colección de Documentos para la Formación Social de Hispanoamérica 1493-1810,* Volumen I, 416.

78 Jeremy Mumford, *Vertical Empire*, 1–2; Karen Graubart, "Containing Law within Walls," 34.

79 See "R.C. Para que los indios se recojan a vivir en pueblos" in Richard Konetzke, *Colección de Documentos para la Formación Social de Hispanoamérica 1493-1810*, Volumen I, 416.

80 See Daniel Nemser, *Infrastructures of Race*, 4–5, 48, 63.

81 See Law 12, Title 1, of Book 6, of the *Recopilación de Leyes para las Indias, 1681*. Content downloaded from https://home.heinonline.org

82 See Law 7, Title 7, of Book 6 of the *Recopilación de Leyes para las Indias, 1681*. Content downloaded from https://home.heinonline.org. The law is based on a decree from 1568.

83 See Law 28, Title 8, of Book 6 of the *Recopilación de Leyes para las Indias, 1681*. Content downloaded from https://home.heinonline.org. The law is based on a decree from 1594.

84 This is particularly significant because it brings into focus the forms of disciplinary power that were developing. As Paul Rabinow explains, Foucault argues that disciplinary power aimed to produce docile bodies through their control in space. See Rabinow, *The Foucault Reader* (New York: Pantheon Books, 1984), 17.

85 See Law 19, Title 3, of Book 6, of the *Recopilación de Leyes para las Indias, 1681*. Content downloaded from https://home.heinonline.org

86 See Law 18, Title 3, of Book 6, of the *Recopilación de Leyes para las Indias, 1681*. Content downloaded from https://home.heinonline.org. Based on a single decree form October 10, 1618.

87 See Law 6, Title 17, of Book 6, of the *Recopilación de Leyes para las Indias, 1681*. Content downloaded from https://home.heinonline.org

88 Magnus Mörner, *La Corona Española y los foráneos en los pueblos de indios de América* (Madrid: Ediciones de Cultura Hispánica, 1999), 121.

89 See Richard Konetzke, *Colección de Documentos para la Formación Social de Hispanoamérica 1493–1810*, Volumen II, Primer Tomo (Madrid: Consejo Superior de Investigaciones Científicas, 1953), 204.

90 See Silvia Federici, *Caliban and the Witch* (New York: Automedia, 2004), 8, 38, 86, 89.

91 The source on which Law 14, Title 13, of Book 6 is based is also the October 10, 1618 instructions. The law summarizes many of the points made in the original instructions. See Richard Konetzke, *Colección de Documentos para la Formación Social de Hispanoamérica 1493–1810*, Volumen II, Primer Tomo, 204, 206, 208.

92 See Law 13, from Title 17, of Book 6 of the *Recopilación de Leyes para las Indias, 1681*. Content downloaded from https://home.heinonline.org

93 See Joanne Rappaport for more on the case of the mestizos who denounced the practice of using indigenous women as wet nurses. Rappaport, *The Disappearing Mestizo*, 137–138.

94 Larissa Brewer-García, "Bodies, Texts, and Translators: Indigenous Breast Milk and the Jesuit Exclusion of Mestizos in Late Sixteenth-Century Peru," *Colonial Latin American Review* 21, no. 3 (2012): 371.

95 Max Hering Torres, "Purity of Blood. Problems of Interpretation," in *Race and Blood in the Iberian World*, edited by Max S. Hering Torres, María Elena Martínez, David Niremberg (Berlin: Lit Verlag, 2012), 18; María Elena Martínez, *Genealogical Fictions*, 56; Joanne Rappaport, *The Disappearing Mestizo*, 19; Emilie L. Bergmann "Milking the Poor: Wet-nursing and the Sexual Economy of Early Modern Spain," in *Marriage and Sexuality in Medieval and Early Modern Iberia*, edited by Eukene Lacarra Lanz (London: Routledge, 2002): 90–108.

96   Larissa Brewer-García, "Bodies, Texts, and Translators," 371–372.
97   Qtd. in Joanne Rappaport, *The Disappearing Mestizo*, 19.
98   Jan Mohamed, "Sexuality on/of the Racial Border," 109.
99   Robert Bernasconi, "Crossed Lines," 216.
100 See Law 4, Title 4, Book 7 of the *Recopilación de Leyes para las Indias, 1681.* Content downloaded from https://home.heinonline.org
101 Ibid.
102 For more on the history of *recogimiento* also see Nancy Van Deusen, *Between the Sacred and the Worldly: The Institutional and Cultural Practice of* Recogimiento *in Colonial Lima* (Stanford: Stanford University Press, 2001).
103 Qtd. in Daniel Nemser, *Infrastructures of Race*, 65.
104 Daniel Nemser, *Infrastructures of Race*, 67.
105 For more on the prohibition on the ordination of mestizos see Larissa Brewer-García, "Bodies, Texts, and Translators"; Felipe E. Ruan, "Andean Activism and the Reformulation of Mestizo Agency and Identity in Early Colonial Peru," *Colonial Latin American Review* 21, no. 2 (2012).
106 Daniel Nemser, *Infrastructures of Race*, 67.
107 Kathryn Burns, "Gender and the Politics of Mestizaje: The Convent of Santa Clara in Cuzco," *The Hispanic American Historical Review* 78, no. 1 (1998): 19, 25.
108 Kathryn Burns, "Gender and the Politics of Mestizaje," 21.
109 Kathryn Burns, "Gender and the Politics of Mestizaje," 25.
110 Kathryn Burns, "Gender and the Politics of Mestizaje," 20–21, 24.
111 Kathryn Burns, "Gender and the Politics of Mestizaje," 21, 25, 27, 28.
112 See "R.C. Que los hijos de españoles habidos en indias y andan fuera de su poder sean recogidos" in Richard Konetzke, *Colección de Documentos para la Formación Social de Hispanoamérica 1493-1810,* Volumen I, 147.
113 Robert C. Schwaller, *Géneros de Gente,* 70.
114 See "R.C. Que los hijos de españoles habidos en indias y andan fuera de su poder sean recogidos" in Richard Konetzke, *Colección de Documentos para la Formación Social de Hispanoamérica 1493-1810,* Volumen I, 147.
115 Ibid.
116 See "R.C. Que se recojan los mestizos y mestizas que andan perdidos" in Richard Konetzke, *Colección de Documentos para la Formación Social de Hispanoamérica 1493-1810,* Volumen I, 328.
117 Ibid.
118 See decree from January 15, 1569, in Encina's *Cedulario Indiano.* Accessed online: https://babel.hathitrust.org/cgi/pt?id=inu.32000004954873&view=1 up&seq=372&q1=569
119 Ibid.
120 Felipe Ruan argues that in the 1560s mestizos began to be conceived as morally deviant and corrupt social subjects in the viceroyalty. See Ruan "Andean Activism," 211. Similarly, Larissa Brewer-García shows that prejudices toward mestizos in the late 1570s evidence the identification of mestizo bodies "as materially different from Old Christian bodies." See "Bodies, Texts, and Translators," 375.
121 Magnus Mörner, *La Corona Española*, 113.
122 See Law 21, Title 3, Book 6 of the *Recopilación de Leyes para las Indias, 1681.* Content downloaded from https://home.heinonline.org
123 Ibid.
124 See decree from July 12, 1600, in Richard Konetzke, *Colección de Documentos para la Formación Social de Hispanoamérica 1493-1810,* Volumen II, Primer Tomo, 64.

125 See decree from May 2, 1563, in Richard Konetzke, *Colección de Documentos para la Formación Social de Hispanoamérica 1493-1810,* Volumen I, 400.
126 Ibid.
127 See decree from May 8, 1581, in Richard Konetzke, *Colección de Documentos para la Formación Social de Hispanoamérica 1493-1810,* Volumen I, 535–536.
128 See Law 21, Title 3, Book 6 of the *Recopilación de Leyes para las Indias, 1681.* Content downloaded from https://home.heinonline.org
129 See decree from November 25, 1578, in Richard Konetzke, *Colección de Documentos para la Formación Social de Hispanoamérica 1493–1810,* Volumen I, 513.
130 See decree from January 10, 1589, in Richard Konetzke, *Colección de Documentos para la Formación Social de Hispanoamérica 1493–1810,* Volumen I, 599.
131 See decree from January 10, 1589, in Richard Konetzke, *Colección de Documentos para la Formación Social de Hispanoamérica 1493–1810,* Volumen I, 598.
132 Antonio Feros, *Speaking of Spain,* 72.
133 Orlando Bentancor, *The Matter of Empire,* 35.
134 Solórzano Pereira, *Política Indiana,* Libro II, Tomo I (Madrid: Ediciones Atalas 1972 [1647]), 447.
135 Solórzano Pereira, *Política Indiana,* Libro II, Tomo I, 445. More on the origins of the term *mestizo,* see Ruth Hill, "*Casta* as Culture," 231–259.
136 Solórzano Pereira, *Política Indiana,* Libro II, Tomo I, 446–447.
137 Solórzano Pereira, *Política Indiana,* Libro II, Tomo I, 445.
138 Solórzano Pereira, *Política Indiana,* Libro II, Tomo I, 447.
139 Archivo General de la Nación. Indiferente Virreinal, Caja 1847, 6926/6, Expediente 006.
140 Archivo General de la Nación. Instituciones Coloniales, Indios, Volumen 2, 15043/943. Expediente 944.
141 For more on the evolution of Uruapan as a "pueblo de indios" see Oziel Ulises Talavera Ibarra, "El dominio racial de los no indígenas en Uruapan: ocupación del espacio y del territorio," in *Del Territorio a la Arquitectura en el Obispado de Michoacán,* edited by Carlos Salvador Paredes Martínez, Guadalupe Salazar González, Catherine Rose Ettinger, Luis Alberto Torres Garibay (Morelia: Universidad Michoacana de San Nicolás de Hidalgo, 2008), 115–135.
142 Archivo General de la Nación. Instituciones Coloniales, Indios, Volumen 4, 15045/645. Expediente 650.
143 See Michel Foucault, *The History of Sexuality: An Introduction, Volume I.* Trans. Robert Hurley (Vintage Books, 1990), 38.
144 See Ann Laura Stoler, *Race and the Education of Desire: Foucualt's History of Sexuality and the Colonial Order of Things* (Duke University Press, 1995), 40.

3 Felipe Guaman Poma de Ayala's Endorsement of Segregation

A Plea for Racially-Qualified Life

Felipe Guaman Poma de Ayala's *El primer nueva corónica y buen gobierno* has rightly become one of the most canonical Andean texts and iconic visual representations from the colonial period. The unique manuscript consists of 1,189 pages—398 of which are line drawings—and it offers an ambitious, bold, and wide-ranging reflection on pre-conquest indigenous societies and the devastating impact of Spanish colonization. The text was completed in 1615 (then amended in 1616),[1] and according to its self-described indigenous author, it is the product of 30 years of labor that was concluded when Guaman Poma was 80 years old.[2] The text's genre eludes easy classification, but it has been variously described by critics as a letter-chronicle, an autoethnography, and a "crónica india."[3] It is mostly written in Spanish, but it also has passages in Latin, Quechua, and Aymara, as well as fragments of songs, sermons, and didactic dialogues, including a fictional dialogue between Guaman Poma and the King of Spain.[4] The illustrated manuscript is currently housed at Danish Royal Library in Copenhagen, and most experts believe that it was donated to the library by Cornelius Pedersen Lerche, who served as the Danish ambassador to Spain during the 17th century.[5]

Guaman Poma's intention was to publish his *Nueva corónica* (as it is commonly known), and he designed it as if it were a printed book, including by giving his line drawings the look of woodblock prints.[6] For nearly 300 years, however, the manuscript remained buried away and undetected at the Royal Library. It is unclear, but unlikely, that it was ever read by its main intended addressee: King Philip III.[7] It was not until 1908 that it was re-discovered by the German anthropologist and Orientalist Richard Pietschmann at the Danish Library, and, since then, it has received increasing academic attention.[8] During the 1980s and 1990s, Guaman Poma's work was largely interpreted through the analytical lenses of the consolidating fields of postcolonial and subaltern studies,[9] and, more recently, it has been hailed by critics like Walter Mignolo as a hallmark text to understand and theorize the genealogy of decolonial thought.[10] In 2001, the manuscript was also digitized by the Royal Library—making it widely accessible to

DOI: 10.4324/9781003145196-4

the broader public— and, in 2007, it was recognized by UNESCO for its documentary heritage as part of the "Memory of the World Program."[11]

One of the reasons why the *Nueva corónica* has gained worldwide recognition and continues to be the object of extensive academic scholarship is that, as Rocío Quispe Agnoli suggests, it offers readers a seemingly inexhaustible array of themes to explore.[12] The text begins by establishing Guaman Poma authorship and noble genealogy, it spells out the author's intentions, and it establishes his unambiguous embrace of Christianity— which decisively informs and frames the entire narrative. The content is then organized around a number of titled sections, which include a biblical account of the development of Andean societies up to the period of Inca rule,[13] a section on the Spanish conquest, a series of reflections on good government and justice that features the author's most biting critique of ongoing abuses by colonial officials, a brief section on the history of blacks, and the aforementioned fictional dialogue between Guaman Poma and King Philip III in which the author transgressively ventriloquizes the sovereign's voice to solicit his advice on how to reform the colonial government.

Guaman Poma's erudition has also been the subject of a number of recent studies. The *Nueva corónica* displays the author's knowledge of European discourses, and scholars have established that Guaman Poma was deeply familiar with Spanish codified law,[14] made conscious references to European literary and visual practices,[15] and was well versed in contemporary political discussions, including some of Bartolomé de las Casas most radical arguments in favor of indigenous land restitution.[16] The author was likewise knowledgeable of Andean history as passed down through oral accounts and *khipus*,[17] and he at times made reference to pre-Hispanic poetic and dramatic traditions in Quechua.[18] Augusta Holland further argues that Guaman Poma's drawings may have been influenced by Asian visual forms that circulated in the Americas as a result of the transpacific trade routes opened up by the Manila-Acapulco Galleon.[19]

Longstanding enigmas about Guaman Poma's biography are another reason why the *Nueva corónica* continues to attract scholars' attention. We know that he was born sometime after the Spanish conquest, but specialists' estimates on the exact date of his birth are far from definitive, ranging from 1535 to 1567.[20] The date of his death is likewise unknown. The last extant historical record of his life is a letter from February 14, 1615, addressed to King Phillip III, in which Guaman Poma informs the monarch that has written "una corónica o historia general."[21] In the brief letter, he states that his *corónica* offers a supplemental account of European history by taking into account the indigenous perspective, which he purports to represent by authorizing his discourse as a type of native informant: "para que los historiadores de V. Mgd. puedan tener mas entera luz de la que yo entiendo."[22] He also urges the King to take action by highlighting the horrid mistreatment of Andean natives, who he says are treated worse than enslaved Africans:

a solo V. Mgd. incumbe el mirar por ellos como su rey Y señor natural que es dellos y se duela de sus miserias y calamidades y malos tratamientos y peores pagas que continuamente resciuen en general de todo genero de gente, tratándolos peor que a esclauos uenidos de Guinea que aun a estos los tratan mejor por costarles el precio que pagan por ellos.[23]

As mentioned, the letter is the last record we have of Guaman Poma's life, but, as Rolena Adorno compellingly argues, codicological evidence suggests that the author made the final revisions for his *Nueva corónica* no earlier than at the beginning of 1616, so the end of his life could not have logically occurred before then.[24]

Guaman Poma's family background and dramatic decrease in social status are other noteworthy aspects of his life. As he repeatedly states in the *Nueva corónica*, as well as in the 1615 letter, he was the descendant of pre-Hispanic royal dynasties: the Yarovilca on his father's side, and the Inca on his mother's.[25] His positionality as a pre-conquest native elite is critical to understand the author's often ambivalent views about the conquest, which he represents as a period of lawlessness driven by Spaniard's greed,[26] but which he also fails to condemn since he acknowledges that his own father, Martín Guaman Mallque, aided Spanish conquistadors during the colonization period.[27] For most of his life, Guaman Poma also served Spanish colonial authorities in different capacities. In his youth, he worked for the Spanish priest Cristóbal de Albornoz during the latter's fierce campaign to extirpate indigenous idolatries and destroy the indigenous resistance movement known as the Taqui Oncoy.[28] Guaman Poma expressly approved of the work carried out by Albornoz, and, as Adorno argues, his "youthful participation in the missionary church's campaigns to root out native Andean religions was a defining feature of his life experience."[29] Later in his life, he also collaborated with the Mercedarian Spanish priest and missionary Martín de Murúa. Murúa was working on an illustrated history of Peru, and we know that Guaman Poma composed many of the color drawings that we find in the two existing copies of the manuscript: known as the *Getty* and the *Galvin* versions of *Historia general del Pirú*.[30] Guaman Poma likely worked for Murúa between 1596 and the end of 1600, and his artistic mastery was decisively shaped by this experience.[31]

Between 1590 and 1600, Guaman Poma was also actively involved in a longstanding land litigation between his family and a group of Chachapoya indigenous from the city of Huamanga (modern-day Ayacucho).[32] The dispute was over an extensive amount of land in the valley of Chupas, which Guaman Poma's family claimed belonged to them.[33] In one of the series of court documents in which Guaman Poma was directly involved, he presents himself as "Casique Prinçipal" and "governador de los yndios."[34] He also accuses both the Chachapoyas and Spaniards of unjustly taking over his family's land, and he boldly demands restitution.[35] Despite his tireless efforts, however, Guaman Poma and his family ultimately lost the dispute.[36] He was personally accused of falsely presenting himself as a *cacique* and of using the honorific title Don, while his opponents claimed that he was in fact a humble Indian whose real name was Lázaro. On December 19, 1600, a criminal sentence was imposed on Guaman Poma: he was sentenced to 200 public lashes, and he was condemned to 2 years of exile from the city of Huamanga and its six-league radius.[37] As Pablo Macera puts it, "fue entonces que Guamán Poma vino a menos y perdió posiciones políticas, sociales y económicas.... De cacique y mediano propietario se convirtió en un indio trashumante, que vivía a salto de mata, quizás bajo seudónimo."[38] According to Adorno, moreover, it was only after 1600 that Guaman Poma actually began writing his *Nueva corónica,* once he had no other legal recourse and all other avenues of social participation had been essentially foreclosed.[39]

A final point to note about Guaman Poma's biography is that he experienced firsthand the ambitious General Resettlement campaign launched by Viceroy Francisco de Toledo in 1569, which, as noted in the previous chapter, relocated more than a million indigenous subjects into *reducciones.*[40] As Jeremy Mumford contends, Guaman Poma "agreed wholeheartedly with the principle of the Resettlement" and even though he did not use the term, "he embraced the idea of the 'two republics.'"[41] Indeed, Guaman Poma's illustrated manuscript offers an extensive textual and visual commentary on the project of indigenous segregation, and it provides incomparable insight to understand its uneven implementation and multilayered implications. This aspect of the *Nueva corónica*, however, has received insufficient academic attention.[42] By focusing on Guaman Poma's unequivocal endorsement of indigenous segregation, this chapter works to develop current scholarship on the *Nueva corónica.*

In the first section of the chapter, I argue that Guaman Poma's comments on indigenous segregation offer crucial insight to understand how he envisions Indian towns according to the dualistic structure of the two-republic model. I also show that he conceptualizes boundaries in terms of space, jurisdiction, and reproductive sex between differently racialized groups. I further contend that his comments evince the fact that, while the author recognized that mestizaje was a central feature of colonial society, he nevertheless insisted on the viability of indigenous segregation by forcefully discouraging further reproduction of mixed-ancestry groups and by insisting that those groups live and labor among Spaniards. In the second section, I analyze Guaman Poma's consistent emphasis on fostering indigenous population growth. I show that his endorsement of segregation is articulated as a plea for the preservation of racially qualified life, and I consider the implications that this formulation has for how the author politicizes and seeks to regulate indigenous women's reproductive capacities.

The Endorsement of Segregation in the Context of Mestizaje

> *Por esta causa y ley, hordenansas deste rreyno, lo mande echar de las prouincias y pueblo de yndios deste rreyno a los dichos españoles, mestisos, negros y mulatos, zangahígos y que se uayan a las dichas ciudades. Aunque sea casado con yndias, se le lleuen a sus mugeres los dichos españoles y mestisos y mulatos.*
>
> Guaman Poma[43]

Guaman Poma's views on indigenous segregation are expressed in numerous passages and line drawings that appear interspersed throughout the *Nueva corónica*. While many of his comments often overlap and at times express contradictory positions, they can be analytically grouped in relation to two main sets of arguments that he develops. Each of these sets of arguments illustrates the way in which the author envisions segregation in the context of mestizaje, and they call attention to the way in which he conceptualizes boundaries on the basis of presumed socio-racial differences between 'Indians' and the rest of colonial society. By offering a discursive analysis of Guaman Poma's views on segregation that highlights some of its key conceptual implications, this section develops the claim that ongoing processes of mestizaje not only solidified his understanding of racial difference, they also enhanced the author's perceived need for greater spatial regulation based on racial ascription.

The first set of arguments that can be grouped to understand Guaman Poma's views on segregation has to do with his comments on socio-spatial and jurisdictional organization. To begin with, it is important to point out that the author envisions colonial space according to the dualistic structure of the two-republic model. He refers repeatedly to *pueblos de yndios* and *reducciones*, sometimes using the terms interchangeably, and he uses the expression "pueblos de españoles" at least once.[44] He also alludes to a sense of bounded territory in relation to Indian towns, like when he specifies the minimum distance of one league ("una jornada") that should be kept between Indian towns and the rest of colonial society.[45] Geography and law further intersect in his vision of Indian towns as he describes the municipal self-government, or *cabildo*, in charge of the town's juridico-political administration. He visually illustrates a range of indigenous officials in positions of power that evince some level of autonomy—including *alcaldes, regidores, alguaciles, escriuanos*, and *pregoneros*—and he explains their roles, ideal conduct, as well as some of their moral failings and how to punish them.[46] He also stresses that Spanish *corregidores* and priests often interfere in the *cabildo's* affairs, including by unjustly punishing indigenous officials.[47]

Toledo's role in instituting the policy of *reducciones* and enforcing segregationist laws is further stressed by Guaman Poma as part of his account of the socio-spatial and jurisdictional organization under Spanish colonialism.

In his section on good government and justice, he offers an account of the different viceroys of Peru, and he praises Antonio de Mendoza and Andres Hurtado de Mendoza as good Christian rulers who cared for the indigenous.[48] The author makes no mention of the fact that both viceroys attempted to introduce segregationist measures—the first by expanding the strategy of mestizo *recogimiento* from colonial Mexico to Peru, the second by trying to implement the policy of *reducciones*—[49] and, instead, he focuses on the decisive role played by Toledo. He describes Toledo as "rreducidor y poblador destos rreynos deste Pirú"[50] and he praises his legal ordinances banning non-ingenuous subjects from residing in "Indian towns." As he states, "tiene mandado que ningún becino, comendero de yndios, ni entrase español ni mestizo ni mulato ni negro en sus pueblo ni tierras ni en sus término, cino que fuesen a las ciudades a ueuir ellos."[51] He also describes this order as "una de las santas cosas en seruicio de Dios y de su Magestad y bien de los pobres yndios."[52] The author reiterates this stance close to the end of the *Nueva corónica* when he again emphasizes that Toledo explicitly prohibited Spaniards, mestizos, and *mulatos* from living among the indigenous.[53] He also adds that Toledo occasionally ordered and oversaw the removal of "mestisos, mulatos y españoles"[54] from Indian towns, and he appeals to existing legislation to emphasize yet again that "españoles, mestisos, negros y mulatos, zangahígos" should be expelled from said communities even if they are married to indigenous women.[55] As these examples illustrate, as Rolena Adorno confirms, Guaman Poma is unambiguous in praising Toledo for his legislation on indigenous segregation.[56]

The views expressed above are also indicative of the way in which Guaman Poma insists on segregation while acknowledging mestizaje as a central feature of colonial society. This is further confirmed by one of the earliest passages in which Guaman Poma discusses the need to segregate the indigenous. In a section on pre-Hispanic juridical organization, he praises the system of laws that were established under Inca rule, and he claims that Viceroy Francisco de Toledo's tried to incorporate some of those laws as he expanded and reformed the colonial government: "Y uista estas dichas hordenansas el señor don Francisco de Toledo, bizorrey destos rreynos, se enformó esta ley y hordenensas antiguas, sancado dellas las mejores."[57] The section consists primarily of the author's account of pre-Hispanic practices, but Guaman Poma occasionally weaves in comments about what he perceives as problems with the present state of affairs under Spanish colonial rule. Specifically, he makes two comments about the moral failings of Spaniards who sexually abuse indigenous women and contribute to the reproduction of *mestizos*.[58] He also endorses "reducing" Indians in segregated towns:

> para el seruicio de la coro[na] rreal de su Magestad, de nuestro señor rrey don Felipe el terzero, monarca del mundo, aumente yndios y se rredusca en sus pueblos y multiplique yndios. Y deje de multiplicar

mestisos, cholos, mulatos, sanbahigos, cin provecho de la corona rreal; antes para mal que bien salen casta de *biquna* [vicuña] y de *taruga* [venado de altura], que no sale del padre ni de la madre, mala gente en gran daño de la corona rreal y de los pobres yndios deste rreyno.[59]

The passage introduces many of the key arguments that Guaman Poma returns to time and again throughout the *Nueva corónica*. First of all, he refers to King Phillip III as "nuestro señor rrey," which is indicative of the way in which he accepts the monarch's authority over indigenous subjects.[60] He also asserts that promoting native demographic growth is a service to the King, which serves to authorize his consistent plea for the preservation of indigenous lives. In contrast, he explicitly argues that the demographic growth of *mestisos, cholos, mulatos,* and *sanbahigos* should be dissuaded, and he categorically describes these groups as "mala gente." In both cases, he explicitly politicizes life on the basis of racial difference by advocating for opposite strategies on how to manage what he presents as different population groups.

By likening the growth of mixed-ancestry groups to two types of undomesticated animals (the *vicuña* and the *taruga*), Guaman Poma also highlights the disadvantages of mixed-ancestry reproduction. He does so, on the one hand, by associating these groups with the unregulated spatial mobility of undomesticated animals, which again serves to differentiate them from the indigenous, since, as he advocates, the latter can and should be concentrated in segregated towns. On the other hand, as Adorno and John Murra point out in a note about this passage,[61] the comparison to undomesticated animals is meant to call attention to the issue of tribute payment. While *mestizos* were exempt from paying tribute, the Spanish Crown passed a royal decree in 1574 making tribute mandatory for all free blacks, including *mulatos* and *zambahigos*.[62] Yet, as Ronald Escobedo Mansilla explains, the execution of this law in colonial Peru soon ran into problems, among other things because *mulatos* and other free blacks did not always have a stable place of residency, which complicated the collection of tribute. In the case of *zambaigos*, moreover, colonial authorities were unsure if they should pay tribute as *indios* or as *negros* given their mixed ancestry.[63] By alluding to these issues, Guaman Poma establishes a sharp contrast between what he presents as the advantages of fostering indigenous population growth and the disadvantages of mixed-ancestry reproduction.

Later on, the author elaborates on the question of mixed-ancestry tribute in a telling passage that illustrates how he problematizes mestizaje while still accepting it as a fact of colonial life and still affirming indigenous segregation. He writes:

Que el cholo y sanbahigo pague el pecho y tributo y a de acudir a todos los seruicios personales en este rreyno. Porque del todo es yndio fino, que no se a de entender de la casta de precipal sin título, que el cholo ya no tiene cosa de español. Y en esto tiene la culpa y pecado su padre, maldición de Dios, hijo en el mundo de mala fama, mestizo y cholo, mulato, zanbahigo. Para ser bueno criatura de Dios, hijo de Adán y de su mujer Eua, criado de Dios, español puro, yndio puro, negro puro. Estos y sus desendientes mestizos y mulatos o mestizas, mulatas, chola, zanbahiga, uno ne nebguno no queden en los pueblos de los yndios, que an de estar en las ciudades y uillas, aldeas deste rreyno.[64]

The passage begins and ends with two assertions that contradict one another. In the initial lines, Guaman Poma states that *cholos* and *sanbahigos* should pay tribute and perform labor services, and he ambiguously uses the expression "yndio fino" in an apparent reference to both. He thus associates these groups with Indians, which suggests that he accepted that these groups could live as Indians in a manner comparable to what Joanne Rappaport argues about the "disappearing mestizos" who lived in native communities and were "entered into the tribute rolls, effectively becoming 'Indians.'"[65] In the final line, however, he affirms categorically that *mestizos/as, mulatos/as, chola,* and *zanbahiga,* should be expelled from Indian towns and go to cities. He does add a gender specification about *cholas* and *zanbahigas* but does not elaborate on the point. He also appeals to a discourse about blood purity when he affirms that, to be good Christians, Spaniards, Indians, and blacks should not be mixed. The statement, particularly in relation to his other comments, evinces the way in which his formulation of purity is uttered and made meaningful as a result of his understanding of a racially mixed society. In other words, it illustrates the way in which the notion of mestizaje works to reify, rather than undermine, notions of racial purity.[66]

Another set of arguments that Guaman Poma makes about socio-spatial organization in relation to segregation concerns his assertions about the ongoing reliance on indigenous labor power outside of "Indian towns" and the presence of enslaved *negros* in said communities. In terms of the ongoing reliance on indigenous labor power, Guaman Poma concedes that natives may temporarily serve in mines, but he opposes the use of their labor power in cities and Spanish households. Commenting on the first of these issues, he states:

> Que en las dichas minas y plazas de este rreyno, en acauando la dicha *mita* [prestación de trabajo] lo que le fuere mandado de los meses que cirua, acauando de ella a los yndios que ciruiere y los que ayudare, hijos, mujer o ermano, luego le eche de la dicha ciudad o uilla o minas.[67]

The passage comes from the final page of a section titled "Capítulo de los mineros," and it is uttered after the author details a long list of abuses suffered by "yndios pobres" in the mines—including brutal physical punishments carried out by Spaniards, mestizos, and Indians in positions of power;[68] sexual abuse of the indigenous women who accompany their husbands or brothers to serve in the mines;[69] and various forms of labor exploitation.[70] Guaman Poma denounces these abuses and calls for reforms, but he nevertheless accepts that the indigenous' temporary service in mines is an irrevocable fact of colonial labor relations. He also stresses, as evinced in the passage quoted above, that the indigenous should leave those spaces after completing their work. Though he does not explicitly state that they should go back to *pueblos de yndios*, this issue is clarified by a subsequent sentence where Guaman Poma writes that only Spaniards and blacks should live in cities: "que en las ciudades y uillas sólo los españoles y señoras, negros an de biuir."[71]

The author's ideal vision of cities as non-indigenous spaces is also evident in comments where Guaman Poma insists that Indians should not be allowed to work in cities and Spanish households. As he writes:

> Que los yndios de rrecoger en sus pueblos por la sédula rreal de su Magestad, se deue guardarse muy bien en este rreyno para el aumento y seruicio de Dios y de su Magestad. Y ací se deue castigar en todo el rreyno que no ayga yndio ni yndia en las ciudades y en casa de español ni señora, yndio, yndia, muchacho ni *china* [criada] en sus casas y *chacaras* [sementera], qui se lo quite.[72]

Here, Guaman Poma again advocates for spatially gathering "yndios" in segregated towns by appealing to the Crown's interests, and he vaguely references royal legislation on the matter to justify his position. He also tacitly acknowledges the reliance on indigenous labor power in cities and Spanish households, but, instead of conceding this point as another aspect of colonial labor relations, he insists on greater regulation—including punitive measures—to help ensure that the indigenous stay in segregated towns. His arguments are consistent with the type of legislation discussed in Chapter 2, and, though he does not specify what royal decree he is referring to, his discourse evinces that he knew segregationist edicts from the period well.

The author later reiterates that the indigenous should not be allowed to work in cities. In the opening pages of the section on colonial geographies, he asserts:

> En las dichas ciudades, uillas, aldeas que no cirua ningún yndio [ni] yndia ni muchacho ciruan en las minas a su Magestad y que [...] cirua de los negros y negras un millón y de sus hijos mes[tizos] y cholos, mestisas, mulatos, zanbahígos y mulatas que ay [m]uchos millones y que se ciruan entre ello como en Castilla.[73]

In this case, the author justifies his position by again conceding that indigenous laborers may serve in the mines, which preempts any association of *yndios* with idleness. He also describes cities as populous and racially diverse areas, quantifying with hyperbole the number of blacks and mixed-ancestry groups whose labor could be harnessed there. His rhetoric thus provides additional support to his claim that the indigenous should not work in cities by rendering the use of their labor there as redundant. The final lines of the passage also help clarify that the implicit beneficiaries of the labor power of blacks and mixed-ancestry groups in cities are Spaniards. In other words, even though the author recognizes that cities are populated by racially diverse groups, he still associates those areas with Spanish power and jurisdiction.

In the passages analyzed thus far, Guaman Poma argues that blacks should live in cities, and he includes this group inconsistently in the statements he makes about segregationist laws barring non-indigenous subjects from living in Indian towns. The author does, however, make a number of comments where he affirms that enslaved blacks may be allowed to work in Indian towns under certain conditions. Specifically, he concedes that, since Spanish priests were allowed to live in native communities, that dispensation also applied to black slaves owned by priests. On this point, though, he stipulates that only one married black couple should be allowed to serve priests: "Que un padre, cura dotrinante pueda tener sólo un negro esclabo cazado con su negra esclaba."[74] The emphasis on allowing only married black couples to work in Indian towns is reiterated later on:

> Que los dichos negros en los pueblos de los yndios, que nenguno de ellos no meta corregidor ni comendero, padre ni cacique prencipal, cino fuere casado con su ygual negra. Y se fuere casado con yndia lo eche fuera de pa prouincia, so pena de cien pesos para la cámara.[75]

In the latter case, the presence of enslaved blacks in Indian towns is attributed to the actions of various colonial officials, including priests, but he is consistent in arguing that only married black couples should be allowed to live among the indigenous. The justification for Guaman Poma's position is clarified when the author states that, while married black couples should marry "their equals" as a precondition for their presence in Indian towns, black men who marry indigenous women should be expelled from the province. He thus endorses marriage (and therefore reproductive sex) between "equals," while problematizing reproductive relations between differently racialized groups.

In his analysis of the representation of black subjects in the *Nueva corónica,* Eric Vaccarella further argues that Guaman Poma offers several reasons to justify his insistence on marriages between blacks, including associating marriage with a good Christian lifestyle.[76] He also shows that Guaman Poma's positive depiction of blacks is reserved for images of black couples, while images in which black men appear alone are represented negatively. Commenting specifically on an image in which a black *criollo* slave is portrayed trying to seduce an indigenous woman by offering her silver, Vaccarella contends that the man's behavior is associated with carnal sins and sexual immorality.[77] He also adds that Guaman Poma's condemnation of the black man's sexual behavior is framed as more than a moral issue, and should in fact be read as a concern with the reproductive effects of unions between blacks and Indians. As Vaccarella puts it:

> Sin duda, la cuestión de la conducta sexual de los negros representa una preocupación moral para Guaman Poma, pero su mayor inquietud parece radicar en las consecuencias biológicas de la unión sexual entre indios y negros, es decir, el mulatismo.[78]

This analysis provides additional insight to understand Guaman Poma's insistence that only married black couples should be allowed to live in Indian towns, and it brings into focus the way in which his apprehension about mixture informs his representations of racial difference. Even though Guaman Poma never uses the term *mestizaje*, it is evident that his illustrated manuscript offers a range of reflections in which notions of purity and mixture are explicitly articulated in relation to the perceived problem of reproductive sex between differently racialized groups.

The second set of arguments that can be analytically grouped to understand Guaman Poma's views on segregation, pertains to what he says about the regulation of movement based on racial ascription and the imperfect implementation of the policy of *reducciones*. In addition to advocating for punitive measures to ensure that indigenous subjects stay in "Indian towns" and not labor in cities, the author discusses a number of reasons why the indigenous are leaving said communities; he regularly describes those who leave as "yndios ausentes," "yndios cimarrones," and "uagamundos;" and he proposes a series of actions to prevent this from happening further. Among the reasons he gives, he highlights different forms of abuses carried out by colonial officials. For one, in the section on miners discussed above, he asserts that Indians are leaving their communities to avoid being physically mistreated in the mines: "De todos estos dichos agrauios se ausentan de sus pueblos por no yr a las dichas minas a padeser tormento y matirio y por no padeser en aquel ynfierno aquellas penas y tormento de los demonios."[79] As the passage indicates, Guaman Poma is unambiguous in describing the mines as infernal spaces. Yet, because he also concedes that indigenous laborers were obliged to temporarily serve there as subjects of the Spanish King, his comment calls attention to the way in which he tries to align his problematization of indigenous flight with the economic interests of the Spanish Crown. This is confirmed by a later passage in which Guaman Poma plainly states that one of the main problems with Indians who leave their communities is that there is nobody left to pay tribute and serve in the mines: "Y ací, como uen estos yndios ausentes, se salen otros yndios de sus pueblos y no ay quien pague el tributo ni ay quien cirua en las dichas minas."[80] The statement evinces the way in which Guaman Poma appeals to the economic interests of the Spanish Crown, and it foregrounds the fact that Indian towns under Spanish colonial governance were intentionally designed to help extract indigenous labor power and tribute more efficiently, a point which Guaman Poma both understood and accepted.[81]

Another form of abuse that is stressed by Guaman Poma to illustrate why indigenous subjects are leaving segregated communities appears in the section he devotes to Spanish priests. Priests are represented as having close physical contact with the indigenous, and, though the author never advocates explicitly for prohibiting them from residing in Indian towns, he repeatedly refers to priests as "bad examples,"[82] and he offers an extensive textual and visual commentary on systematic abuses, including sadistic forms of punishment and rampant sexual abuse of indigenous women.[83] I discuss these issues in greater detail in the second section of the chapter, but, for now, it is important to consider how he links these abuses to the perceived problem of indigenous flight. In one of many passages on the topic, he writes:

> Que los dichos padres de las dotrinas son tan soberbiosos y coléricos y muy atreuidos que se toman con las justicias y españoles soldados y con los caciques principales y con los yndios pobres y con las yndias como borracho, cin temor de Dios y de la justicia. ...Y ancí destrue todo el rreyno con color de llamarse propietario. Y no ay rremedio en todo el rreyno. Y ancí por ellos se ausenta los yndios, yndias.[84]

Guaman Poma's use of rhetoric works to indict priests' behavior primarily on moral grounds. He describes their moral failures as two types of cardinal sins ("son soberbiosos y coléricos"), and he claims that they conduct themselves as if they did not fear God. The passage thus works to diminish their authority as representatives of the Catholic church, which undermines the main reason they were allowed to be in Indian towns: namely, indigenous Christianization. While the author stops short of claiming that the general rule banning Spaniards from residing in Indian towns should also apply to priests, he does state that their actions are one of the reasons why the indigenous are leaving said communities. He thus suggests that priests' behavior is not only putting the Christianization mission in jeopardy but is also further contributing to socio-spatial disorder.

The perceived problem of indigenous flight from Indian towns is also used by Guaman Poma to call for stricter forms of regulation on their mobility. In the passages above, the term "yndios ausentes" is used to call attention to a pattern of movement that is presented as the result of systematic abuses, but it is also deployed to argue for reforms that are cast as ultimately beneficial to the colonial state. It is also noteworthy that Guaman Poma uses the expression "yndios o yndias cimarrones" to describe individuals who leave said communities. The term "cimarrones" was typically used to describe runaway slaves, and by using it as an adjective to characterize Indians who leave segregated towns, he sanctions their "recapture" as a lawful measure to ensure that segregation was properly enforced. In one of the instances where he uses the expression, he suggests that indigenous *caciques* should be responsible for "gathering" runaway Indians: "Que los dichos caciques principales que se hagan rrecoger a sus yndios o yndias cimarrones de sus *ayllos*."[85] His statement is again compatible with what we find in royal legislation on segregation, and it confirms his familiarity with this body of laws. Later on, Guaman Poma also claims that some indigenous subjects who leave their *reducciones* change their appearance to avoid being recognized by their *caciques*, and he appeals to a discourse about vagrancy to highlight the perceived problem of unregulated mobility:

> Ues aquí, cristiano, cómo no se an de ausentarse los pobres yndios y salir de sus reducciones con tanta molestia en este rreyno.... Que los dichos yndios deste rreyno que no puedan tener en los llanos su bestido y trage de algodón, ací yndio como yndia, porque se ausentan, dexando de pagar el tributo que deue a su Magestad y por no seruir en las dichas minas y otras obligaciones que deuen. Y ací se muda de áuito porque no le connosca sus caciques principales ni sus parientes y andan echos uagamundos.[86]

The passage again foregrounds the way in which he appeals to the economic interests of the Spanish Crown to authorize his discourse, and it illustrates the emphasis that Guaman Poma places on visually distinguishing Indians to prevent the inconveniences he associates with vagrants. As these different examples show, Guaman Poma explicitly advocates for enhanced forms of spatial regimentation aimed at ensuring that Indians remained spatially concentrated as a distinct and identifiable population group.[87]

As part of his endorsement of spatial regulation based on racial ascription, Guaman Poma also emphasizes repeatedly that mixed-ancestry groups should not be allowed to live in Indian towns. The passages where he develops this argument stress that Spaniards should likewise be excluded from those communities, but they offer particular insight to understand how he viewed segregation in the context of mestizaje. In addition to the comments in which Guaman Poma endorses Toledo's ordinances and actions banning non-ingenuous subjects from residing in Indian towns (described above), the author advocates for greater forms of internal policing designed to deal with the reproductive effects of sex between differently racialized groups. He writes:

> Ques muy justo y seruicio de Dios y de su Magestad en este rreyno de que los españoles no se puede poblar junto con los yndios en las ciudades ni en las uillas, aldeas, ni uaya [a] morar nengún español ni española ni mestizo ni mulato ni zambaigo ni cholo. Ci fuere española o

mestiza o mulata que fuere casado con yndio en estre rreyno, que haga los dichos españoles sus pueblos fuera de los yndios en una jornada, ya que no fuera una legua. Y si pariere mestiza, chola, lo lleue a la ciudad por escándalo de ellas.[88]

In the first part of the passage, Guaman Poma reiterates that *yndios* should not live in cities with Spaniards, and he specifies that Spaniards, *mestizos, mulatos, zambaigos,* and *cholos,* should likewise not be allowed to reside among the indigenous. His comments again evince the fact the author recognized that mestizaje was a central feature of colonial society, and they illustrate the way in which he sought to address the potential challenge that racial mixture posed for the project of indigenous segregation by advocating for excluding mixed-ancestry groups from Indian towns. On this point, Guaman Poma actually went beyond what is stipulated in segregationist laws by insisting that *mestizos* and *zambaigos* should also be excluded. As discussed in Chapter 2, royal legislation stipulated possible exemptions for *mestizos* and *zambaigos* who were born in Indian towns, but, in this passage, the author advocates for banning both groups.[89] Though the author is at times inconsistent on this issue—including in the passage discussed earlier in which he concedes that *cholos* and *sanbahigos* may sometimes be allowed to live as Indians—his views are indicative of how he tried to grapple with the effects of mestizaje by insisting on greater regulation of people's movement based on racial ascription.

In the second part of the passage quoted above, it is also noteworthy that Guaman Poma inverts conventional gender dynamics associated with mestizaje by referring specifically to cases in which Indian men are engaging in reproductive relations with non-indigenous women. He presents these unions as stable marriages rather than fleeting or forceful relationships, but he still casts them as problematic. He does so, on the one hand, by arguing that indigenous men who marry outside their socio-racial group should be expelled from Indian towns. In this case, the regulatory logic that informs his views about how people's movements should be policed according to racial ascription is redeployed internally as he begins to stipulate cases in which natives can also be banished from Indian towns based on their marriage and reproductive choices. On the other hand, by describing the reproductive effects of these relations as a scandal, and by insisting that the mixed-ancestry children born of these unions should be taken to cities, Guaman Poma discloses his consistently negative views about mestizaje while still offering a solution to the perceived problem.[90] Both arguments, moreover, are presented as punitive measures intended to dissuade these actions from happening further. The passage also offers critical insight to understand how Guaman Poma conceptualizes boundaries. His view of Indian towns is clearly articulated in terms of a delimited territory, which he expresses when he specifies the minimum distance of one league that should be kept between those communities and the places where he believed Spaniards and mixed-ancestry groups should live. Yet his views also indicate that he envisions boundaries as a reproductive/racial divide between Indians and all other groups, which is why he advocates for greater forms of regulation aimed at deterring reproductive sex between the indigenous and other groups. In other words, Guaman Poma envisions the racial border as always/already a sexual reproductive border.

A final point that is important to consider in regard to Guaman Poma's views on segregation is that, while he unequivocally embraces segregationist efforts, he did at times criticize how the policy of *reducciones* was being carried out. The author points out that Toledo's General Resettlement campaign disrupted indigenous land tenure practices and contributed to their demographic decline. He also denounces Toledo for resettling the indigenous haphazardly in *reducciones* that did not always have the adequate conditions, and he complains that many of the designated areas were far from where the indigenous had cultivated plots on which they depended for their subsistence:

> [Toledo] hizo rreducir y poblar a los yndios, algunos en buena parte, algunos en mala parte, como la suerte cayó. Y por ello se desbarataron los yndios de su querencia por tener las sementeras muy lejos y tienen los yndios.[91]

He also states that he personally witnessed a case in which the judge in charge of overseeing the process of relocating the indigenous into *reducciones* burned the dwellings in which they previously lived and reproduced:

> Y uide en el año de 1609 años un jues rrecogedor de los yndios ausentes que abía enviado su Magestad. Este dicho juez quemaua los citios adonde se poblauan y multiplicauan la gente y los echaua a sus reducciones, para que se acauaran en las reducciones de morir y acauarse, de despoblarse la tierra y perder su Magestad su hazienda que tiene en este rreyno en los yndios.[92]

In this passage, Guaman Poma explicitly associates the *reducciones* with indigenous demographic decline, and he appeals to the interests of the Spanish Crown by suggesting that if the natives were to disappear the King would lose a key source of revenue and labor power. While Guaman Poma is thus consistent in praising Toledo for segregationist laws banning all non-indigenous subjects from residing in Indian towns, he nevertheless pointed out flaws with the material implementation of the *reduccciones*.

The author's ambivalent and often contradictory positions on segregation resist facile interpretations and continuously challenge scholars. As this analysis shows, however, Guaman Poma's endorsement of segregation is a major topic in his *Nueva corónica*, and, as such, it merits greater scrutiny than what it has thus far received. His views are critical to understand how processes of racialization developed in Spanish America in relation to the project of indigenous segregation, and they demonstrate that the context of mestizaje in which segregationist efforts developed not only did not undermine his insistence on the viability of the project, they enhanced his perceived need for greater spatial regulation based on racial ascription.

The Plea for Racially Qualified Life

> Dios y vuestra Magestad no permita que nos acauemos y se despueble su rreyno.
>
> Guaman Poma.[93]

In addition to the two sets of arguments discussed in the previous section, Guaman Poma repurposes and expands the main argument that was used to justify indigenous segregation from the start: namely, the claim that the measure was necessary to ensure indigenous population growth. As shown in the prior two chapters, Vasco de Quiroga first advocated for segregation by stressing that the demographic collapse of the native population caused by colonization could be redressed by physically separating *indios* from Spaniards, and this argument was later developed in segregationist laws and stretched further to account for processes of mestizaje. In *Nueva corónica*, Guaman Poma repeatedly and consistently pleads for the preservation of indigenous lives, and his reflections offer crucial insight to understand how the author politicizes racially qualified life by appropriating that discourse and retooling it from an overtly identitarian position. In this section, I offer an analysis of Guaman Poma's insistence on the need to foster indigenous population growth, I argue that his views are based on a homogenizing conceptualization of *yndios* as a distinct socio-racial group, and I consider the implications that this formulation has for how the author politicizes indigenous women's reproductive capacities.

In the fictional dialogue between Guaman Poma and King Philip III that we find in the latter half of the *Nueva corónica*, the author highlights the topic of indigenous demographic growth by opening with four questions that are exclusively devoted to this issue. Guaman Poma first sets up the dialogue by stating that his intention is to inform the sovereign, and he describes himself as the grandson of the King of Peru ("nieto del rrey del Pirú").[94] He also affirms that he wishes he could see the King face to face ("uerme cara en cara y hablar"), but he adds that he is unable to travel so far because he is old and sick.[95] He further states that the sovereign should thank him for his service, which he says took him thirty years of labor and compelled him to leave his family and property.[96] The fictional dialogue epitomizes the way in which the author seeks to establish an unmediated conversation between the King and himself, and it foregrounds the critical importance that the topic of indigenous demographic growth has in his writing.

In the first two questions of the fictional dialogue, Guaman Poma ventriloquizes the King's voice to inquire about indigenous demographic growth before the arrival of the Spaniards. First, the King asks: "Don Felipe, autor Ayala, dime cómo antes que fuese *Ynga* auían multiplicado los yndios de este rreyno."[97] Here, the King's narrative voice refers to himself as an Inca, which works to establish his authority on Andean terms. He also addresses Guaman Poma's character with the utmost respect by using the honorific *don,* and by explicitly describing him as an author.[98] Similarly, the King asks in his second question: "Dime, don Felipe Ayala, en aquel tienpo, ¿cómo ubo tantos yndios en tiempo de los *Yngas*?."[99] In this case, the use of *don* again underscores the way in which Guaman Poma seeks to elevate his social standing by having none other than the Spanish King legitimate his disputed noble status. The rhetorical strategy in both cases works to authorize Guaman Poma's discourse as a qualified author who can inform the King, and as a nobleman worthy of having a direct hearing with him.

The response that Guaman Poma offers in the dialogue offers preliminary insight to understand the author's views on the matter. In response to the first question, Guaman Poma states that the chief reason why the kingdom was well populated prior to the arrival of the Spaniards is that there was a properly functioning hierarchical government that organized labor efficiently: "Digo a vuestra Magestad que en aquel tienpo auía un rrey y principales. Dencansadmente seruía al rrey y sacaua oro y plata y seruía en sementeras y ganados y sustentaua fortalezas."[100] In response to the second question, he again underscores the fact that hierarchical organization based on the sole authority of the "*Ynga* rrey" was critical to the sense of order that, for him, characterized Andean societies prior to the conquest.[101] Three other aspects that Guaman Poma mentions are that there was a well-enforced system of laws, a leisurely organization of labor that allowed its subjects to subsist and "multiply," and societal gender norms that allowed women to stay in pre-conquest communities, which, as he says, ensured that indigenous men had "mugeres suyas."[102] His second response also evinces a quantifying logic that is clearly displayed when the author offers precise numbers on the size of the indigenous population that lived in pre-conquest communities, which he states ranged from 1,000 to 100,000.[103] Both replies, moreover, are indicative of the way in which the regulation of life at the level of collectivities is presented by the author as a central feature of juridico-political power.

Guaman Poma's views on indigenous reproduction prior to the Spanish conquest can also be contextualized by considering some of the comments he makes about pre-Hispanic sexual and gender norms. In the initial sections of the *Nueva corónica* where he talks about pre-conquest Andean societies, he argues that female virginity was highly regarded, and he emphasizes that indigenous women were neither adulteresses nor whores: "De cómo a sus mugeres no se halló adúltera ni auía puta....De cómo se casauan uírgenes y donzellas y lo tenían por onrra de ellos y la uirginidad te [sic] de edad de treynta años."[104] He also claims that indigenous population growth was not an issue before Spaniard's arrival. Specifically, he affirms that *yndios* used to reproduce like ants ("como hormiga multiplicaron");[105] he states that indigenous men had multiple women who swelled the land with people ("Y tenían muchas mugeres y multiplicaron y hinchieron la tierra de gente y ancí multiplicaron muy muchos yndios en este rreyno");[106] and he references past sexual practices as a model for the future ("Mira qué tanta zuma de yndios pudía auer en el rreyno").[107] Guaman Poma also establishes a sharp contrast between pre- and post-conquest sexual and gender norms. He argues that before colonization adultery and pre-marital sex were grave offenses punishable by death.[108] In contrast, he asserts that Spaniards are responsible for introducing adultery and other mortal sins to Andean societies: "Todo lo malo adulterio y otros pecados mortales trajo concigo los dichos cristianos."[109] As these examples illustrate, Guaman Poma underscores the importance of pre-Hispanic disciplinary sexual and gender norms as part of his reflections on indigenous population growth.

As the fictional dialogue between King Philip III and Guaman Poma progresses, the author further asserts that colonial sexual practices are contributing to indigenous demographic decline. He also proposes a series of reforms based on the assumption that fostering racially qualified life is in alignment with the sovereign's interests. In the third and fourth questions of the dialogue, the King's narrative voice shifts from inquiring about the past to ask instead about the present and future. The King asks: "Dime, autor, ¿cómo agora no multiplica los yndios y se hazen pobres?," followed by, "Dime, autor, ¿cómo multiplicará la gente?."[110] Guaman Poma's answer to the first question focuses solely on what he presents as the problematic sexual appropriation of indigenous women by Spanish men. He states:

> Lo primero, que no multiplica porque todo lo mejor de las mugeres y donzellas lo toman los padres dotrinantes, comenderos, corregidores y españoles, mayordomos, tinientes, oficiales criados de ellos. Y ancí ay tantos mesticillos y mesticillas en este rreyno. Con color de decille manzebado le toma y quita a las mugeres y a sus haziendas de los pobres. De todo lo dicho, de tanto agrauio y daño, se ahorcan ellos propios como los yndios Changas en Andaguayllas. Está un serrillo lleno de yndios, yndias. Quiere murir una ues que no uerse en tanto daño.[111]

In the first half of the passage, Guaman Poma openly denounces Spanish priests and other officials for "taking" indigenous women and virgins, sometimes, as he states, by appealing to false pretenses. The enunciation is written from a male perspective—including when he makes a value judgment about how Spaniards appropriate the "best" of women— and it discloses some of the patriarchal values that inform the author's thinking— including by presenting women as helpless victims and by equating the appropriation of women to the seizure of property. The reproductive effects of these unions are further highlighted by the author when he explains that these relations are the reason why there are so many *mestizos/as* in the kingdom. His use of the diminutive *mesticillos/mesticillas* is somewhat ambiguous in this case, but other passages indicate that he uses it to refer to infants. The inclusion of this point is also indicative of the way in which he correlates mestizaje with indigenous demographic decline. In the latter part of the passage, he further stresses that the sexual appropriation of indigenous women has led to cases of mass suicide, which adds an additional dimension to his problematization of this practice.

In response to the fourth question about how to ensure indigenous "multiplication" in the future, Guaman Poma offers a series of prescriptive measures. First, he states that priests, *encomenderos, corregidores*, and other Spaniards should live as Christians as commanded by the King. What he means by this is clarified when he adds that they should stop engaging in sexual relations with indigenous women. As he puts it "dexen gozar sus mugeres y haciendas y los dexe sus donzellas."[112] This formulation is again articulated from a male perspective, and, more specifically, from an indigenous male perspective, since the implicit collective subject whose interests Guaman Poma purports to represent are the indigenous men whose women are being appropriated. The use of the possessive to describe the women further discloses the author's patriarchal views. Guaman Poma also recommends harsh punishments for Spaniards who are not good Christians and impede indigenous men from "enjoying their women": "Y sean castigados grauemente y quitados de los oficios y beneficios."[113] The final point he makes— which is the only one that does not focus on perceived moral shortcomings associated with sex—is that the indigenous should not be burdened by so many kings and legal authorities who claim to have jurisdiction over them: "Y no ayga tantos rreys y justicias sobre ellos y los dexen multiplicar."[114] Here, his expressed views help clarify the earlier emphasis on Inca organization that we see in his response to the first two questions of the dialogue, and it foregrounds the fact that, for Guaman Poma, one of the key problems of colonial governance was that competing colonial authorities—whom he describes as "tantos rreys"—undermined the sovereignty of the Spanish King.

In Guaman Poma's reflections on indigenous population growth, *yndios* are clearly homogenized as a distinct socio-racial group. Indeed, the author deliberately deploys the Spanish socio-racial label even though he sometimes recognizes that there are significant ethnic, linguistic, and cultural differences among the various indigenous groups that populated the Americas prior to colonization. He also includes himself in that group, as shown in the epigraph for this section, when he pleas for racially qualified life from an overtly identitarian position: "Dios y vuestra Magestad no permita que nos acauemos y se despueble su rreyno."[115] In the opening questions of the dialogue, the Kings' narrative voice likewise assumes that *yndios* are a distinct and identifiable population, and by having the King's character inquire what he can do to foster their growth, Guaman Poma aligns the fictive sovereign's interests with his own personal plight for the preservation of indigenous lives. In an earlier passage, the author also directly appeals to the interests of the actual Spanish King when he states that fostering indigenous reproduction is critical for the prosperity of his kingdom:

> Con ello amentará y multiplicará y con ello primeramente será seruido Dios y su Magestad. Será rrico, ciendo este rreyno rrico y prouecho del padre y del corregidor y comendero. Auiendo rriquesas en la tierra, todos se prouechará, mucho más su Magestad deste rreyno.[116]

The role of the Spanish King in fostering racially qualified life is thus consistently stressed by Guaman Poma, both by depicting him as a fictional character who is keenly interested in indigenous demographic growth and by appealing to his economic interests as one of the main historical addresses of the *Nueva corónica*.

By insisting on the need to foster indigenous reproduction as a racialized collectivity, Guaman Poma also implicitly politicizes indigenous women's procreative capacities. He does so by highlighting that indigenous women's reproductive relations with non-indigenous men are having an adverse effect on the growth of the population. Indigenous women's bodies are represented by Guaman Poma as key vessels of demographic change, and, because he both sanctions and presents the regulation of life at the level of collectivities as a central feature of juridico-political power, he advances a conceptualization of power's hold over life premised on sexual difference and the regulation of women's reproductive capacities. Specifically, he calls for indigenous men to exert greater disciplinary control over indigenous women's bodies as a means to foster racially qualified life.

Throughout the *Nueva corónica*, Guaman Poma decries reproductive relations between differently racialized people, and he stresses in particular that Spaniard's sexual appropriating of indigenous women is hindering native population growth and is contributing to the reproduction of *mestizos/as*. As noted above, in the fictional dialogue with the Spanish King, he denounces Spanish men who seize indigenous women and dispossess indigenous men of their "property," and he identifies Spanish priests, *encomenderos*, and *corregidores* as the main perpetrators of this offense. Guaman Poma also makes this argument repeatedly in earlier passages,[117] including in the section where he first highlights Toledo's role in instituting the *reducciones*. He writes:

> Y cómo se perderá la tierra y quedará solitario y despoblado todo el rreyno y quedará muy pobre el rrey. Por causa del dicho corregidor, padre, comendero y demás españoles que rroban a los yndios sus haziendas y tierras y casas y sementeras y pastos y sus mugeres e hijas, por ací casadas o donzellas, todos paren ya mestisos y cholos. Ay clérigo que tiene uey[n]te hijos y no ay rremedio.[118]

Here the author again associates Spaniard's sexual appropriating of indigenous women with native depopulation, which helps frame his denunciation of the practice not merely as a moral offense but rather as a transgression of the Spanish King's political and economic interests. The trope of theft that is used to characterize Spaniard's sexual affront also works to displace the subject of victimhood since indigenous men are represented as the victims of robbery while indigenous women's bodies are simply cast as one of the objects being seized, with no indication of their subjectivity. Guaman Poma's representation of indigenous women in this passage is also narrowly circumscribed in relation to their reproductive capacities. He depicts them as the child-bearers of *mestisos* and *cholos*, and he uses this to emphasize that their reproductive relations with non-indigenous men are a critical factor to understand the changing demographics of colonial society.

The author also elaborates on the passage above in a subsequent segment that is included immediately after he praises Toledo's legal ordinances banning non-indigenous subjects from residing in Indian towns. Though he explicitly states that Toledo's segregationist legislation applies to Spaniards, *mestizos, mulatos,* and blacks, his comments focus specifically on the benefits of preventing Spanish men from residing in Indian towns:

> Porque no rresultase daños y males entre los yndios, que dellos rresultaría alsamiento y se enseñarían malos uicios. Y los dichos españoles estarían amancebados y haría casta maldita de mestisos. Y no multiplicarían los dichos yndios tiste rreyno, y les forsarían sus mujeres e hijas y se enseñarían uellacos y no obedecerían a sus caciques principales y se harían haraganes y ladrones, *yanaconas*, bachelleres y las mugeres, grandes putas.[119]

As evinced, Guaman Poma associates the presence of Spanish men in native communities with different forms of reproductive relations that he says are hindering indigenous population growth.

On the one hand, he suggests that if Spaniards were allowed to live among the indigenous, they would engage in sexual cohabitation practices (*amancebamiento*). He does not specify if he envisions these relations as consensual, forced, or coerced, but he nevertheless characterizes them as negative by describing their reproductive effects as a "casta maldita." On the other hand, he claims that if Spaniards were allowed to reside in Indian towns, indigenous women would be sexually abused. In this case, he does qualify the nature of the relations by describing them as forced. Yet, instead of representing indigenous women as victims of sexual violence, he describes them as great whores ("grandes putas").

The characterization of indigenous women as whores is also expressed in a number of additional passages and visual illustrations where Guaman Poma denounces their rape. In one passage, he accuses Spanish *corregidores* and priests (among other colonial officials) of roaming around trying to look at indigenous women's naked bodies, or, as he puts it, "la güergüenza de las mugeres."[120] He also claims that some priests would dress up as Indians, and wander all night so they can enter indigenous' homes and gaze at the naked bodies of virgins.[121] His representation of the lustful officials is further developed into a legal argument when he states that they act lawlessly and accuses them of rape: "Y andan rrobando sus haciendas y fornican a las cazadas y a las doncellas los deuirga."[122] While Guaman Poma does not use the word *estupro* in this passage, he does clarify in a later passage that taking a woman's virginity through coercion is a form of *estupro*; in his words: "del uirgo con doncella o doncel uírgenes, estupro."[123] As Lee M. Penyak and Asunción Lavrín explain, the term *estupro* was used in Spanish legal codes to describe rape, though sometimes the word was used to refer to the act of sexually forcing a female, while other times it was used to describe cases in which a man coerced or tricked a female virgin into having intercourse.[124] Guaman Poma's definition of rape is thus consistent with what we find in Spanish legal codes from the period. It is remarkable, though, that while he indicts Spanish men for raping indigenous women, he nevertheless describes raped women as whores. As he states in the immediate sentence after decrying the priests and *corregidores* for taking indigenous women's virginity: "Y así andan perdidas y se hazen putas y paren muchos mesticillos y no multiplica los yndios."[125] The author thus condemns Spaniard's sexual abuse of indigenous women, but at the same time he denigrates the women by calling them whores, and he again correlates the reproductive effects of these relations with indigenous demographic decline.

Similarly, Guaman Poma claims in another passage that raped indigenous women are whores. He writes: "Que los dichos encomenderos en los pueblos de yndios ellos o sus hijos, ermanos, mayordomos desuirgan a las doncellas y a las demás les fuerza a las casadas. Y así se hacen grandes putas las yndias."[126] In this case, as in the passage described above, the author's characterization of indigenous women indicates that the author uses the term as an insult rather than a description of a commercial sexual relationship. In the illustration analyzed in the previous section, where a black *criollo* slave is depicted trying to seduce an indigenous woman by offering her silver, the woman is also described as an "yndia puta,"[127] but, as Valérie Benoist argues, the image does suggest a type of commercial exchange between the two figures because silver is used to coerce the woman into having sex.[128] In contrast, when Guaman Poma states in the passage above that raped indigenous women are "grandes putas," there is no indication of an economic transaction. He nominally invokes the business of prostitution—which, as Eukene Lacarra Lanz explains, was legally sanctioned by both the Spanish monarchy and church though not always clearly defined—but what he problematizes is rape as a form of ongoing colonial violence.[129] By likening the victims of rape to prostitutes, and by using that qualifier as an insult, however, not only does the author ignore important differences that were made in legal codes on the matter, but he also ascribes some level of blame to rape survivors while demeaning women who sell their bodies for economic reasons and coercions.

The reproductive effects of Spaniard's sexual abuse of indigenous women are also stressed by Guaman Poma to further the argument about how the rise of the *mestizo* population is correlated with native demographic decline. In his section on priests, he develops the claim that many clerics have fathered multiple *mestizos/as* despite their vows on celibacy,[130] and he suggests that while priests' children are abundantly reproducing, the indigenous population continues to decline:

> En el año de 160[0] uide en el pueblo de Tiaparo en la prouincia de los Aymarays un clérigo dotrinante con color de dotrinalle y llamarse propietario, como estaua rico, el encomendero o los españoles o los caciques principales no lo podían echar de la dotrina. Y ací se uan acauando los yndios en este rreyno y no ay rremedio. De multiplicar, más multiplicó los padres que los yndios en este rreyno. Con color de la dotrina ajuntaua a las yndias solteras y a los solteros los echaua de la doctrina…. Tenía *acllaconas* [escogidas] y a éstas les hazía trauajar con las demás biudas, ajuntaba con color de decir amancebadas…. Después os espantáys, señoría, cómo no multiplica los yndios. Ci sólo un padre tiene doze hijos, y todas las donzellas por muger que no le dexa, ¿cómo a de multiplicar? Y lo rreparte las biejas, aunque por sus pecados tiene un hijo o dos uastardos, se a de desemular porque es criatura de Dios. Y estos hijos llevó una harria de mesticillos niños, niñas. Una mula llebó says y otro, otros seis…Y ací es muy justo que consagre sus casas y sea bendito, que muger ninguna entre. Y ací multiplicará y que no ajunte a las mugeres ni soltera ni biuda, niña. Y ancí multiplicará los pobres yndios de Dios y de su Magestad.[131]

I quote the passage at length because it illustrates many of the key points that Guaman Poma emphasizes consistently throughout the *Nueva corónica*. First, he claims that priests use religious indoctrination as an excuse to sexually abuse indigenous women. Since he reluctantly accepts the presence of priests in Indian towns, he also underscores that priests who employ native women in their houses end up engaging in sexual cohabitation practices with them. He further associates these actions with the reproduction of *mestizos/as,* and he contrasts priests' prolific progeny to what he describes as a consistent decline of the indigenous population. Moreover, Guaman Poma authorizes his discourse as an eyewitness, and he explicitly addresses the Spanish King to again suggest that ensuring indigenous reproduction is in line with his political and economic interests.

The passage above is also preceds by a line drawing that depicts the reproductive effects of priests' relations with indigenous women.[132] The composition of the illustration first draws viewers to the center of the image, where a mule carrying a packsaddle with six infants *mestizos/as* appears in the foreground. The ornamental letters at the top of the drawing also create the visual effect of a funnel, drawing further attention to the representation of *mestizos/as*. Though the text reads "hijo de los padres dotrinantes mesticillos y mesticillas," the infants' gender is not always clearly distinguishable. What is visibly accentuated are the infants' expressions and gestures: the one in the right front corner appears frightened, behind him/her is another who looks puzzled or angered, and there are two who are raising their index fingers to the sky. Most are looking straight at the viewer, but the one on the left raising his finger looks in the direction of the Spanish priest as if trying to get his father's attention. In the middle ground, Guaman Poma visually distinguishes between a Spanish and an indigenous man by meticulously drawing the difference in their attires, by presenting the former as bearded and the latter as beardless, and by establishing a social hierarchy between the indigenous laborer who is on foot and the Spanish priest who sits elevated on a horse and is commanding the labor transaction.

Valerie Benoist argues that Guaman Poma consistently introduces his arguments pictographically to direct the reader to particular messages that he then textually develops.[133] In this case, though, the ornamental text in the drawing includes a piece of information that is neither mentioned nor developed in the longer textual explanation of the image. Namely, the indication that the indigenous mule driver in the drawing is taking the six infant *mestizos/as* to the city of Lima. As noted in the first section of the chapter, Guaman Poma repeatedly states that *mestizos/as* and other mixed-ancestry groups should live in cities instead of Indian towns, but this argument is not developed in the pages that follow the drawing. In the illustration, moreover, there is no indication of who the infants' mother or mothers are, and the scene suggests that it is the priest's prerogative to decide what to do with his progeny. This works to sever any connection to their mother/s—since their *mestizo/a* children are being taken away from them to Lima—and it validates the type of arguments that were used to justify *mestizo* integration into the Spanish Republic, including the claim that *mestizos/as* were either orphans or "lost" among the Indians. In contrast, in the passage analyzed above Guaman Poma specifies that indigenous women who are in close physical proximity with priests are the reason why *mestizos/as* are reproducing while the indigenous are not. Though he does not elaborate on the women's subjectivity, he does at least mention them, which works as a tacit acknowledgment that they are living mothers whose children are being taken away to the city. As mentioned in Chapter 2, segregationist laws made exceptions for *mestizos* and *zambaigos* who were born in "Indian towns," but in the drawing, Guaman Poma reiterates his insistence that *mestizos* should not be allowed to live among the Indians, even if that meant separating children from their mothers.[134] In both the text and the illustration indigenous women's bodies are again rendered as vessels of demographic change, which politicizes their reproductive capacities but gives them no say over their children. The interplay between text and image thus suggests that Guaman Poma does not solely use his illustrations to introduce messages that he then textually develops but rather to present supplemental information that he does not always elaborate on.

Guaman Poma's patriarchal views on women's role in reproduction are also reflected in comments he makes about how indigenous men should be able to exert greater disciplinary control over their bodies as a means to foster racially qualified life. Specifically, he asserts that one of the roles of indigenous *caciques* is to ensure that Spanish men do not sexually abuse native women: "Un cacique prencipal defiende a los yndios.... Defiende del tragenar uino y texer rropa y amasar y hazer chicha y forsar de sus mugeres, hijas, donzellas de toda la prouincia."[135] Later on, he also writes that another reason why the indigenous leave the *reducciones* is that Spanish men appropriate indigenous women and interfere in their affairs so that indigenous men have no other recourse to defend "their" women:

> Que los dichos yndios por qué causa y rrazón salen de los dichos sus pueblos: Porque les quita a sus mugeres y hijas los dichos corregidores, o el dicho escriuano, el dicho padre y su ermano el comendero y sus hijos y mayordomos para sus seruicios y mansebas....De la defensa de sus hijos o hijas lo tienen en odio. Y por ello le castiga a los dichos pobres yndios. Con estos agrauios se ausentan y se uan a otras prouincias y así se despuebla los pueblos y se acauarán de despoblarse en todo este rreyno....Con este tanto trauajo y desuentura y ocupaciones y molestia se ausentan los dichos yndios de sus pueblos y rreducciones en todo este rreyno.[136]

As shown, he claims that Indian men who try to defend "their" women are hated by colonial officials and are punished harshly for trying to do so. He also links indigenous' men inability to "protect" women with indigenous demographic decline. His politicization of indigenous lives is premised on an understanding of sexual difference that is indissociable from women's reproductive capacity, and, as part of his plea for racially qualified life, he sanctions and demands greater regulation of women's reproductive bodies.

As these examples illustrate, Guaman Poma consistently problematizes reproductive sex between differently racialized people, and, as part of this, he advocates for greater regulation of indigenous women's reproductive capacities. In the fictional dialogue with the Spanish King, the initial theme of the dialogue shifts after the opening questions to cover a arrange of other topics, but Guaman Poma's emphasis on indigenous population growth is consistently woven into the conversation. In particular, it is expressed as part of the author's endorsement of segregation. About midway through the dialogue, the King's voice reacts emotively to Guaman Poma's account of indigenous demographic decline: "me aués contado tantas cosas lastimosas."[137] He also asks the author how to remedy the situation: "¿cómo se podrá rremediar?."[138] In his response, Guaman Poma focuses on two key points. On the one hand, he reiterates that Spaniards should live as Christians and marry their own kind: "Digo vuestra Magestad que todos los españoles uiuan como cristianos, procuren de casarse con su calidad ygual señora y dexen a las pobres yndias multiplicar y dexen sus pociciones de tierras y casas."[139] His answer is consistent with his earlier problematization of Spanish-indigenous reproductive relations, but he elaborates on this point by sanctioning marriages between people of equal "calidad" that works to explicitly differentiate the natives based on these criteria. On the other hand, Guaman Poma also argues that the indigenous should be "reduced" in segregated communities, allotted arable land and pastures, and granted their own jurisdiction: "Y ací conbiene que vuestra Magestad, como rrey *Ynga*, le mande dar título y posición de que se rredusca y pueble y se le dé sementeras y pastos y jurisdicción y propedad que tenía aquellos que piciyyan."[140] Thus his response evinces the way in which his problematization of Spanish-indigenous reproductive relations is intertwined with his views about segregation. His overarching aim is to emphasize the need to foster the reproduction of the indigenous population, and, for him, the way to achieve that goal is to discourage reproductive sex between differently racialized people through spatial and jurisdictional separation.

The endorsement of indigenous segregation that we find in Guaman Poma's dialogue with the King is again reiterated in the last few pages of the section. He writes:

> Es muy gran serbicio de Dios nuestro señor y de vuestra Magestad y aumento de los yndios deste rreyno que no estén ningún español, mestizo, cholo, mulato, zanbahígo, casta de ellos, cino fuere casta de yndio, que a todos les eche a chicos, grandes, casados.[141]

The passage again indicates that Guaman Poma was familiar with official legislation on segregation. His insistence that non-indigenous groups be expelled from Indian communities is further justified by his appeal to a discourse about caste that works to differentiate between those whom he includes in the label "casta de yndio" and the rest of the listed groups, which he presents as socio-racially distinct from Indians. The passage, moreover, again foregrounds the fact that Guaman Poma viewed segregation as a necessary measure to ensure indigenous population growth. The fictional dialogue between Guaman Poma and the King thus allows us to recognize that one of the main reasons why Guaman Poma endorsees segregation is because he saw the project as necessary for fostering racially qualified life.

Notably, in the fictional dialogue with the King, Guaman Poma does not mention disease as a major cause of the indigenous' demographic decline. Earlier in the *Nueva corónica,* he does talk about measles and smallpox in passages where he discusses the death of the Inca Huayna Capac, and the 1586 earthquake that devastated Lima when Fernando de Torres y Portugal was viceroy.[142] Yet, as Alex M. Klohn and Philippe Chastonay suggest, while the effects of diseases were well known by Guaman Poma, he never focuses on this issue as part of his reflections on indigenous depopulation.[143] Instead, his comments about indigenous population decline evince the way in which he politicizes reproductive sex between differently racialized people, and they foreground the fact that the regulation of indigenous women's reproductive capacities is tied to his broader political project of how to reform the colonial government.

Conclusion

El primer nueva corónica y buen gobierno Guaman offers a firsthand account of how the project of indigenous segregation was carried out in the Andes. Guaman Poma not only endorsed segregationist measures, but he also justified them by appealing to the same type of rhetoric that we find in juridical discourses from the period. The text also brings into focus the way in which notions of racial difference were developing and being articulated in relation to segregationist projects. Throughout the text, Guaman Poma uses terms like *casta*, *linaje*, and *cristiano de sangre* to establish marked distinctions between the different socio-racial groups that were part of Andean colonial society—including Spaniards, *criollos*, Amerindians, *mestizos*, mulattos, Jews, Moors, *cholos*, *zambaigos*, and black Africans (both enslaved and free).[144] He also talks about different "géneros de personas,"[145] and he occasionally uses skin color to make distinctions between different groups, including in a passage in which he describes indigenous groups as "blanquícimos como españoles."[146] While there is no systematic account of mestizaje in the *Nueva corónica*, Guaman Poma consistently problematizes reproductive sex between differently racialized people, and it is around this problematization that differences between groups of people are largely articulated and made meaningful. His emphasis on fostering racially qualified life, moreover, is presented as part of a broader argument about the need to manage reproductive relations, and, as part of this, he repeatedly advocates for greater "protection" and regulation of indigenous women's procreative capacities.

Guaman Poma's consistent denunciation of how Spanish men are sexually appropriating indigenous women is also decisively tied to his own lived experience. For one, as the author explains in the opening pages of the *Nueva corónica*, he had a *mestizo* half-brother named Martín de Ayala. For the most part, Guaman Poma represents *mestizos* in highly negative terms—including when he characterizes them as a "casta maldita"—[147] but, in the case of his half-brother, he consistently praises him and describes him as a "mestizo sancto."[148] This is significant because Martín de Ayala was conceived by Guaman Poma's mother, Juana Curiocllo Coya, who had a relationship with the Spanish conquistador Luis Davalos de Ayala. Though there are many enigmas about the nature of this relationship—including whether it was forced or consensual, and whether or not it happened before Guaman Poma's mother married his father—this personal background adds a level of complexity to his demeaning characterization of indigenous women who engage in reproductive relations with Spanish men, including his description of raped women as whores.[149] Moreover, Guaman Poma also states that the Spanish priest and missionary Martín de Murúa, whom he collaborated with, tried to, as he puts it, appropriate "his woman": "Mira, cristiano, todo a mí se me a hecho, hasta quererme quitar mi mujer un flayre merzenario llamado Morúa en el pueblo de Yanaca."[150] Guaman Poma's reflections about the need to "protect" indigenous women, including through better enforcement of segregation, are thus informed by his own lived experience, and they cannot be disentangled from his consistent plea for racially qualified life. While there are numerous ongoing enigmas about these issues, his personal experience certainly informs his oeuvre and enriches this and future readings of it.

Notes

1 Rolena Adorno, "Los textos manuscritos de Guaman Poma (I) La preparación de la *Nueva corónica* para la imprenta," in *La memoria del mundo inca: Guaman Poma y la escritura de la* Nueva corónica, edited by Jean-Philippe Husson (Fondo Editorial de la Pontifica Universidad Católica del Perú, 2016), 50.

2 Felipe Guaman Poma de Ayala, *El primer nueva corónica y buen gobierno*, edited by John V. Murra, Rolena Adorno (Siglo Veintiuno, 2006 [1615]), 962[976]. Guillermo Lohmann Villena, "Una carta inédita de Huamán Poma de Ayala," *Revista de Indias* 6 (1945): 326. Juan M. Ossio, among others, questions that Guaman Poma was 80 years old when he completed his illustrated manuscript. See "Mito e historia en torno a la fecha de nacimiento de Guaman Poma de Ayala," in *La memoria del mundo inca: Guaman Poma y la escritura de la* Nueva corónica, edited by Jean-Philippe Husson (Fondo Editorial de la Pontifica Universidad Católica del Perú, 2016), 147–148.

3 Rolena Adorno, "Racial Scorn and Critical Contempt: Review of *Nueva corónica y buen gobierno*," *Diacritics* 4, no. 4. (1974): 5; Mary Louise Pratt, "Arts of the Contact Zone," *Modern Language Association* (1991): 35; Mercedes López-Baralt, "Un ballo in maschera: Hacia un Guaman Poma multiple," *Revista de Crítica Literaria Latinoamericana* 21, no. 41 (1995): 76; Rocío Quispe Agioli "Escribirlo es nunca acabar: cuatrocientos cinco años de lecturas y silencios de una *Opera Aperta* colonial andina," *Letras: Revista de Investigacion de la Facultad de Letras y Ciencias Humanas* 91, no. 133 (2020): 6. Mauro Mamani Macedo also affirms that Guaman Poma's text "constituye la biblia del indigenismo." See "Introducción," in *Guamán Poma de Ayala: las travesias culturales*, edited by Mauro Mamani Macedo (Facultad de Letras y Ciencias Humanas Universidad Mayor de San Marcos, 2016), 9.

4 Ralph Bauer, "'EnCountering' Colonial Latin American Indian Chronicles: FelipeGuaman Pomade Ayala's History of the 'New' World," *American Indian Quarterly* 25, no. 2 (2001): 274.

5 Rolena Adorno, "A Witness unto Itself: The Integrity of the Autograph Manuscript of Felipe Guaman Poma de Ayala's *El primer nueva corónica y buen gobierno*," in *New Studies of the Autograph Manuscript of Felipe Guaman Poma de Ayala's* Nueva corónica y buen gobierno, edited by Rolena Adorno,

Ivan Boserup (Museum Tusculanum Press, 2003): 20–21; Rolena Adorno, "Introduction," in *Unlocking the Doors to the Worlds of Guaman Poma and His* Nueva corónica, edited by Rolena Adorno, Ivan Boserup (The Royal Library Museum Tusculanum Press, 2015), 10–11.

6 Jesper Nielsen and Mettelise Fritz Hansen, "Dedications and Devils: Comparing Visual Representations of in Early Colonial Mesoamerican Sources and Guaman Poma's *Nueva corónica*," in *Unlocking the Doors to the Worlds of Guaman Poma and His* Nueva corónica, edited by Rolena Adorno, Ivan Boserup (The Royal Library Museum Tusculanum Press, 2015), 238; Rolena Adorno, "Los textos manuscritos de Guaman Poma," 43, 57.

7 Gregory Khaimovich argues that the use of bilingualism in the *Nueva corónica* suggests that King Phillip III was not the only addressee of the manuscript. See "In Search of the Background for the Bilingualism of *El primer nueva corónica y buen gobierno*," in *Unlocking the Doors to the Worlds of Guaman Poma and His* Nueva corónica, edited by Rolena Adorno, Ivan Boserup (The Royal Library Museum Tusculanum Press, 2015), 205.

8 Rolena Adorno, "Introduction," 11.

9 For a review of how Guaman Poma's oeuvre was read by Latin American postcolonial, subaltern, and deconial scholars see Olimpia E. Rosenthal, "Guamán Poma and the Genealogy of Decolonial Thought," *Journal of Commonwealth and Postcolonial Studies* 6, no. 1 (2018): 64–85.

10 See Walter Mignolo, "Delinking," *Cultural Studies* 21, no. 2–3 (2007): 460; Mignolo, "El pensamiento Decolonial: Desprendimiento y Apertura. Un manifiesto," in *El giro decolonial. Reflexiones para un diversidad epistémica más allá del capitalismo global*, edited by Santiago Castro-Gómez, Ramón Grosfoguel (Siglo del Hombre Editores, 2007), 28; Walter Mignolo,"Preamble: The Historical Foundation of Modernity/Coloniality and the Emergence of Decolonial Thinking," in *Companion to Latin American Literature and Culture*, edited by Sara Castro Klaren (Wiley-Blackwell Publishing, 2008), 17. For a critique of Latin American decolonial studies see Abraham Acosta, "Unsettling Coloniality: Readings and Interrogations," *Journal of Commonwealth and Postcolonial Studies* 6, no. 1 (Spring 2018): 3–16.

11 Quispe Agioli, "Escribirlo es nunca acabar," 6.

12 Quispe Agnoli, "Escribirlo es nunca acabar," 7.

13 For Guaman Poma's biblical account of the different Andeans groups who preceded the Incas, see *El primer nueva corónica* 22[22], 23[23], 24[24[25]. Rolena Adorno interprets this representation as one of Guaman Poma's strategies to establish that the indigenous descended directly from the biblical progenitors. See Rolena Adorno "The Depiction of Self and Other in Colonial Peru," *Art Journal* 49, no. 2 (1990): 113.

14 Regina Harrison, "Guaman Poma: Law, Land, and Legacy," in *Unlocking the Doors to the Worlds of Guaman Poma and His* Nueva corónica, edited by Rolena Adorno, Ivan Boserup (The Royal Library Museum Tusculanum Press, 2015), 144.

15 Jesper Nielsen and Mettelise Fritz Hansen, "Dedications and Devils: Comparing Visual Representations of in Early Colonial Mesoamerican Sources and Guaman Poma's *Nueva corónica*," in *Unlocking the Doors to the Worlds of Guaman Poma and His* Nueva corónica, edited by Rolena Adorno, Ivan Boserup (The Royal Library Museum Tusculanum Press, 2015), 233–268; Audrey Prevotel, "A Central Aspect of the Intellectual, Religious, and Artistic Context of the *Nueva corónica: Lives of Saints*," in *Unlocking the Doors to the Worlds of Guaman Poma and His* Nueva corónica, edited by Rolena Adorno and Ivan Boserup (The Royal Library Museum Tusculanum Press, 2015), 331–353.

16 José Cardenas Bunsen, "Manuscript Circulation, Christian Eschatology, and Political Reform: Las Casas's *Tratado de las doce dudas* and Guaman Poma's *Nueva corónica*," in *Unlocking the Doors to the Worlds of Guaman Poma and His* Nueva corónica, edited by Rolena Adorno and Ivan Boserup (The Royal Library Museum Tusculanum Press, 2015), 77. Guaman Poma talks about restitution in *El primer nueva corónica*, 526 [540].

17 Ralph Bauer, "'EnCountering' Colonial Latin American Indian Chronicles," 274; Galen Brokaw, "The Poetics of Khipu Historiography: Felipe Guaman Poma de Ayala's 'Nueva corónica' and the 'Relación de los quipucamayos," *Latin American Research Review* 38, no. 3 (2003): 116.

18 Jean-Philippe Husson, "A Little Known but Essential Element of the Cultural Context of the *Nueva corónica*: Felipe Guaman Poma de Ayala's Native Sources," in *Unlocking the Doors to the Worlds of Guaman Poma and His* Nueva corónica, edited by Rolena Adorno and Ivan Boserup (The Royal Library Museum Tusculanum Press, 2015), 163–187.

19 Augusta Holland, "Importancia de los enanos y corcovados en la *Nueva corónica*," in *La memoria del mundo inca: Guaman Poma y la escritura de la* Nueva corónica, edited by Jean-Philippe Husson (Fondo Editorial de la Pontifica Universidad Católica del Perú, 2016), 273, 274, 283.

20 Juan M. Ossio estimates that Guaman Poma was born between 1562 and 1567. See "Mito e historia," 151. Others place his birth in 1535 based on the author's own account of being 80 years old in 1615. See Ossio for a review of this scholarship.

21 Guillermo Lohmann Villena, "Una carta inédita," 326.

22 Guillermo Lohmann Villena, "Una carta inédita," 326, 327.

23 Guillermo Lohmann Villena, "Una carta inédita," 327.

24 Rolena Adorno, "Los textos manuscritos de Guaman Poma," 50.

25 Guaman Poma, *El primer nueva corónica*, 5[5], 6[6], 15[15], 16[16] 736 [750], 758 [772], 902 [916]; Guillermo Lohmann Villena, "Una carta inédita," 326. See also Mercedes López-Baralt, "Un ballo in Maschera," 89; Rolena Adorno, "The Depiction of Self and Other in Colonial Peru," *Art Journal* 49, no. 2 (1990): 113.

26 Guaman Poma, *El primer nueva corónica*, 374[376], 380[382], 386[388], 389[391], 391[393], 395[397], 397[399], 399[401].

27 Guaman Poma, *El primer nueva corónica*, 736[750], 903[917]. See also José Carlos de la Puente Luna, "El capitán, el ermitaño y el cronista. Claves para establecer cuándo nació el autor de la *Nueva corónica y buen gobierno*," in *La memoria del mundo inca: Guaman Poma y la escritura de la* Nueva corónica, edited by Jean-Philippe Husson (Fondo Editorial de la Pontifica Universidad Católica del Perú, 2016), 136.

28 For more on The Taqui Onqoy, see Sabine MacCormack, "Pachacuti: Miracles, Punishments, and Last Judgment: Visionary Past and Prophetic Future in Early Colonial Peru," *The American Historical Review* 93, no. 4 (1988): 982; Sara Castro-Klaren, "Dancing and the Sacred in the Andes: From the 'Taqui-Oncoy' to 'Rasu Niti'" *Dispositio* 14, no. 36/38 (1989): 169–185. For more on Cristóbal de Albornoz and his campaign to extirpate indigenous idolatries, see Pierre Duviols, "Cristóbal de Albornoz. Instrucción," in *Fábulas y mitos de los incas*, edited by Henrique Urbano, Pierre Duviols (Historia 16, 1989). For more on Guaman Poma's involvement with Albornoz, see Jean-Philippe Husson, "Prólogo," in *La memoria del mundo inca: Guaman Poma y la escritura de la* Nueva corónica, edited by Jean-Philippe Husson (Fondo Editorial de la Pontifica Universidad Católica del Perú, 2016), 20; Juan M. Ossio, "Mito e historia," 152. For Guaman Poma's comments about Albornoz see *El primer nueva corónica*, 676 [690].

29 Rolena Adorno, *The Polemics of Possession in Spanish-American Narrative* (Yale University of Press, 2007), 26.
30 See Juan M. Ossio, "Inca Kings, Queens, Captains, and *Tocapus* in the Manuscripts of Martín de Murúa and Guaman Poma," in *Unlocking the Doors to the Worlds of Guaman Poma and His* Nueva corónica, edited by Rolena Adorno and Ivan Boserup (The Royal Library Museum Tusculanum Press, 2015), 291–330; Ivan Boserup, "Los textos manuscritos de Guaman Poma (II): Las etapas de la evolución del manuscrito *Galvin* de la *Historia general del Perú* de Martín de Murúa," in *La memoria del mundo inca: Guaman Poma y la escritura de la* Nueva corónica, edited by Jean Philippe Husson (Fondo Editorial de la Pontifica Universidad Católica del Perú, 2016), 61–115.
31 Rolena Adorno, "Los textos manuscritos de Guaman Poma," 43.
32 Rolena Adorno, *Writing and Resistance in Colonial Peru* (University of Texas Press, 2000), xxii–xxiii. Gregory Cushman also points out that the Humanga hertland was "one of the most ethnically diverse regions in all of South America." See "The Environmental Contexts of Guaman Poma: Interethnic Conflict over Forest Resources and Place in Huamanga, 1540-1600," in *Unlocking the Doors to the Worlds of Guaman Poma and His* Nueva corónica, edited by Rolena Adorno and Ivan Boserup (The Royal Library Museum Tusculanum Press, 2015), 106.
33 Pablo Macera, "Introducción," *Phelipe Gvaman Poma de Aiala. Y no ay remedio,* edited by Elías Prado Tello y Alfredo Prado Prado (CIPA Centro de Investigación y Promoción Amázonica, 1991), 28; Elías Prado Tello and Alfredo Prado, "Presentación," in *Phelipe Gvaman Poma de Aiala. Y no ay remedio,* edited by Elías Prado Tello and Alfredo Prado Prado (CIPA Centro de Investigación y Promoción Amázonica, 1991), 15.
34 See *Expediente Prado Tello,* 55 v. in Elías Prado Tello and Alfredo Prado Prado, *Phelipe Gvaman Poma de Aiala,* 172; Gregory Cushman, "The Environmental Contexs," 111.
35 Elías Prado Tello and Alfredo Prado Prado, *Phelipe Gvaman Poma de Aiala,* 172–173.
36 Pablo Macera, "Introducción," 31.
37 Rolena Adorno, *Writing and Resistance,* xxxvi–xxxvii. As Adorno explains, we do not know if the corporal punishment was carried out, but his banishment from Huamanga certainly was.
38 Pablo Macera, "Introducción," 26.
39 Rolena Adorno, "Textos imborrables: Posiciones simultaneas y sucesivas del sujeto colonial." *Revista de Crítica Literaria Latinoamericana* 21, no. 41 (1995): 38; Rolena Adorno, *Writing and Resistance,* xvii. Other critics maintain that Guaman Poma started to work on his illustrated manuscript since 1587. See Mónica Morales, *Reading Inebriation in Early Colonial Peru* (Ashgate, 2012), 78; Ralph Bauer, "'EnCountering' Colonial Latin American Indian Chronicles," 274.
40 Jeremy Mumford, *Vertical Empire: The General Resettlement of Indians in the Colonial Andes* (Duke University Press, 2012), 1–2, 119.
41 Jeremy Mumford, *Vertical Empire,* 144, 152.
42 Although Guaman Poma's views on segregation have not been the object of a sustained study, several scholars have made brief remarks on the subject. See José Cardenas Bunsen,"Manuscript Circulation," 80; Mercedes López Baralt, *Ícono y conquista: Guamán Poma de Ayala* (Ediciones Hiperión, 1988), 297; John V. Murra, "Waman Puma, Etnógrafo del mundo Andino," in *El primer nueva corónica y buen gobierno,* edited by John V. Murra and Rolena Adorno (Siglo Veintiuno, 2006), xix; Rolena Adorno, "Los textos manuscritos de Guaman

Poma," 48; Raquel Chang-Rodriguez, "Coloniaje y conciencia nacional: Garcilaso de la Vega Inca y Felipe Guamán Poma de Ayala," *Cahiers du monde hispanique et luso-brésilien*, no. 38 (1982): 42; Jeremy Mumford, *Vertical Empire*, 143–156; Sara Vicuña Guengerich, "Virtuosas y corruptas: Las mujeres indígenas en las obras de Guamán Poma de Ayala y el Inca Garcilaso de la Vega," *Hispania* 96, no. 4 (2013): 673; Irene Silverblatt, "Family Values in Seventeenth-Century Peru," in *Native Traditions in the Postconquest World*, edited by Elizabeth Hill Boone and Tom Commins (Dumbarton Oaks, 1998): 75.

43 Guaman Poma, *El primer nueva corónica*, 1117 [1127].

44 For evidence of passages where he uses the expressions *pueblos de yndios* and *reducciones* interchangeably see Guaman Poma, *El primer nueva corónica*, 857 [871], 869 [883], 872 [886], 873 [887]. He also uses the term *pueblo de españoles* in 996[1004].

45 Guaman Poma, *El primer nueva corónica*, 533 [547].

46 See Guaman Poma, *El primer nueva corónica*, 793 [807]–815 [829]. In this section, he also mentions the figure of the *capac apo*, who he describes as an indigenous administrator in charge of "todos los bienes de la comunidad y *sapci*." See 809 [823]. For more on the meaning and importance of *sapci*, see Jose Carlos de la Puente Luna "That Which Belongs to All: Khipus, Community, and Indigenous Legal Activism in the Early Colonial Andes," *The Americas* 72, no. 1 (2015): 19–54; Frank Salomon, "Guaman Poma's *Sapci* in Ethnographic Vision," in *Unlocking the Doors to the Worlds of Guaman Poma and His* Nueva corónica, edited by Rolena Adorno and Ivan Boserup (The Royal Library Museum Tusculanum Press, 2015), 355–396. For more on Guaman Poma's representation of the indigenous *cabildo*, see Jeremy Mumford, *Vertical Empire*, 146–148.

47 See Guaman Poma, *El primer nueva corónica*, 571 [585], 586 [600], 654 [668]. For an analysis of the visual representation of a black man punishing an indigenous *alcalde*, as instructed by a Spaniard, see Rachel Sarah O'Toole, *Bound Lives: African, Indians, and the Making of Race in Colonial Peru* (Pittsburgh: University of Pittsburgh Press, 2012), 160.

48 Guaman Poma, *El primer nueva corónica*, 437[439], 439[441]. For more on the omissions and mistakes in Guaman Poma's account of the viceroys, see Rolena Adorno and John V. Murra, "Notas aclaratorias," in Guaman Poma, *El primer nueva corónica y buen gobierno* (Siglo Veintiuno, 2006), notes 438, 446 on page 1144.

49 For more on Antonio de Mendoza's strategy of mestizo integration, see Nemser, *Infrastructures*, 73–74. For more one Andres de Mendonza's attempt to implement the *reducciones*, see Alejandro Málaga Medina, "Las reducciones en el Perú durante el gobierno del Virrey Toledo," *Kollasuyo: revista de estudios bolivianos* 87 (1974): 48; Jeremy Mumford, *Vertical Empire*, 50.

50 Guaman Poma, *El primer nueva corónica*, 445 [447].

51 Guaman Poma, *El primer nueva corónica*, 446 [448].

52 Ibid.

53 Guaman Poma, *El primer nueva corónica*, 1116 [1126].

54 Ibid.

55 Guaman Poma, *El primer nueva corónica*, 1117 [1127].

56 Rolena Adorno, "Los textos manuscritos," 48.

57 Guaman Poma, *El primer nueva corónica*, 193 [195].

58 Guaman Poma, *El primer nueva corónica*, 224 [226], 230 [232].

59 Guaman Poma, *El primer nueva corónica*, 213 [215].

60 Raquel Chang-Rodrínguez confirms that Guaman Poma accepted the authority of the Spanish Crown. See "Coloniaje y conciencia nacional," 42.

61 Rolena Adorno and John V. Murra, "Notas aclaratorias," note 215 for page [215], on page 1135.

62 See Joanne Rappaport, *The Disappearing Mestizo: Configuring Difference in the Colonial New Kingdom of Granada* (Duke University Press, 2014), 11; Ronald Escobedo Mansilla, "El tributo de los zambaigos, negros y mulatos libres en el virreinato peruano," *Revista de Indias* 41 (1981): 43–46.

63 Ronald Escobedo Mansilla, "El tributo," 46.

64 Guaman Poma, *El primer nueva corónica*, 526 [540].

65 Joanne Rappaport, *The Disappearing Mestizo*, 10.

66 Joshua Lund, *The Impure Imagination. Toward a Critical Hybridity in Latin American Writing* (University of Minnesota Press, 2006), 15.

67 Guaman Poma, *El primer nueva corónica*, 533 [537].

68 Guaman Poma, *El primer nueva corónica*, 525 [529], 526 [530].

69 Guaman Poma, *El primer nueva corónica*, 526 [530], 532 [536].

70 Guaman Poma, *El primer nueva corónica*, 528 [532], 530 [534], 532 [536].

71 Guaman Poma, *El primer nueva corónica*, 533 [537].

72 Guaman Poma, *El primer nueva corónica*, 843 [857].

73 Guaman Poma, *El primer nueva corónica*, 997 [1005].

74 Guaman Poma, *El primer nueva corónica*, 574 [588].

75 Guaman Poma, *El primer nueva corónica*, 710 [724].

76 Eric Vaccarella's "Estrangeros, uellacos, santos y rreys: la representación de los negros en la obra de Felipe Guamán Poma de Ayala," *Revista Iberoamericana* LXVIII, no. 198 (2002): 21. For additional analyses of the representation of blacks in Guaman Poma see Rachel Sarah O'Toole, *Bound Lives*, 160; Valerie Benoist, "La conexión entre casta y familia en la representación de los negros dentro de la obra de Guarnan Poma," *Afro-Hispanic Review* 29, no. 1 (2010): 35–54; Larissa Brewer-García, *Beyond Babel: Translations of Blackness in Colonial Peru and New Granada* (Cambridge Univeristy Press, 2020): 195–198.

77 Eric Vacccarella, "Estrangeros, uellacos, santos y rreys: la representación de los negros en la obra de Felipe Guamán Poma de Ayala." *Revista Iberoamericana* LXVIII, no. 198 (2002): 22.

78 Ibid.

79 Guaman Poma, *El primer nueva corónica*, 527 [531].

80 Guaman Poma, *El primer nueva corónica*, 1128 [1138].

81 For more on Toledo's role in organizing the labor system in mines, see Jeremy Mumford, *Vertical Empire*, 96.

82 Guaman Poma, *El primer nueva corónica*, 568 [582], 569 [583] 857 [871], 857 [871], 872 [886].

83 Guaman Poma, *El primer nueva corónica*, 566 [580].

84 Guaman Poma, *El primer nueva corónica*, 578 [592]. For additional examples in which Guaman Poma links indigenous flight with priest's behavior see 571 [585], 572 [586]. He also makes a similar claim in relation to absuses by other colonial officials, see 581 [595], 797 [811], 857 [871], 869 [883], 873[887], 872 [886].

85 Guaman Poma, *El primer nueva corónica*, 773 [787]. Mumford also argues that *caciques* were responsible for insuring that the Andean population stayed in the *reducciones*, see *Vertical Empire*, 97–98.

86 873 [887]. For other instances where he uses the expression "yndios cimarrones" see 872 [886], 888 [902].

87 For more on Guaman Poma's views on restricting indigenous mobility, see Jeremy Mumford, *Vertical Empire*, 154.

88 Guaman Poma, *El primer nueva corónica*, 533 [547].

89 See Law 21, Title 3, Book 6 of the *Recopilación,* as well as my analysis of the 1589 decree on which the law is partly based in Chapter 2. For other examples in which he calls for banning Spaniards and mixed ancestry groups form Indian towns, see *El primer nueva corónica* 524 [528], 533 [547], 816 [830], 977 [995].

90 As Rolena Adorno confirms, "Guaman Poma's resounding condemnation of *mestizaje* constitutes one of the basic premises of his work's conceptualization." See Rolena Adorno, *Writing and Resistance,* xli. For a different account of Guaman Poma's views on mestizaje see also Juan Carlos Estenssoro Fuchs, "Los colores de la plebe: razón y mestizaje en el Perú colonial," in *Los cuadros del mestizaje del virrey Amat y la representación etpnografica en el Perú colonial,* edited by Natalia Majluf (Museo de Arte de Lima, 2000). See also Rocío Quispe Agnoli, "Mestizos (in)deseables en el Perú colonial tempran," *Revista de Crítica Literaria Latinoamericana* XLIII, no. 86 (2017): 127–150.

91 Guaman Poma, *El primer nueva corónica,* 445 [447]. See also Guaman Poma, *El primer nueva corónica,* 951 [965].

92 Guaman Poma, *El primer nueva corónica,* 578 [592]. For more on the location of reducciones, see also Jeremy Mumford, *Vertical Empire,* 148.

93 Guaman Poma, *El primer nueva corónica,* 981 [999].

94 Guaman Poma, *El primer nueva corónica,* 962 [976].

95 Ibid.

96 Ibid.

97 Ibid.

98 For more on Guaman Poma's use of the term *don,* see Rocío Quispe Agnoli, "Yo y el otro: identidad y alteridad en la 'Nueva Corónica y Buen Gobierno,'" *MLN* 119, no. 2 (2004): 233.

99 Guaman Poma, *El primer nueva corónica,* 962[976].

100 Ibid.

101 Ibid.

102 Ibid.

103 Ibid.

104 Guaman Poma, *El primer nueva corónica,* 59 [59]. For additional textual evidence see Guaman Poma, *El primer nueva corónica,* 67 [67], 70 [70], 73 [73]. For more on Guaman Poma's representation of women prior to colonization, see Sara Vicuña Guengerich, "Virtuosas y corruptas: Las mujeres indígenas en las obras de Guamán Poma de Ayala y el Inca Garcilaso de la Vega," *Hispania* 96, no. 4 (2013): 673–674.

105 Guaman Poma, *El primer nueva corónica,* 58 [58].

106 Guaman Poma, *El primer nueva corónica,* 71 [71].

107 Guaman Poma, *El primer nueva corónica,* 61 [61].

108 According to Guaman Poma, adultery was punished by stoning to death, and pre-marital sex by hanging the perpetrators by their hair until they eventually perished. See *El primer nueva corónica,* 306 [308], 307 [309], 308 [310], 309 [311]. For more on concepts of female virginity under the Incas, see also Irene Silverblatt, *Moon, Sun, and Witches: Gender Ideologies and Class in Inca and Colonial Peru* (Princeton University Press, 1987): 85, 102.

109 Guaman Poma, *El primer nueva corónical,* 224 [226].

110 Ibid.

111 Guaman Poma, *El primer nueva corónica,* 962 [976], 963 [977].

112 Guaman Poma, *El primer nueva corónica,* 963 [977].

113 Ibid.

114 Ibid.

115 Guaman Poma, *El primer nueva corónica,* 981 [999].

116 Guaman Poma, *El primer nueva corónica*, 810 [824].

117 For additional examples in which Guaman Poma talks about how Spanish priests appropriated indigenous women see Guaman Poma, *El primer nueva corónica* 598 [612], 646 [660].

118 Guaman Poma, *El primer nueva corónica*, 446 [448].

119 Ibid.

120 Guaman Poma, *El primer nueva corónica*, 504[508].

121 Ibid.

122 Ibid.

123 Guaman Poma, *El primer nueva corónica*, 616 [630].

124 See Asunción Lavrín, "Sexuality in Colonial Mexico: A Church Dilemma," in *Sexuality and Marriage in Colonial Latin America*, edited by Asunción Lavrín (University of Nebraska Press, 1992), 70, 71; Lee M. Penyak, "Incestuous Natures: Consensual and Forced Relations in Mexico, 1740–1854," in *Sexuality and the Unnatural in Colonial Latin America*, edited by Zeb Tortorici (University of California Press, 2016), 175.

125 Guaman Poma, *El primer nueva corónica*, 504 [508]. This is also accompanied by a visual representation in 503 [507].

126 Guaman Poma, *El primer nueva corónica*, 553 [567].

127 Guaman Poma, *El primer nueva corónica*, 709 [723].

128 Valerie Benoist, "La conexión entre casta y familia en la representación de los negros dentro de la obra de Guarnan Poma," *Afro-Hispanic Review* 29, no. 1 (2010): 47.

129 Eukene Lacarra Lanz, "Changing Boundaries of Licit and Illicit Unions: Concubinage and Prostitution," in *Marriage and Sexuality in Mediaeval and Early Modern Iberia*, edited by Eukene Lacarra Lanz (Routledge, 2002), 183–187.

130 On two occasions, Guaman Poma explicitly states that, by cohabiting with women, priests are violating the Santo Concilio, see *El primer nueva corónica,* 230 [232], 565 [579]. He is referring to the Tercer Concilio Limense, which was held between 1582 and 1583 in the city of Lima. For more on the Tercer Concilio Limense, see Francesco Leornardo Lisi, *El tercer concilio limense y la aculturación de los indígenas sudamericanos* (Ediciones Universidad de Salamanca, 1990). For more on Guaman Poma's role in the Concilio see Rocío Quispe Agnoli "Yo y el otro: identidad y alteridad en la 'Nueva Corónica y Buen Gobierno,'" *MLN* 119, no. 2 (2004): 235–236.

131 Guaman Poma, *El primer nueva corónica,* 607 [621].

132 Guaman Poma, *El primer nueva corónica,* 606 [620].

133 Valerie Benoist, "La conexión entre casta y familia en la representación de los negros dentro de la obra de Guarnan Poma," *Afro-Hispanic Review* 29, no. 1 (2010): 37.

134 See Law 21, Title 3, Book 6 of the *Recopilación de Leyes para las Indias, 1681.*

135 Guaman Poma, *El primer nueva corónica*, 498 [502].

136 Guaman Poma, *El primer nueva corónica*, 869 [883]. See also accompanying drawing in 869 [883].

137 Guaman Poma, *El primer nueva corónica*, 966 [984].

138 Ibid.

139 Ibid.

140 Guaman Poma, *El primer nueva corónica*, 967 [985], 968 [986].

141 Guaman Poma, *El primer nueva corónica*, 977 [995].

142 Guaman Poma, *El primer nueva corónica*, 286 [288], 465 [467].

143 Alex M. Klohn and Philippe Chastonay, "Guaman Poma de Ayala's 'New Chronicle and Good Governmnet: A Testimony on the Health of the

Indigenous Populations in XVIth Century Peru," *Hygiea Internationalis: An Interdisciplinary Journal of the History of Public Health* (2015): 151.

144 For examples of how Guaman Poma appeals to discourse of purity of blood see *El primer nueva corónica*, 549 [563], 937 [951], 940 [954].

145 Guaman Poma, *El primer nueva corónica*, 949 [963].

146 Guaman Poma, *El primer nueva corónica*, 901 [915]; 902 [916].

147 For more on Guaman Poma's representations of mestizos, see Olimpia E. Rosenthal, "La figura abyecta del mestizo en *El primer nueva corónica y buen gobierno*," *Letras: Revista de Investigacion de la Facultad de Letras y Ciencias Humanas* 85, no. 121 (2014): 31–46.

148 Guaman Poma, *El primer nueva corónica*, 15 [15].

149 For more on Martín de Ayala, see José Carlos de la Puente Luna, "El capitán, el ermitaño y el cronista. Claves para establecer cuándo nació el autor de la *Nueva corónica y buen gobierno*," in *La memoria del mundo inca: Guaman Poma y la escritura de la* Nueva corónica, edited by Jean-Philippe Husson (Fondo Editorial de la Pontifica Universidad Católica del Perú, 2016), 119, 121; Juan de Ossio "Mito e historia en torno a la fecha de nacimiento de Guaman Poma de Ayala" in *La memoria del mundo inca...*, 151, 154; Rocío Quispe Agnoli, "Mestizos (in)deseables en el Perú colonial temprano." *Revista de Crítica Literaria Latinoamericana* XLIII, no. 86 (2017): 147.

150 Guaman Poma, *El primer nueva corónica*, 906 [920]. See also 647 [661] for additional comments on Murúa.

4 Aldeamento and the Politicization of Racially Qualified Life in Nóbrega's Writing from Brazil

The Jesuit missionary Manuel da Nóbrega (1517–1570) played a critical role in shaping the course of Brazil's colonization in ways that can be productively analyzed in relation to the history of segregation in Spanish America. For one, he helped introduce the policy of indigenous *aldeamento*, which can be situated as part of the same genealogy of spatial concentration that informs the policy of *congregación* or *reducción* in the context of Spanish America.[1] Both projects decisively transformed prior models of sociospatial organization, and both contributed, in different ways, to the gradual homogenization of *indios/as* as a meaningful category of group identity.[2] In Brazil, Nóbrega's initial plan to evangelize the natives was premised on the Jesuit's missionary ideal of itinerancy, but local demands gradually lead him to emphasize the need to physically fix and concentrate diverse indigenous groups in missionary villages, known as *aldeamentos* or *aldeias*.[3] In 1554, Nóbrega and his fellow Jesuit José de Anchieta founded the first *aldeamento* in Piratininga (modern-day São Paulo), near a native community led by the indigenous leader Tibiriçá.[4] By 1558, the governor Mem de Sá forcefully expanded the practice of resettling diverse indigenous groups in sedentary communities throughout the Brazilian coast, with Nóbrega's support and cooperation, officially launching the policy of *aldeamento*, which would continue until the beginning of the 19th century.[5]

On a material level, the policy of *aldeamento* involved the relocation of thousands of indigenous subjects from different communities and backgrounds, in some cases captured through forceful military campaigns known as *descimentos*.[6] The residents of *aldeamentos*, known as *índios aldeados*, were also subjected to a disciplinary regime implemented by the Jesuits to Christianize and "civilize" indigenous subjects. They were likewise compelled to work, both within the *aldeamentos* for the communities' self-subsistence and, for pay, for the Portuguese colonists and Crown in the defense of the territory, public works, and, increasingly, in sugar plantations (or *engenhos*) as the sugar economy expanded in the 1580s.[7] The location of *aldeamentos* tended to be close to the colonial settlements, partly as a way to streamline the access to indigenous labor power, but, in some cases, like the *aldeamento* in Piratininga, they were also built near

 DOI: 10.4324/9781003145196-5

native communities and were supported by native leaders like Tibiriçá.[8] The project of *aldeamento*, moreover, as John Manuel Monteiro argues, not only offered a reserve of free laborers to build the nascent colonial economy but also affected prior models of land tenure. As Monteiro contends, each *aldeamento* had a sizable territory granted through royal *sesmarias*, which already implied a radical redefinition of property rights for the prior occupants of the territory who were "donated" land to work for their self-subsistence while restricted to live in areas determined by the colonizers, and which, in turn, opened up access to additional lands previously occupied by indigenous groups.[9] Within these bound spaces, as Charlotte de Castelnau-L'Estoile further shows, the movement for *índios aldeados* was closely regulated and any absence from the *aldeamento* had to be authorized by the Jesuits and other internal authorities, partly to prevent residents from fleeing.[10]

The administration of *aldeamentos* was largely left to the Jesuits, who were charged with the spiritual administration of the residents, but were also, from the start, involved in the juridico-political and economic administration of the communities. In the "Estatuto das aldeias" (1558) by Mem de Sá, the governor circumscribes the role of Jesuit priests in *aldeias* in terms of their missionary role, but the distribution of administrative powers within the communities is left unclear. As Castelnau-L'Estoile points out, the governor foresees some level of municipal autonomy since he stipulates that a *tronco* and *pelourinho* should be installed in *aldeais*—both forms of public punishment were previously restricted to Portuguese colonial settlements. He also calls for the nomination of a *meirinho* in each *aldeia*, that is, an indigenous authority invested with lower judiciary power to administer punishment for lower offenses.[11] From the beginning, then, the policy of *aldeamentos* stipulated the presence of Jesuit priests in the communities and granted some level of autonomy to indigenous authorities. The "Estatuto das aldeias," however, is not precise on the point of who was to oversee the administration and distribution of labor both within the communities and for the compulsory, remunerated work, outside the communities.[12]

The administration and distribution of labor in *aldeamentos* was a major point of contention between the Jesuits and Portuguese colonists, and this played a critical role in shaping processes of racialization in colonial Brazil. To begin with, it is critical to note that *aldeamento* was based on a segregationist logic premised on the need to spatially separate *índios* from *brancos*.[13] In Nóbrega's initial articulations of the project, he explicitly calls for segregating these groups: "porque temos por certo que quanto mais apartados dos Brancos, tanto mais crédito nos têm os Índios."[14] Here, Nóbrega highlights skin color as a key marker of distinction, and he nominally homogenizes diverse native groups as *índios*. While his use of these socio-racial labels merits particular scrutiny—as will be shown in this chapter—the passage illustrates the racializing distinctions that, from the start, informed how *aldeamento* was envisioned. In subsequent laws, the presence of *brancos* in *aldeais* was explicitly prohibited, except for Jesuit priests and in cases where the administration of justice was left to a *procurador de índios*, or the temporal governance to the *capitão de aldeia*.[15] A law from 1611 also stipulates that the location of *aldeamentos* should be situated at a distance from white settlements (or "povoamentos brancos"), though this represents a departure from earlier tendencies to locate them near the Portuguese colonists to ensure the "civilizing" mission and facilitate the extraction of indigenous labor power.[16]

Aldeamento also developed in a context in which indigenous enslavement was massively practiced, and this setting is critical to understand both the different ways in which diverse native groups were racialized in Brazil and the sharp tensions that existed between the Jesuits and Portuguese colonists over the use of *índios aldeados'* labor power. Indeed, the enslavement of diverse indigenous groups in Brazil can be traced to the earliest years of Portuguese colonization, and, though it was categorically prohibited in laws from 1609 and 1680, the said laws were later reversed, and natives' enslavement continued until the mid-18th century.[17] Though Nóbrega's views on indigenous slavery oscillated, his initial insistence on segregating *índios* from *brancos* was largely tied to his denunciation of native enslavement in São Vicente, and, as the policy of *aldeamentos* evolved in the second half of the 16th century, missionary *aldeias* were increasingly presented in contradistinction to slavery.[18] As Castelnau-L'Estoile argues, the policy of *aldeamento* was envisioned as an alternative to slavery inspired by what was happening in Spanish America.[19] *Aldeamento* also introduced a crucial juridical distinction between *índios aldeados* and enslaved natives. As Maria Regina Celestino de Almeida explains, *índios aldeados* were integrated into colonial society as subjects of the Portuguese King, and special legislation was issued to protect them from enslavement while still ensuring that colonists could extract their labor power efficiently.[20] At the same time, since native groups continued to be massively enslaved—particularly with the expansion of the sugar economy in the 1580s—the term *índio* came to be used almost exclusively to refer to native groups within *aldeamentos,* while the term *negros da terra* was used to designate enslaved natives.[21]

This context in turn helps illuminate the sharp tensions that existed between the Jesuits and Portuguese colonists regarding the administration and distribution of *índios aldeados* for public works and temporary labor in places like *engenhos.* In her analysis of the various laws that governed the distribution of laborers from *aldeias*, Beatriz Perrone Moises shows that, while some laws stipulated that two-thirds of the residents from *aldeamentos* should be used in services outside the communities, other laws stated that half the residents should be allocated for said work. She also points out that laws consistently emphasized that their work should be remunerated and temporary; for instance, some laws specify that *índios aldeados* should work for a maximum of 6 months per year outside their communities in alternating periods of 2 months.[22] Since, for the most part, the administration and distribution of *índios aldeados'* labor power were controlled by the Jesuits, Portuguese colonists bitterly complained that the missionaries claimed to protect the natives but were actually making them work for the Jesuit's own economic benefits.[23] Moreover, many colonists repeatedly argued that they preferred to negotiate directly with indigenous laborers from *aldeias* rather than through the Jesuits' mediation.[24] It is also critical to note that colonists manipulated marriage and reproduction to try to keep *índios aldeados* in their properties. The most common practice was that of marrying them to enslaved women from their properties, and, though serval laws stipulated explicitly against this, the tactic ensured the reproduction of the colonists' slave holdings since, according to the Roman legal principle of *partus sequitur ventrem*, the legal status of enslaved children followed that of their mothers.[25]

A final point that is important to stress about the development of the policy of *aldeamentos* is that its trajectory was influenced by various forms of indigenous resistance.[26] Among other events, there was a large-scale indigenous insurrection known as the Santidade de Jaguaripe, which was organized in the recôncavo Baiano sometime between 1580 and 1585.[27] As Ronaldo Vainfas explains, the leader of the movement was an indigenous figure known as Antônio who had fled from a Jesuit *aldeamento* and helped hundreds of natives escape from *engenhos* and *aldeias*.[28] For the Jesuits, as Castelnau-L'Estoile notes, the Jaguaripe revolt was highly disconcerting because it suggested a certain level of failure in their missionary efforts and their inability to prevent *índios aldeados* from leaving the communities.[29] Nevertheless, as Celestino de Almeida argues and Charlotte de Castelnau-L'Estoile corroborates, *aldeamento* gradually contributed to the homogenization of diverse native groups as *índios* who came to share a common experience, and, over time, this influenced the way in which many indigenous subjects came to revindicate a sense of common identity for their own advantages, specifically since *aldeamentos* represented an alternative to slavery.[30]

Analyzed in relation to the segregationist dual republic model in Spanish America, the policy of *aldeamento* thus allows us to recognize some of the similarities and differences in terms of how colonial socio-spatial reorganization helped shape processes of racialization. While in Spanish America segregationist projects developed in a context following the abolition of indigenous slavery in 1542, in colonial Brazil the policy of *aldeamento* was established in a setting in which the enslavement of diverse native groups was massively—if unevenly—practiced until the mid-18 century.[31] As noted, this created a crucial juridical distinction between *índios aldeados* and *negros da terra*, and this in turn created a schism in terms of how diverse native groups were racialized in Brazil. Like in Spanish America, though, the policy of *aldeamento* did contribute to the homogenization of diverse indigenous groups as *índios*, including through laws that governed the circulation of movement based on racial ascription. Nóbrega's writing offers incisive insight to understand the initial phases of this process of racialization, and it is critical to understand how *aldeamento* was first justified.

Nóbrega's writing and actions can also be productively examined in relation to the history of segregation in Spanish America because they help bring into focus a broader pattern of colonial governance increasingly staked on the regulatory management of life. Starting in 1532, King João III started to emphasize the need to populate the Brazilian colony, and, in 1549, as the monarchy moved to secure its territorial control, a series of biopolitical measures were introduced to foster the growth of the Portuguese population. Specifically, a series of institutional practices developed to facilitate the transportation of Portuguese penal exiles—many of them women—and female orphans to the colonies to meet the populating needs of empire building while simultaneously taking care of—and making productive use of—the increasing number of destitute individuals in Portugal.[32] Timothy Coates describes these practices as a system of forced and state-sponsored colonization, respectively, and he argues that the implementation of the system is indicative of the growing power of the early modern state and of the increasingly intrusive relation between the state and its subjects.[33]

Nóbrega's writing offers a reflection of these broader developments, and it evinces the way in which he directly contributed to the institutionalization of the practice of sending Portuguese women to the colonies. Starting in 1549, Nóbrega discussed the matter with Simão Rodrigues, the co-founder of the Society of Jesus who had a close relationship with King João III.[34] He did so again in a letter from 1550 also addressed to Rodrigues, where he explicitly states that if the King's intention is to populate the land, then Portuguese orphan women and prostitutes should be sent to the colony.[35] By 1551, the first group of female orphans arrived, and an additional four groups of women were subsequently sent.[36] In Brazil, the practice was discontinued in 1608/1609,[37] but women continued to be sent to other Portuguese colonies in Asia and Africa until the first half of the 18th century.[38] Nóbrega also wrote two additional letters on the topic, addressed directly to King João III, where he explicitly frames the issue as a request informed by an existing practice rather than as a tentative suggestion. In his writing on the topic, Portuguese women's reproductive capacities are explicitly instrumentalized as a means to foster racially qualified life, and an analysis of this aspect of his work helps foreground the way in which processes of racialization are shaped by the differential ways in which women's reproductive capacities have been historically regulated.

In this chapter, I offer a historically contextualized analysis of Nóbrega's writing that highlights his role in shaping both the policy of *aldeamento* and the system of state-sponsored colonization that institutionalized global traffic in Portuguese women. In the first section, I present an account of how Nóbrega influenced the reorganization of colonial space. I begin with a brief overview of the process of colonial socio-spatial reorganization in

Brazil, and I emphasize that Nóbrega's arrival in the colony was part of a much broader shift in colonizing tactics introduced by the Portuguese Crown to secure its territorial control and ensure long-term population growth. I further show that Nóbrega's representation of indigenous groups shifted dramatically over the course of three key periods in his writing in which he helped pave the way for the policy of *aldeamento,* and I point to some of the ways in which the policy contributed to colonial processes of racialization.

In the second and third sections, I examine Nóbrega's repeated requests for Portuguese women to be sent to the colony. I offer a discursive analysis of Nóbrega's letters on the topic, and I show that his repeated request for Portuguese women is part of a broader concern with the regularization of reproductive relations between differently racialized groups. I further discuss the network of institutions that were set up in Portugal to temporarily house and ultimately ship the women overseas, I consider the disciplinary regulations and gender assumptions on which these institutions were premised, and I contextualize how some of the major shifts that were happening in Portugal in regard to poverty and how to make productive use of the increasing number of destitute and economically "surplus" populations influenced the system of forced and state-sponsored colonization. I also highlight the conceptual implications of this case, both for thinking about how the politicization of life at the level of collectivities influences processes of racialization, and how this intersects with the ways in which differently racialized women's reproductive capacities have been historically regulated and instrumentalized.

The Colonial Reorganization of Space and the Shift Toward *Aldeamento*

In Brazil, the process of socio-spatial reorganization ushered in by colonization differed significantly from what happened in Spanish America. After the Portuguese first landed in Brazil on April 23, 1500, their presence along the Brazilian coast remained sparse and intermittent.[39] In the early years, fortified trading posts (or *feitorias*) were set up along the coast, but they had few year-round Portuguese colonists. They were also impermanent settlements that followed a non-contiguous pattern determined by commercial interests and navigational accessibility. The main economic activity at the time centered on the commercialization of Brazilwood, and, in the municipality of São Vicente enslaved natives were also a major commodity.[40] As Pasquale Petrone puts it, São Vicente was initially set up as a "feitoria de escravos."[41]

Between 1532 and 1549, the Portuguese Crown tried to secure its territorial control over the region by implementing a system of proprietary grants. The move was meant to contest other foreign incursions, particularly by the French and Dutch, and it was initially supported by King João III.[42]

The captaincy system (as it is known) consisted of dividing the Brazilian coast into fifteen hereditary captaincies assigned to 12 men who, in turn, assumed the responsibility of protecting, settling, and developing their respective territorial grants.[43] As Stuart Schwartz explains, the captaincy system provided the first administrative structure for the settlement of the colony.[44] The men who were granted captaincies (known as *donatários*) tended to belong to the nobility or were military or state functionaries associated with Portugal's early colonization campaigns in India and Africa.[45] Individual *donatários* provided the main juridico-political structure, and they had power over a range of issues, including the authority to found settlements and award land grants. They also had jurisdiction over civil and criminal matters, which, in the case of the latter, could involve decisions over the death penalty for slaves.[46]

The organization of the captaincies also implied that the economic enterprise of colonization was largely left to the individual *donatários*, effectively shifting the economic burden onto them. The majority turned to sugar production early on, and they increasingly relied on indigenous chattel slavery.[47] By 1540, many of the captaincies were already exporting sugar, and, while some *donatários* had their own funds to develop sugar production, others turned to foreign investment, particularly by Florentine bankers and Dutch merchants.[48] The organization of space during this period was thus largely driven by commercial activities centered on sugar production. Large *engenhos* were built on properties obtained through royal concessions, and the generalized model of land use was oriented toward export sugar production.[49]

Another important aspect of the captaincy system is that it was intended to help populate the colony. In 1532, the influential royal adviser Diego Gouveia wrote a letter to King João III in which he explicitly addresses the need to populate the land. In the letter, Gouveia is precise in quantifying the reproductive effects of sending Portuguese colonist to Brazil, and as Carlos Alberto de Moura Ribeiro Zeron points out, the sovereign followed his advice closely.[50] Indeed, a few months later King João III wrote a letter to the *donátario* Martim Afonso de Sousa as the latter was preparing to assume power in the captaincy of São Vicente. In the letter, the monarch explicitly highlights the importance of populating the colony: "seria meu serviço povoar-se toda esta costa do Brasil."[51] By the 1540s, however, it was clear that the captaincy system was not working as the Crown intended.[52] Various indigenous groups actively resisted Portuguese incursions, and, as the war intensified, many colonists feared that control over the colony would soon be lost. As the Portuguese colonist Luís de Góis expresses in a letter from 1548 addressed to King João III: "Se Vossa Majestade não assistir logo essas capitanias, não só perderemos nossas vidas e mercadorias como também perderá Vossa Majestade a terra."[53] In response to these different concerns, and again counseled by Gouveia who by then viewed the captaincy system as ineffective and dangerously tied to private capital, the King was again compelled to shift tactics. He did so by assuming colonization as a royal project and by appointing Tomé de Sousa as the first governor-general of Brazil.[54]

The arrival of the Tomé de Sousa as the first governor-general of Brazil, on March 29, 1549, marked the beginning of a new colonizing tactic adopted by the Portuguese Crown.[55] Major changes were introduced on a political and administrative level, and the organization of space was decisively transformed to reflect the changing power dynamics. For one, the move implied a greater administrative centralization of power in Bahia, and it entailed the transference of metropolitical bureaucratic systems to the colony.[56] The construction of the city of Salvador da Bahía as the new capital also decisively transformed the built environment, visually inscribing the new colonial order.[57] The expedition that accompanied De Sousa is further revealing of the political and religious reorientation that was beginning to take place. It included the largest armed force up to that point, numerous colonists and penal exiles (*degredados*), civil and military functionaries, and, notably, the first Jesuit mission under the command of Nóbrega.[58] Nóbrega's main role was to Christianize the indigenous— partly to legitimate the occupation of the territory— but his writing and actions demonstrate that he also actively intervened in, and helped shape, the new colonizing model.[59]

One of the major ways in which Nóbrega helped shape the contours of Portuguese colonization in Brazil is by decisively influencing the shift toward the policy of *aldeamento*. In Nóbregra's writing, there are three distinct periods that clearly illustrate the transition to the policy, and his reflections offer critical insight to understand the circumstances and ideological justification that propelled the project forward. In his earliest writing, comprising the letters he wrote between 1549 and 1552 and based on his experience in different sites in Northeast Brazil, his missionary approach consisted of having the Jesuits disperse themselves along the Brazilian coast to proselytize.[60] As the leader of the Jesuits' first missions in the New World, chosen for the position by the co-founder of the Society of Jesus Simão Rodrigues,[61] Nóbrega's main aim was to Christianize the indigenous, and his early letters are characterized by a general sense of optimism about this endeavor. He depicts the various indigenous groups of Brazil as docile and malleable subjects who have no previous knowledge of God and are, as he puts it, eager to be Christianized: "desejam ser cristãos como nós".[62] He also acknowledges the differences between the various native groups of Brazil, for instance when he describes them as "gentios de diversas castas,"[63] and he variously uses terms like *gentios, índios da terra*, and *negros/as da terra* to nominally mark distinctions in status between them. In particular, he uses the term *negro/a* to convey a person's enslaved status, and many of his early letters reflect both the context of indigenous slavery in which he was operating and the way in which he helped shape juridical discussions on the topic. His writings from the first period are also addressed to highly influential figures: including Simão Rodrigues, who co-founded the Society of Jesus and was the Provincial for the Portuguese Jesuits; the Spanish canonist and theologian Martim de Azpicueta Navarro, who participated in some of the most prominent juridical debates about the occupation of the Americas, first in the University of Salamanca and later in the University of Coimbra; and King João III himself, who, as indicated above, sought to exert greater royal control over the Brazilian colony.[64] Though the information conveyed to these various figures at times varies and is often framed differently depending on the intended audience, there is a consistent set of arguments developed by Nóbrega that allows us to identify some of the main ways in which he helped shape the trajectory of Brazil's colonization through the reorganization of space.

In the very first letter that Nóbrega wrote from Brazil, dated April 10, 1549, and addressed to Simão Rodrigues, it is clear that one of the guiding assumptions of his missionary efforts is premised on a distinction between the Portuguese colonists and the indigenous inhabitants. He describes the land as peaceful, and he quantifies the number of colonists who lived in the walled settlement of Vila Velha, originally founded by the *donatário* Francisco Pereira Coutinho: "Achamos a terra em paz e quarenta ou cinquenta moradores na povoação."[65] He also outlines his missionary approach by stating that he will begin preaching to the colonists in the still-under-construction capital of Salvador, while another Jesuit will begin proselytizing to the natives: "Eu prego ao Governador e à sua gente na nova cidade que se começa, e o Pe. Navarro à gente da terra."[66] As the letter continues, Nóbrega further outlines his differential approach to ensure indigenous Christianization:

> Temos determinado ir viver com as Aldeas como estivermos mais assentados e seguros, e aprender com elles a lingoa, e i-los doctrinando pouco a pouco.... Nós todos três confessaremos esta gente, e depois spero que irá hum de nós a huma povoação grande, das mayores e melhores desta terra, que se chama Pernambuco.[67]

As the passage indicates, Nóbrega's initial plan for Christianization is premised on the assumption that previously established indigenous settlements would be beneficial to the Jesuits' conversion efforts. In contrast to the rhetoric about indigenous dispersion that we find in Vasco de Quiroga's writing about Mexico, Nóbrega presumes that the indigenous already lived in tight-knit communities, and he suggests that their residents will welcome the preachers and help guarantee their security. His description of Pernambuco as a large and great indigenous settlement that can be used to disseminate the Jesuits' ideas also suggests that he was not initially looking to transform existing forms of socio-spatial organization, but rather to use that organization to further the missionaries' objectives. As Alida Metcalf confirms, Nóbrega's initial plan was to have the Jesuits "disperse themselves along the coast of Brazil" as part of his initial evangelization approach.[68]

A few months later, Nóbrega again reiterates his plan to have the Jesuits preach in existing *aldeias* in two additional letters. In the first, dated August 9, 1549, and again addressed to the Jesuit Provincial Rodrigues, he states:

> e está logo hi huma Aldea perto, onde nós começamos a baptizar, em a qual já temos nossa habitação. Está sobre ho mar, tem agoa ao redor do Collegio, e dentro dele tem muito lugar para hortas e pomares; hé perto dos christaos asi velhos como novos. Somente me põem hum inconveniente o Governador: nom ficar dentro na Cidade e poder aver guerra com ho gentio, ho que me parece que nom convence, porque os que am-d'estar no Collegio am-de ser filhos de todo este gentio....E quando agora nós andamos lá, e dormimos e comemos, que hé tempo de mais temor, e nos parece que estamos seguros, quanto mais depois a terra mais se povoar.[69]

Similarly, he writes a day later to the canonist and theologian Martim de Azpicueta Navarro:

> Começamos a visitar as suas Aldeias quatro companheiros que somos, e a conversar com eles familiarmente, apresentando-lhes o Reino de Céu se fizerem o que lhes ensinarmos....desejam ser cristãos como nós, e só o impede o trabalho de os apartar de seus maus costumes, no que agora e todo nossso estudo; e já, glória de Deus, nestas Aldeias que visitamos aqui, ao redor da cidade, se tiram muitos de matar e comer carne humana...Aonde chegamos somo recebidos com muito amor, mormente dos meninos a quem ensinamos.[70]

In both cases, the *aldeias* that Nóbrega refers to are represented as communities that openly welcome the Jesuits and are near Portuguese settlements, and they again suggest that Nóbrega's initial missionary approach did not seek to intervene in existing forms of socio-spatial organization. The indigenous *aldeias* that Nóbrega alludes to in these passages were not, however, as permanent as he suggests. Most of the native villages that were close to Portuguese settlements in Bahia were large multifamily lodges made of straw, and they were frequently moved because of agricultural practices based on slash-and-burn methods.[71] These villages, like others in Brazil, were organized by kin and clan, and their loose gatherings in temporary villages varied significantly from the type of cities found in pre-conquest Mexico and Peru.[72] As Metcalf suggests, moreover, the Jesuits would soon learn that the impermanence of the settlements hindered the process of Christianization, since, every time the villages split or moved, the Jesuits had to reinitiate their labors.[73]

Notably, while Nóbrega did not initially seek to transform existing indigenous forms of socio-spatial organization, he did propose a different practice premised on a spatial logic of concentration. Specifically, in the first letter that he writes directly to King João III, dated September 14, 1551, he presents a concrete plan to spatially gather the children of Portuguese colonists whom he says are "lost" in the wilderness among the natives. He writes:

> Quasi todos tem negras forras do gentio e quando querem se vão para os seus....Ho sertão está cheo de filhos de christãos grandes e pequenos, machos e femeas, com viverem e se criarem nos costumes do gentio....Vam-se ajuntando os filhos dos christãos que andão perdidos pollo sertão, e já são tirados alguns e espero no Senhor que os tiraremos todos.[74]

Here, Nóbrega suggests that reproductive relations between Portuguese colonists and indigenous women were widespread, including, as he puts it, with free native women or *negras forras*. I will discuss this aspect of his work and its implications in greater detail in the following section, but for now, I want to emphasize that the prevalence of sexual relations between Portuguese men and diverse indigenous women is referenced early on by Nóbrega to justify a concrete plan to deal with the reproductive effects of these unions. In particular, Nóbrega justifies physically removing the sons and daughters of Christians whom he says are "lost" among the natives by appealing to the same type of rhetoric that was used to sanction the integration of "lost" *mestizo* children into the Republic of Spaniards. Like early Spanish legal discourses about *mestizos*, Nóbrega is also precise in describing the group as "filhos de christãos," which works to sever any connection to their mothers and further justifies integrating them into Portuguese colonial society. His writing also makes clear that the act of physically gathering this group of people—which he presents as an identifiable segment of the population but does not yet describe as *mestiços*—is an ongoing practice with a foreseeable end point: "os tiraremos todos." This aspect of Nóbrega's discourse further allows us to recognize the way in which he begins to experiment with spatial practices of gathering (*recolhimento*) as part of his broader vision on how to bring order to colonial society.

Between 1553 and 1556, Nóbrega moved to the southern province of São Vicente (in the modern-day state of São Paulo), and it is then that he began advocating for and rehearsing spatial practices of concentration designed to ensure indigenous Christianization. His move was largely a result of his disagreements with the bishop Pedro Fernandes Sardinha, who arrived in Salvador in June of 1552 and openly questioned some of the tactics adopted by the Jesuits.[75] Nóbrega had sharp disagreements with the bishop, and, shortly after his arrival, he decided to leave Bahia and concentrate his efforts in the southern province of São Vicente. Writing from São Vincente in February of 1553, he lists his grievances against the bishop manifesting just how stark their differences were: "o Bispo leva outros modos de proceder com os quais creio que não se tirarão pecados e se roubará a gente de quanto dinheiro puderem ganhar, e se destruirá a terra....A evitar pecados não veio, nem se evitarão nunca."[76] Noting the bishop's lax stance on sins, and corrupt ways to profit, Nóbrega emphasizes that nothing less than the destruction of the land is at stake. His move to São Vicente was his way of dissociating from what he saw as a doomed project, but, as Leite rightly points out, it is also a moment that, retrospectively, can be characterized as a type of "interregnum" that marks a critical shift in Nóbrega's writing and actions.[77]

During his period in São Vicente, Nóbrega's letters evince a marked shift in his approach to indigenous Christianization. Materially, this shift is exemplified by his socio-spatial experiments in Piratininga—where he first started physically gathering diverse native groups—and it is driven by two central concerns. First, he justifies his new approach by appealing to the same type of rhetoric about the colonists' bad example that we see in segregationist discourses about Spanish America. In a letter from March 10, 1553, he writes to his Jesuit superior: "segundo o nosso parecer e experiência que temos da terra, esperamos fazer muito fruto, porque temos por certo que quanto mais apartados dos Brancos, tanto mais crédito nos têm os Índios."[78] The optimism that is evident in the first part of the passage is premised on his conviction that segregation is necessary. He further strengthens his claim by referencing his knowledge and prior experience, and, as noted in the introduction, he both highlights skin color rather than religion as a key marker of distinction and nominally homogenizes diverse native groups as *índios*. Nóbrega also correlates the need for separation with the Jesuits' ability to maintain their reputation and credibility among the indigenous, and this rhetorical move helps him underscore the importance of keeping physical distance between what he presents as discretely different groups of people.

Significantly, existing Portuguese settlements in the captaincy of São Vicente had developed partly as a result of economic profits from the indigenous slave trade, and such activities had established a network of coerced social relations that brought these groups into close proximity. In the letter quoted above, Nóbrega denounces the prevalence of indigenous slavery in these settlements, and he suggests that the injustice of the practice is one of the reasons why the indigenous do not trust the Portuguese:

Os homens desta costa, e principalmente desta Capitania, os mais têm índios forçados, que reclamam liberdade e não sabem mais do judicial que virem a nós como pais e valedores, alcolhendo-se à Igreja....De maneira que por falta de justiça, eles ficam cativos e os seus senhores em pecado mortal, e nós perdemos o crédito entre toda a gentilidade.[79]

He emphasizes later in the letter that he had not seen similar levels of enslavement elsewhere, and he urges Simão Rodrigues to discuss the matter with the King.[80]

In his letters from São Vicente, Nóbrega also begins to recognize the limitations of the Jesuits' rehearsed approach to preaching in indigenous villages. It is this second concern that prompts him to begin experimenting with the creation of alternative settlements where the indigenous could be spatially gathered under the watchful supervision of the Jesuits. Nóbrega had traveled to São Vicente in the company of the governor-general Tomé de Sousa, who was at the time undertaking his visitation of colonial possessions in Brazil, but the governor insisted that, after preaching, the Jesuits had to return to Portuguese settlements, and this issue was becoming a point of contention between them.[81] Nóbrega writes:

> Disse-nos o Governador que podemos ir pregar o Evangelho e voltar às Capitanias e povoações dos cristãos....E vale pouco ir-lhes pregar e voltar para casa, porque, ainda que dêem algum crédito, não é tanto que baste a os desarraigar dos seus velhos costumes...E por isso, não sendo para viver entre eles, não se pode fazer fundamento de muito fruto.[82]

In this case, the question of physical distance is presented as a major obstacle for the Jesuits' missionary efforts. His insistence that Jesuits must be allowed to live among the indigenous for the sake of continuity is, however, strictly reserved for members of the religious order. As a partial compromise with the governor, but firmly adhering to his own convictions, Nóbrega thus advocates for the reorganization of colonial space based on a segregationist logic.

In letters from June and October of 1553, Nóbrega discusses the initial process of creating *aldeias* where various indigenous groups could be spatially gathered and separated from the Portuguese colonists. In a missive from June, he addresses a member of the overseas council in Lisbon and discusses existing and future projects. Talking about Piratininga, where Nóbrega, José de Anchieta and the indigenous leader Tibiriçá had compelled three indigenous groups to relocate into a single settlement, Nóbrega writes: "E pelo Campo [de Piratininga], daqui doze léguas, se querem ajuntar três povoações numa, para melhor aprenderem a doutrina crista e mostram grande fervor e desejo de aprender e de que lhes preguem."[83] In the *aldeia* of Piratininga, the indigenous lived from subsistence farming, and they allowed their children to be educated and indoctrinated by the Jesuits.[84] In the letter from June, Nóbrega also insists on the importance of going further inland given the better disposition and "quality" of the indigenous:

> E considerando a qualidade destes gentios...assentamos ir cem léguas daqui a fazer uma casa, e nela recolher os filhos dos gentios e fazer ajuntar muitos índios em uma grande cidade, fazendo-os viver conforme à razão, o qual não fora muito difícil, pelo que da terra já havemos sabido e vemos por experiência.[85]

Similarly, in a letter from October 1553 to King João III, Nóbrega further emphasizes consistent points to further justify the missionary's projects to spatially-fix diverse native groups: he insists that the indigenous in the area have a single chief whom they follow, and he stresses that they do not practice cannibalism.[86] As these passages indicate, and as José Eisenberg confirms, these experiments in Campos de Piratininga were Nóbrega's first attempts to physically concentrate indigenous groups in mission-style villages under Jesuit supervision, and they are critical to understand the shift toward the policy of *aldeamento*.

In July 1556, Nóbrega returned to Bahia. Hearing that bishop Sardinha had been recalled to Portugal and that the new governor-general, Duarte da Costa, had defeated indigenous groups who had waged war against the colonists, Nóbrega considered it an auspicious time to resume his conversion efforts in the region.[87] In a letter he wrote some years later, he recounts that, as part of his plans to resume his Christianization mission there, he had asked Da Costa to first congregate two indigenous villages that had recently been subjected.[88] Da Costa rejected his petition, arguing that the process of forcibly resettling indigenous groups in *aldeias* was expressly against royal orders. Nevertheless, things would soon change.[89] Not only was Da Costa deposed shortly afterward—among other things for his inability to prevent French invasions in territories that were claimed by Portugal—bishop Sardinha was shipwrecked on his way back to Lisbon and cannibalized. Between 1556 and 1557, Nóbrega retreated to the village of Rio Vermelho and wrote extensively. His health was failing, and in a letter from September 1557, after listing a series of things that needed to be done, he concludes:

> Portanto, se deve lá trabalhar por nos mandarem socorro logo, ao menos de hum Provincial e alguns Padres e Irmãos que ajudem, porque a mi devem-me já de ter por morto porque ao presente fico deitando muyto sangue pola boca.[90]

The passage helps convey Nóbrega's overt pessimism during this period. It clearly expresses his hopeless views on his deteriorating health, and it presents the missionary project in Brazil as in need of urgent reform.

In the following years, Nóbrega's representation of indigenous groups changed dramatically, and, though he continued to favor practices of spatial concentration, he started to advocate for forcefully subjecting native groups to achieve his missionary objectives. These arguments are developed by Nóbrega in two main texts: a Socratic dialogue titled *Diálogo sobre a conversão do gentio* (1556), which is considered by some as the first literary piece written in Brazil, and a letter from 1558 known as *Plano Civilizador*, which provides the main official ideological justification for the policy of *aldeamento*.[91] Both texts evince Nóbrega's increasing pessimism about the prospects of Christianizing the indigenous, but they also show

how Nóbrega had begun to reframe the question of conversion as part of a broader problem of colonial governance. In this sense, as Rafael Chambouleyron argues, Nóbrega's role in the colony cannot be circumscribed solely in relation to his missionary efforts but should instead be considered as part of a broader shift in power dynamics that are critical to understand the consolidation of the Portuguese colonial state.[92]

In his analysis of *Diálogo sobre a conversão do gentio,* José Eisenberg argues that the piece offers Nóbrega's reflections on how to reform the missionary project and that it follows the Spanish debates about the rights of conquest in the New World.[93] On the one hand, he suggests that Nóbrega's dialogue is similar to Las Casas' *Argumentum Apologiae* in that it tries to systematize an argument favoring the continuation of religious missions in the New World. As Eisenberg stresses, though, Nóbrega never questioned the legitimacy of the conquest, and his piece does not have the explicitly political emphasis of Las Casas' influential text, a version of which he read in the Valladolid debate with Juan Ginés de Sepúlveda.[94] On the other hand, he points out that there is a remarkable similarity between Nóbrega's dialogue and Sepúlveda's *Demócrates Segundo,* both in form and content.[95] In his analysis, Eisenberg discusses the tension between these two views, and he productively helps reframe existing interpretations of Nóbrega's literary piece. Nevertheless, his contribution overlooks the centrality of the question of space in Nóbrega's *Diálogo,* and this ends up undermining his most incisive point about the way in which the dialogue attempts to solve the central dilemma over whether evangelization should be done through force or persuasion.

The narrative structure of the dialogue, as Eisenberg points out, draws from Ignatious of Loyola's rhetorical model of persuasion through desolation and consolation.[96] The two characters in the piece are both temporary assistants to the Jesuit missionaries (or "coadjutores temporais") based on historical figures: Mateus Nogueira was a translator and interpreter of indigenous languages who had worked with Nóbrega in São Vicente, and Gonçalo Álvares was a blacksmith stationed in Espírito Santo whom Nóbrega met on his way back to Bahia.[97] The characters' overt pessimism about the conversion efforts is evident in the opening lines of the dialogue. Álvares states:

> Por demais é trabalhar com estes! São tão bestiais, que não lhes entra no coração coisa de Deus! Estão tão encarniçados em matar e comer, que nenhuma outra bem aventurança sabem desejar! Pregar a este é pregar em deserto e pedras.[98]

Similarly, Nogueira retorts:

> Ouvi eu já um evangelho a meus Padres, onde Cristo dizia; 'Não deis o Santo aos cães, nem deites as pedras preciosas aos porcos.' Se alguma

geração há no mundo por quem Cristo N. S. isto diga, deve ser esta, porque vemos que são cães em se comerem e matarem, e são porcos nos vícios e na maneira de se tratarem.[99]

The hopeless tone of each of the passages is consistently justified by the Jesuits' demeaning characterization of the indigenous as warring cannibals. Nóbrega had written about cannibalism in earlier letters, but throughout the *Diálogo*, the practice is singled out as a crucial marker of difference, a move likely informed by the recent incident involving bishop Sardinha. As the dialogue progresses, however, a form of consolation is offered, one that presents the prospect of Christianization as contingent upon the forceful subjection and spatial concentration of native groups.

The problem of forceful subjection is the topic most developed in the *Diálogo*. Alvares first introduces this issue after urging Nogueira to tell him why the Jesuits are still hopeful that the indigenous can be converted. He suggests that other Portuguese colonists think that the conversion efforts are pointless unless the indigenous are first subjected and made to accept Christianity through fear: "alguns têm acertado que trabalharmos debalde ao menos até que este gentio não venha a ser mui sujeito e com medo venha a tomar a fé."[100] In response, Nogueira simply poses a question: "E isso que aproveita, se fossem cristãos por força e gentios na vida e nos costumes e vontade?."[101] For Nogueira, then, the central drawback of forceful subjection is that it introduces the problematic possibility of Christian conversion as a performative, and ultimately insincere, form of mimicked behavior. A crucial turning point in their discussion happens when Alvares concedes that, in Portugal, the forceful conversion of Jews was, in retrospect, a mistake: "Conforme a isso não foi bom fazer El-Rei D. Manuel os judeus, cristãos, depois da matança."[102] He is specifically referring to the 1506 Lisbon pogrom, which, revealingly, targeted *conversos,* not Jews, but the conflation of these terms is indicative of the way in which notions of purity of blood inform his discourse.[103] By admitting that, in that case, the use of force was ultimately ineffective he is pressed to consider the differences between these cases, and this opens to a different but interrelated conversation about the nature of the indigenous.

In his initial comments about the indigenous, Alvares presents them as bestial, and he likens preaching to them to proselytizing to inanimate objects like rocks.[104] He also recounts a story of an indigenous boy whom he raised to be a good Christian, but who later ran away and returned to his family. He presents him as an ingrate—appealing rhetorically to the Spanish proverb "cría cuervos y te sacarán los ojos"—and seems to suggest through this anecdote that there is a deterministic difference that even a Christian upbringing cannot help overcome. After the section on subjection, however, having reached an impasse on the question of forceful conversion, Alvares returns to the question of indigenous alterity and asks

Nogueira whether the indigenous have souls. Reprehending him for not knowing better, Nogueira replies:

> Isso está claro, pois a alma tem três potencias: entendimento, memoria, vontade, que todos têm.... Depois que nosso Adão pecou, como diz o salmista, não conhecendo a honra que tinha, foi tornado semelhante à besta, de maneira que todos, assim Portugueses, como Castelhanos, como Tamoios, como Aimurés, ficámos semelhantes a bestas por natureza corrupta, e nisto todos somos iguais.[105]

This is the critical point of inflection in the narrative structure. From this point forward, the negative representation of the indigenous becomes less deterministic, as the affirmation of a common human corruption caused by Adam's fall allows Nogueira to redirect the emphasis of the conversation. The indigenous are not all equated, but rather ethnic and cultural differences are accepted. For Nogueira, the central difference between natives and other converts is that the former lack civility and orderly living. Thus, for him, the reorganization of space becomes the necessary precondition for the Christianization mission to be successful.

In the second part of the *Diálogo*, there are two main points that Nóbrega sets out to establish, if not always without ambiguity. First, the text turns to the question of orderly living as a way to try to circumvent the potential problems of forceful subjection. Going along with Nogueira's assertion about how the indigenous have souls, Alvares nevertheless probes further: "Pois [se] assim é, que todos temos uma alma e uma bestialidade naturalmente, e sem graça todos somos uns: de que veio estes negros serem tão bestiais, e todas as outras gerações, como os romanos e os gregos e os judeus, serem tão discretos e avisados?"[106] In response, Nogueira offers two interrelated explanations. On the one hand, he states: "Terem os romanos e outros gentios mais polícia que este não lhes veio de terem naturalmente melhor entendimento, mas de terem melhor criação e criarem-se mais politicamente."[107] On the other hand, he asserts that the lack of orderly political living among the indigenous is a sign of God's punishment: "lhes veio por maldição de seus avós, porque estes cremos serem descendentes de Cam."[108] Notably, here Nóbrega describes the indigenous as *negros da terra*, and he associates their lack of civility with the Old Testament story that recounts the curse of Ham, a story that was more commonly used to describe black Africans and to justify their enslavement.[109] It is also highly revealing that he consistently appeals to the concept of *polícia*.

As María Elena Martínez explains, the concept of *polícia* was inherited from the Greek term *politeia*, which in classical antiquity was used to discuss the art of administering orderly urban living. Speaking about colonial Mexico, she argues that the classical meaning of the term was regularly deployed by colonial officials but that it also acquired additional connotations as it started being used in reference not only to urban living but also to the issue of colonial governance.[110] As Martínez notes:

> Placing native people *en policía* thus not only meant bringing them under the control of secular authorities but transforming them, through dominant Castilian cultural values and institutions, into rational subjects, into *políticos* or *gente de razón*—a transformation that was considered a prerequisite for full conversion to Christianity. Civilizing and evangelizing were therefore part of a single process, but within Spanish colonial logic, the transmission of (European) culture, the means to *policía humana,* was a necessary precursor to complete transmission of the faith, to *policía divina.*[111]

Though Martínez's argument focuses on 16th-century Mexico, where, admittedly, the process of urbanization was significantly different from what happened in Brazil, her insights are nevertheless highly relevant for thinking about the logic that informs Nóbrega's *Diálogo.*

To begin with, it is important to note that when Nogueira explains to Alvares why the Romans and other groups enjoyed urban orderly living in better *policía,* he does not attribute this to any kind of natural intellectual capacity that the indigenous lack. Rather, he sees it as a result of the sociopolitical environment in which the former were raised, while the latter were condemned to unorderly living because of the Hamitic curse. The tension between Nogueira's competing views on determinism is left unresolved in the dialogue. What this section accomplishes, though, is that it manages to reframe the question of indigenous conversion as a broader problem for colonial governance. Indeed, by invoking the concept of *policía,* Nóbrega subtly reformulates the problem of forceful subjection as an issue for secular colonial authorities. In this way, the ability to bring the indigenous into the fold of colonial society and to reorganize their political communities in orderly *policía* based on Portuguese cultural values and institutions is presented as the necessary precondition for the successful Christianization of the indigenous. When Eisenberg criticizes the conceptual limitations of existing interpretations of the *Diálogo,* he points precisely to how this subtle move allows Nógrega to reconcile the use of force by colonial authorities while at the same time continuing to advocate for conversion through peaceful means of persuasion.[112] Yet by eliding the centrality of the question of space, and in particular how it is articulated in relation to the notion of *policía,* he too overlooks one of the key aspects of Nóbrega's literary piece, which is critical to understand how he helped pave the way for *aldeamento.*

The second major point that Nóbrega hopes to establish through the *Diálogo* turns on the question of the colonists' bad example, and it references the experimental *aldeias* in São Vicente as a possible way forward. For Nogueira, one of the key challenges that Jesuits face is that the indigenous do not trust them. He complains that other colonists deceive and enslave the indigenous, and, speaking sympathetically, he states "E têm razão de se temerem de os quererdes enganar, porque isto é que comumente tratam os maus cristãos com eles."[113] When Alvares points out that, even though the Jesuits speak to them with love, they nevertheless mistrust them, Nogueira retorts: "Porque até agora não têm os Índios visto essa diferença entre os Padres e os outros cristãos."[114] While Nogueira thus tries to justify the indigenous understandable skepticism, he further adds that he has nevertheless met others—both children and adults—who showed clear signs of having genuine faith in God after only brief periods of proselytizing. Specifically, he states that São Vicente is the captaincy where the most meaningful interactions with the indigenous have taken place.[115] To illustrate this point, he recounts two stories. The first is of an old man, Caiubi, who left his village to go live in the aldeia of Piratininga as one of the first settlers, and Nogueira emphasizes the sacrifices he made for his genuine faith in God and his love for the Jesuits.[116] The second story is about a younger indigenous man who died in order to spread the faith in the village of Maniçoba. Both examples reference the early project of *aldeamento* that Nóbrega rehearsed in São Vicente, and they are meant to illustrate the importance and viability of reforming the Jesuits' missionary objectives.

In December 1557, Mem de Sá arrived in Brazil as the new governorgeneral. When Nóbrega heard that the governor had reached Bahía in January 1558, he left his secluded retreat in Rio Vermelho and went to meet him.[117] Mem de Sá was receptive to the Jesuits' ideas on how to reform the missionary system, and, during the first months of 1558, he and Nóbrega worked together on this task.[118] In a letter that Nóbrega wrote a little over a year later, he praises the governor's prudence, virtue, and zealousness, and he enthusiastically recounts what he saw as the positive changes implemented by his new government.[119] In particular, Nóbrega highlights Mem de Sá's systematic approach to physically concentrate diverse indigenous groups:

> Na conversão do gentio nos ajudou muyto, porque fez logo ajuntar quatro ô cinco Aldeas
>
> que estavao derredor da Cidade.... Outra ygreja mandou logo fazer, de S. Joam Evangelista, quatro ô cinco legoas da Cidade onde se ajuntarão outras tantas Aldeas do gentio de Mirangaoba. A terceira mandou fazer onde chamão o Rio de Joanne, esta se chama Sant Spiritus; aqui há mais gente junta que em todas; está sete ou oito legoas da Cidade, perto
>
> da costa do mar. Nestas três ygrejas se faz agora muyto serviço a Nosso Senhor, e o gentio
>
> vay conhecendo que só a Jesu Christo se deve crer, amar e servir.[120]

Here, Nóbrega is describing the policy of *aldeamento* that was launched by Mem de Sá in 1558. The implementation of this system reinvigorated

Nóbrega, and it compelled him to return to the political scene with a new militant zeal. Shortly after the passage above, he writes: "tudo isto se deve a N. Senhor e ao bom zelo do Governador. E des que eu isto vi na terra, comecei a ressuscitar e já não queiro ser ethico [herético] nem morrer."[121] In contrast to the pessimistic outlook that characterizes the period when Nóbrega wrote the *Diálogo*, here the author admits that his earlier disposition bordered on heresy, and he explicitly correlates his renewed sense of vitality with the governor's successful implementation of the new socio-spatial policies.

The *aldeamento* system put in place by Mem de Sá was part of a broader shift in colonial governance that, for secular authorities, was centrally tied to economic and political concerns. For one, it is important to note that with the death of King João III in June of 1557, his brother, cardinal Dom Leão Henriques, assumed the position of regent.[122] Under Henriques, as Eisenberg argues, the economic policies in Brazil underwent a significant reorientation.[123] Henriques abandoned the idea of an economy based on the extraction of minerals—since none had been found up to that point—and he focused instead on the commercialization of wood and export agriculture.[124] The production of sugar was privileged because of its rising value in European markets, and the regent incentivized its cultivation in coastal areas. This economic reorientation in turn deepened existing tensions with indigenous groups, and conflicts over land became a central problem.[125] Colonists complained that the indigenous were attacking their plantations, and, as tensions escalated, Mem de Sá launched a series of military campaigns the likes of which had not been seen before in Bahia. As Metcalf recounts: "The level of violence unleashed by Mem de Sá's military campaigns was devastating….The governor turned horses and ships into weapons, and by targeting villages one by one, he eliminated many formerly independent and powerful Indian chiefs living in Bahia."[126] The campaigns were euphemistically described as indigenous "pacification," and they led to a profound reorganization of socio-spatial relations. Indeed, once autonomous Indian villages were defeated, their residents were relocated to Jesuit *aldeamentos*.[127] Other indigenous groups, like the Caeté, who were accused of cannibalizing bishop Sardinha, were enslaved and the action was justified by presenting the campaign as a "just war."[128] Indeed, as Carlos Alberto de Moura Ribeiro Zeron points out, the war waged against the Caeté, with the consent of the Jesuits, was initially the main source of slaves for the sugar industry.[129] Thus, the military campaigns against the indigenous were directly correlated with the successful implementation of economic reorientation in the second half of the 16th century.[130] It also helped secure lands for the sugar mills and captives to do the labor.[131]

Nóbrega's writing from the period clearly reflects the rising tensions, but in his letter from May 1558, known as the *Plano Civilizador*, he offers the official ideological justification for Mem de Sá's campaigns. The letter is addressed to the Jesuit Provincial Miguel de Torres, and it presents a marked change in the Jesuit's intentionality. For one, Nóbrega writes to Torres as a colleague rather than a superior, since he had recently been promoted to Jesuit Provincial for Brazil. He knows that his proposal no longer depends on the approval of the Jesuits in Portugal—it only needed consent from Rome—but he nevertheless tries to persuade his immediate reader knowing that the material and human resources necessary for the plan's implementation had to come from the metropole.[132] On the other hand, it is notable that in his articulation of the need to spatially concentrate natives in *aldeamentos*, Nóbrega explicitly recommends defeating the indigenous military to achieve this goal.[133] Moreover, he frames the importance of his proposal not so much in terms of how it will help enhance the Christianization mission in Brazil, but rather in terms of the potential profits that it will help generate for the Crown and its subjects.[134]

The need to forcefully subject the indigenous is the central theme of Nóbrega's *Plano Civilizador*. He begins by stating that natives need to be subjected and made to live like the rational subjects they are, and he contends that this can only be achieved through fear and dispossession.[135] As Eisenberg suggests, the legitimization of political authority by consent generated through fear is a salient feature in Nóbrega's text.[136] Nóbrega's argument, however, can also be analyzed in terms of the central claims he makes about the qualification and quantification of life. To begin with, his argument about indigenous subjection depends on his characterization of the indigenous as otherwise irredeemable. Appealing to his years of experience in Brazil, he argues that the nature of the indigenous in Brazil is such that they are more responsive to fear and subjection than to charity.[137] He describes them as "[o] mais triste e vil gentio de todo o mundo,"[138] and he emphasizes their cruelty and bestial customs by referencing recurrently the trope of cannibalism. Nóbrega acknowledges that some Christians had enslaved and mistreated the indigenous, but he emphasizes that other colonists who have never harmed them are unjustly paying for those offenses with their lives. As he puts it: "E são tão cruéis e bestiais, que assim matam aos que nunca lhes fizeram mal, clérigos, frades, mulheres de tal parecer, que os brutos animais se contentariam delas e lhes não fariam mal."[139] His essentialized depiction highlights the indigenous' alterity. The project to congregate them in *aldeias*, is thus, again, like in the *Diálogo*, a project not only about Christianization but also civilizing them by bringing them into the fold of colonial society. It also justifies, for Nóbrega, their exploitation:

> Sujeitando-se o gentio, cessarão muitas maneiras de haver escravos mal havidos e muitos escrúpulos, porque terão os homens escravos legítimos, tomados em guerra justa, e terão serviço e vassalagem dos Indios e a terra se povoará e Nosso Senhor ganhará muitas almas e S.A. terá muita renda nesta terra, porque haverá muitas criações e muitos engenhos já que não haja muito ouro e prata.[140]

The ideological basis that informs Nóbrega's proposal is clearly laid out in this passage. Indigenous slavery is justified by the rhetoric of "just war," the economic incentives for the king are clearly stated, and population growth is associated with his Christianization efforts. All of this, though, as he presents it, depends on indigenous subjection.

In *Plano Civilizador* Nóbrega also makes a series of remarks that evince a concern for the quantification of life. His emphasis on the question of cannibalism is constant throughout the letter, but it serves a particular function here since he correlates it to the low number of Portuguese settlers. As he puts it, "são mais os que morrem que os que vem cada ano."[141] Moreover, he discusses the experimental project of sending destitute settlers from Portugal as part of a plan to populate the colony—in a way that resembles Las Casas' proposal in *Memorial de Remedios* and that points to the use of "surplus" populations in Europe—but he recounts its shortcomings. Most, he says, were unable to support themselves, and they either returned to Portugal or died in Brazil. What is needed instead, he says, are strong men who can control and subject the indigenous.[142]

By April of 1558, shortly before Nóbrega had written *Plano Civilizador*, Mem de Sá had already ordered the congregation of four indigenous villages surrounding Salvador into one large *aldeia*.[143] Several others were created between 1559 and 1561: including the aldeias in São Paulo, São João, Espírito Santo, Santo Antônio, and São Miguel.[144] Within the more controlled environment of the *aldeias*, as Metcalf explains, the Jesuits returned to "their preferred approach: persuasion through teaching, preaching, and conversation."[145] Nóbrega talks about the organization of the aldeias in his *Plano Civilizador*. He discusses how each aldeia had to have a "Protetor dos Índios" who was charged with punishing the indigenous in case of violation of the rules, and who was supposed to protect them from abuses by the colonists.[146] Nóbrega also lists the central laws that indigenous were expected to uphold:

> A lei, que lhes hão-de dar, é defender de comer carne humana e guerrear sem licença do Governador; fazer-lhes ter uma só mulher, vestirem-se pois tem muito algodão, ...tirar-lhes os feiticeiros, mantê-los em justiça entre si e para com os cristãos; faze-los viver quietos sem se mudarem para outra parte, se não for para entre cristãos, tendo terras repartidas para que lhes bastem, e com estes Padres da Companhia para os doutrinarem.[147]

It is notable that cannibalism and non-state-sanctioned warfare are the first prohibitions that Nóbrega lists. It indicates that the consolidating state moved swiftly toward the monopolization of war, and it spells out the fact that the indigenous' submission entailed their loss of sovereignty.[148] The civilizing mission is further evident in the prescriptions to wear clothing, abandon the cultural practice of polygamy, and submit to the indoctrinating supervision of the Jesuits.[149] It is also highly significant that the indigenous' movement is restricted and that this depends on having both to remain within close physical presence to other Christians, as well as on the distribution of lands previously alienated from them.[150]

Not long after their creation, though, *aldeamentos* began to have devastating consequences for the spread of disease.[151] As Metcalf explains, no smallpox epidemic was reported in Brazil before 1562, but shortly after the disease spread, and, in each of the villages, about a third of the indigenous population died.[152] The indigenous had been the primary workforce in Brazil, but, faced with the increasing opposition of the crown to enslavement,[153] the growing demands of the sugar economy, and the disastrous spread of disease, the colonists turned to the labor to be found in the Atlantic slave trade.[154] As Schwartz puts it, it is no accident that the "importation of large numbers of Africans began in the 1570s following the peculiar conjunction of demographic, economic, and political circumstances."[155] Nóbrega witnessed some of the worst phases of the indigenous' demographic decline, but in his writing, he does not develop this topic in any significant way. In contrast to Spanish America, where the indigenous demographic decline was used to justify the policy of *congregación* or *reducción* from the start, in Brazil, the policy of *aldeamento* was only later justified by figures like the Jesuit Pero Rodrigues by appealing to arguments about the perceived need to stabilize and foster indigenous population growth.[156] Indeed, the demographic decline of the native population is *not* what allows us to trace the politicization of racially qualified life in Nóbrega's discourse. For that, I now turn to an examination of his repeated request for Portuguese women and consider how this is tied to his consistent problematization of reproductive relations between differently racialized groups.

The Politicization of Racially Qualified Life in Nóbrega's Letters

> Mande V.A. muitas orfãas... porque são tão desejadas as molheres brancas quá, que quaisquer farão quá muito bem à terra.
>
> Manuel da Nóbrega[157]

In Nóbrega's earliest letters from Brazil, between 1549 and 1552, there is a consistent emphasis on trying to regulate reproductive relations between differently construed groups of people. Early on, he discusses the fact that Portuguese colonists were engaging in widespread polygamous unions with native women of different statuses—including enslaved *negras*— and he directly asks King João III and the theologians from the University of Coimbra for clearer legislation and guidance about marriage in a context of slavery. He also writes four letters requesting that white Portuguese women be sent to the colony, an action that he largely justifies by appealing to the

King's stated intentions to populate the land and which reflected existing practices. This aspect of Nóbrega's writing evinces the way in which the reproductive effects of sex became an object of political reflection and intervention for the nascent colonial state, and it foregrounds the fact that the politicization of life at the level of collectivities not only affected women differentially than men, it was also premised on a distinction between women that is critical to trace colonial processes of racialization.

In order to delineate the conceptual implications of Nóbrega's politicization of reproduction, it is important to begin by considering the racializing distinctions that inform how he describes the sexual practices of Portuguese colonists in Brazil. In his first letter from April 10, 1549, addressed to Simão Rodrigues, he writes: "Spero em N. Senhor fazer-se muito fruito, posto que a gente da terra vive toda em peccado mortal, e nom há nehum que deixe de ter muytas negras das quaes estão cheos de filhos, e hé grande mal."[158] The passage follows an affirmation about how Nóbrega intends to begin preaching to the colonists, and it reveals his optimism about how his intervention as a religious authority will help redress the sexual practices he characterizes as mortal sin. Nóbrega also makes an explicit distinction between, on the one hand, the Portuguese colonists whom he ideologically describes as "gente da terra," and, on the other, enslaved native women whom he describes as "negras."[159] He further emphasizes the reproductive effect of these unions and describes these as a great evil ("grande mal"), but he neither comments on the status of the children born from these relations nor on their place within colonial society. Similarly, in a letter from August 9, 1549, also addressed to Rodrigues, he states: "Nesta terra há hum grande pecado, que hé terem os homens quase todos suas negras por mancebas, e outras livres que pedem aos negros por molheres, segundo ho costume da terra."[160] In this case, Nóbrega again uses the terms *negras* and *negros* to describe the indigenous population, but he acknowledges that some of the women were free and states that the latter had been obtained through relations of coerced exchange with indigenous men. While there are important inconsistencies in terms of how Nóbrega uses the terms *negras/negros* in these early letters, both passages point to his use of socio-racial labels to differentiate between groups of people, specifically in a discourse about reproductive sex.

In the letter from August 9, 1549, Nóbrega also recounts to Rodrigues how Portuguese colonists excuse their sexual practices with various native women of different legal statuses by claiming that there are no marriageable women in the colony. He also uses this issue to frame his first tentative request that women from Portugal be sent to Brazil:

> Todos se me escuão que nom tem molheres com que casem, e conheço eu que casariam si achassem com quem; em tanto que uma mulher, ama de hum homem casado que veo nesta armada, pelejavão sobre ella a quem a haveria por molher.... Parece-me cousa mui conveniente mandar S.A. algumas molheres que lá têm pouco remedio de casamento

a estas partes, ainda que fossem erradas, porque casaram todas muy bem.... De maneira que logo as mulheres terião remedio de vida, e estes homens remediarião suas almas, e facilmente se povoaria a terra.[161]

As evinced, his initial request is presented as a tentative suggestion, and it is framed as a convenient way to address two perceived problems simultaneously. First, he states that he is confident that the Portuguese colonists will marry the women, and he strengthens his claim by referencing an incident of a Portuguese nursemaid who had recently arrived in the colony, and, whom he says, many of the colonists fought over. Second, he emphasizes the social vulnerability of the women he is requesting and suggests that they will find a "remedy" in the colony. At the end of the passage, he reiterates that the measure would be beneficial for both the men and the women, and he adds that it will further ensure that the land is easily populated, which overtly politicizes reproduction.

Nóbrega expands on some of these arguments in later letters in ways that further clarify how he sought to regulate marriage and reproduction, both among the Portuguese and among enslaved natives. On January 6, 1550, he addresses Rodrigues for the second time about sending Portuguese women to the colony:

Se El-Rei determina povoar mais esta terra, é necessário que venham muitas mulheres órfãs e de toda a qualidade ate meretrizes, porque há varias qualidades de homens; e os bons e os ricos casarão com as órfãs; e deste modo se evitarão pecados e aumentará a população no serviço de Deus.[162]

As the passage indicates, Nóbrega's request is first and foremost tied to the question of populating the colony. He articulates his appeal as a response to the king's presumed determination to populate, and he authorizes his views by situating his locus of enunciation in the very colony where said population is at stake. The emphasis on the number of women justifies Nóbrega's suggestion that prostitutes are likewise acceptable, and it adds a sense of urgency to his tone. It also speaks to the social vulnerability of the particular type of women that he targets in his request. It is clear, then, that his petition is organized around a dual objective. On the one hand, it is presented as a plan to help expand the Christian population in the colony. His appeal is expressed as being consistent with the colonial imperative to populate, and it is founded on the assumption that women's reproductive capacities can be made instrumental to such an endeavor. On the other hand, Nóbrega's proposal claims to offer a partial solution to the sinful sexual practices taking place in the colony. His perceived need for women is premised on the dismissal of indigenous women as worthy marriage partners, and it introduces a marked gender distinction that becomes progressively racialized as his views on the matter develop.

In addition to his growing insistence on the need to intervene in the Portuguese colonists' marriage and reproductive practices, Nóbrega also insists on the need to marry enslaved natives among themselves. He writes in a letter from September 13, 1551, addressed to theologians from the University of Coimbra who were debating and counseling the King on a range of juridical issues:

> Os que estão amancebados com suas mesmas escravas, fazemos que casem com ellas e, por ser costume novo a seus senhores, am medo que casando lhes fiquem forras, e não lho podemos tirar da cabeça.... Devia El-Rey de mandar desenganar aos senhores, que nom fiquão forros, porque isto arreceão; que doutra maneira todos os casarião.[163]

Similarly, he writes a day later directly addressing King João III:

> Nestas partes há muitos escravos e todos vivem em pecado com outras escravas. Alguns dos tais fazemos casar, outros areceam fiquarem seus escravos forros e não ousão há casá-los. Seria serviço de Nosso Senhor mandar V.A. huma provisão em que declare nam fiquarem forros casando.[164]

As shown, Nóbrega sanctions marriages among enslaved indigenous by appealing to a religious moral argument about non-marital cohabitation practices as a form of sin.[165] He also makes clear that he has the authority to compel slaves to marry—since, as he states, he has already married many of them—but he recognizes that Portuguese slave owners are impeding his actions out of fear that their slaves will be freed as a result. It is precisely by recognizing his limited authority over the matter that he asks the theologians from Coimbra and the King himself to intervene by issuing legislation to address the slaveholders' apprehensions. What these letters illustrate, then, is not only the way in which Nóbrega actively sought to intervene in the marriage and reproductive practices of the colony, but also how reproduction is framed in his discourse as an issue that concerns both the Jesuits and the nascent colonial state more broadly.

Nóbrega's initial requests for Portuguese women to be sent to the colony also bring into focus the way in which the Jesuit politicizes reproduction to meet the needs of empire building. As shown, in his first letters on the topic addressed to Simão Rodrigues, he emphasizes the need to populate the colony, and he implicitly instrumentalizes Portuguese women's reproductive capacities as a means to achieve said goal. He later develops this topic in two subsequent letters addressed to King João III that further clarify how he politicizes life at the level of collectivities by making racializing distinctions between women. In the letter analyzed above from September 14, 1551, where Nóbrega asks the King for clearer legislation about marriage in

the context of slavery, he also asks the sovereign to send Portuguese women
to the colony. He writes:

> Pera as outras Capitanias mande V.A. molheres órfãs, porque todas
> casarão. Nesta nam são necessárias por agora por averem muitas filhas
> de homeins brancos e índias da terra, as quais todas agora casarão com
> a ajuda do Senhor; e se nam casavam dantes, era porque consentiam
> viver os homens em seus peccados livremente, e por isto nam se curavão
> tanto de casar e alguns deziam que não pecavão.[166]

In this case, Nóbrega acknowledges that some female orphans had already
arrived in the colony, and he specifically requests that future groups be sent
to other captaincies since, as he says, in the village of Olinda (from which he
writes) women are no longer in such dire need considering the high number
of mixed-ancestry women there.[167] Notably, Nóbrega does not use the term
mestiças here; rather, his careful wording emphasizes that these women are
the daughters of *white* men and *índias da terra*, thus highlighting the fact
that the latter are not enslaved. Furthermore, he stresses that these women
are helping ease the alleged women shortage in Olinda and are no longer
consenting to live with men outside of marriage; they have instead adopted
the Portuguese practice of monogamous church-sanctioned marriage. In
other words, in the passage, Nóbrega presents mixed-ancestry women as
worthy marriage partners for the Portuguese colonists, partly because he
explicitly associates them with their white fathers and emphasizes their acceptance of Christianity and Portuguese customs. In later letters, though,
Nóbrega offers a more negative characterization of *mestiços* that illustrates
how he progressively came to differentiate this group as a distinct socio-
racial category. In letters from 1556 and 1561, for instance, he describes
mestiços as different from the Portuguese and more similar to the indigenous in their customs.[168]

In his final letter petitioning orphans, from July 1552, Nóbrega explicitly
specifies the skin color of the women he was requesting. The letter is again
addressed directly to King João III, and he writes:

> Já que escrevi a V. A. ha falta que nesta terra há de molheres com que
> os homens casem e vivão em serviço de N. Senhor apartados dos pec-
> cados em que agora vivem, mande V.A. muitas orfãas e, se não houver
> muitas, venhão de mestura dellas, e quaisquer porque são tão desejadas
> as molheres brancas quá, que quaisquer farão quá muito bem à terra, e
> ellas se ganharão e os homens de quá apartar-se-ão do pecado.[169]

Although the question of sin is present in all of Nóbrega's letters about the
importation of women, in this case, he specifically states that by sending
white women to the colony, Portuguese men will distance themselves from
the sins in which they currently live. These sins, however, are not merely

an issue of polygamy and extra-marital sexual relations. Their conceptualization is further intertwined with a hierarchical gender distinction that privileges Portuguese over indigenous women as ideal marriage and reproductive partners for the colonists. While it is true that Nóbrega also makes hierarchical distinctions between Portuguese women—for instance, when he distinguishes between prostitutes, other wrongdoers, and orphans—the passage above makes clear that, despite the differences among them, the common attribute that makes their presence in the colony so desirable is, as he overtly states, their whiteness. What this indicates is that his petition for women is racially coded, in the sense that the central problem with sexual relations that he identifies is clearly premised on a racialized distinction between the women.[170] His final letter thus helps clarify not only how the politicization of life at the level of collectivities affected women differentially than men—in the sense that the former's reproductive capacities are explicitly instrumentalized for the purposes of populating the land—but it also foregrounds the fact that the Nóbrega's politicization of life is premised on a racializing distinction between white and indigenous women. What we see in his discourse then is an overt politicization of racially qualified life.

As a conceptual framework to think about the significance of Nóbrega's politicization of racially qualified life, Gayle Rubin's theory of the exchange of women offers productive insight. Rubin's central intervention is that she proposes a reconceptualization of the genealogies of gender oppression from the perspective of exchange rather than production. For her, the central insight of Claude Lévi-Strauss's theory of kinship is that it allows us to recognize the ways in which marriage systems and socially organized forms of sexuality function within an economy of exchange; specifically, of exchange in women.[171] Rubin criticizes the tendency to explain gender oppression as a result of a specific mode of production—for example, an analysis of capitalism that only consider production—and she argues that this fails to account for the ways in which what she terms sex/gender systems like kinship organize social formations in the first place. She recognizes that kinship formations are always part of broader social systems tied to specific economic and political arrangements, but she highlights the fact the domestication of women as products of exchange—and the organization of sexuality and gender that develops from this exchange—is constitutive of those same economic and political arrangements, which are, in turn, intricately tied to gender oppression.[172] As Rubin puts it, in an economy of exchange where women are gifts rather than exchange partners, "women are in no position to realize the benefits of their own circulation. As long as the relations specify that men exchange women, it is men who are the beneficiaries of the product of such exchanges—social organization."[173] Rubin admits that men are of course also trafficked, most notably as slaves, but never just as men. Women, on the other hand, as she says, "are transacted as slaves, serfs, and prostitutes, but also simply as women."[174] This assertion urges us to think about the ways in which women's role in social reproduction operates in relation to exchange rather than production, and it allows us to recognize the ways in which systems of exchange influence the development of economic and political social formations where the organization of sexuality and gender are a constitutive part of those formations. This conceptual framework is highly productive for thinking about Nóbrega's petition for white Portuguese women, and it can be further contextualized and developed by considering the global exchange of white women that informs Nóbrega's repeated requests.

As órfãs d'el Rei and the Politicization of White Women's Reproductive Capacities

In 1551, three orphaned sisters arrived in Brazil: Catarina, Joana, and Micia Baltasar Lobo de Sousa. The sisters' father, Baltasar Lobo de Sousa, had lost his life as a member of the Portuguese armada while working to secure imperial trade routes in what is known as the *Carreira da India*. His daughters were granted royal dowries as a way to posthumously reward their father's service to the Crown by sending them to Brazil with express orders from King João III that they marry "pessoas principais da terra."[175] In July 1553, a second group of nine women reached the colony—the largest in the case of Brazil—and a third group of six orphans arrived in April of 1557. For the fourth group that arrived in 1561, there are almost no extant records, and for the fifth that reached Brazil sometime between 1608 and 1609, there is a single record stating that the captain and the pilot of the ship transporting the orphans, Sebastião Martins, and his brother, were arrested and sent back to Portugal to be judged for the abuses they perpetrated against the orphans.[176]

These groups of women are known as *órfãs d'el Rei*,[177] and they were part of a broad imperial project that Timothy Coates describes both as a system of "state-sponsored colonization," and "a marriage scheme" between male colonial authorities and metropolitan institutions.[178] Orphan girls who qualified for the perceived distinction of being selected as an *órfã d'el Rei* were relatives of men who had lost their lives serving the Portuguese crown in different colonizing campaigns. The women were selected in Portugal, housed temporarily in transitory shelters whose mission was to instill the gendered values that the crown wanted them to uphold, and they were eventually shipped overseas after first being awarded an imperial dowry meant to incentivize colonists to marry them.[179] As an imperial scheme, the case of *as órfãs d'el Rei* is also noteworthy because of the institutional mechanisms that were set up to facilitate this global exchange of women.[180] In tandem with the campaign of forced colonization through penal exiles, the practice of sending orphan women to the colonies worked toward similar objectives but did so through a strategy of state-sponsored, rather than forced, colonization. This was accomplished by, first, identifying two groups of single women who, because of their social and economic vulnerability, were seen as ideal candidates for assistance. By helping them, the state could address a metropolitan social problem while simultaneously helping advance its own empire-building ambitions. The two groups of women selected were orphans and reformed prostitutes.[181] Reformed prostitutes became the focus of reformers as a result of the Council of Trent since the state started paying greater attention to marriage and family values as a way to discourage alternate sexual expressions, including prostitution and homosexuality.[182] Orphans, on the other hand, had long been seen as a particularly vulnerable group that was at the mercy of charitable institutions and the state. There was an ever-increasing number of orphans in Portugal, and local *misericórdias* directed and sponsored many of the orphanages in Portugal.[183] In fact, the Santa Casa da Misericórdia was one of the principal organizations behind this colonizing effort, and it acted in conjunction with some of the most powerful institutions in the kingdom. This suggests that the assistance of orphans in Portugal—which was itself not a new phenomenon—was critically reconfigured during this period so that, as Ana Isabel Marques Guedes suggests, the king could still fulfill his sovereign obligations of protecting this vulnerable group while simultaneously taking advantage of their potential as "demographic capital."[184]

The institutional regulations of the orphanages that governed the lives of the orphans prior to their transportation overseas also offer additional insight into the process of subjectification that shaped the agents who were at the center of this colonial project. The Recolhimento do Castelo, for instance, which was the most important shelter that the Santa Casa da Misericórdia helped establish in Lisbon, clearly functioned as part of a larger strategy for colonization.[185] It was a place for the disciplining of bodies. Specifically, for the inculcation of heteronormative gender roles. The institution's stated mission was to prepare women for marriage, and the limited training and instruction that the orphans received reflected this overarching goal. For one, the women were only taught certain trades like cooking and embroidering that were clearly based on assumptions about the sexual division of labor and that prepared them exclusively for domestic work. Moreover, the fact that the Recolhimento did not prioritize teaching women to read or write is suggestive of the gendered assumptions that informed the institution's position on how to engender "ideal" marriageable women. The texts that were available for those who were already literate, or that were routinely read aloud for those who were not, were scrutinized by administrators who were charged with burning any books considered to be profane or potentially detrimental. The most common texts that the orphans read or heard were stories about married female saints and marriage manuals like João de Barros' *Espelho de casados*, which emphasizes the harmonious gendered division of labor and the gendered organization of social space.[186] Notably, the Recolhimento also required proof of blood purity for admission, which meant that women of Jewish, Muslim, or mulatto backgrounds were barred from entering.[187]

The women's daily routines at the Recolhimento and other orphanages were likewise highly structured, and deviations from expected behavior often involved corporal punishments. The orphans were required to rise at five o'clock from Easter until September, and at six during the winter months.[188] Their actions were then standardized according to set schedules, and they were expected to participate in all stipulated activities, including being present when any of the women were nearing death to "animá-lá nessa passage."[189] The controls over women's bodies were central to the disciplining mechanisms of the institutions. When rules were not followed, standard punishments included food restrictions and, in more severe cases, the use of wooden stocks to restrict their movement, a punishment known as *o tronco* that was most often used to discipline enslaved people.[190] Among the documented cases of disciplinary misconduct, Coates recounts an incident in which two women were punished for having a suspicious friendship: "uma amizade de má suspeita."[191] This indicates that same sex-desire was likewise carefully supervised, and it speaks to the way in which the historical formation of norms influences the structuring of affect and desire even when, as Judith Butler points out, "sexuality is never fully re-ducible to the 'effect' of this or that operation of regulatory power."[192]

As physical enclosures, the function of these orphanages further reso-nates with Foucault's arguments about the intricate relation between disci-pline and space. Not only were the orphans prohibited from having contact with people from the exterior, but their physical confinement also ensured that the disciplinary measures described above could operate more effec-tively at the micro level of architectural space.[193] Moreover, we can think of these institutions as spaces of confinement where, similar to what Foucault describes for a different historical context, certain elements of the popu-lation deemed unproductive could be reincorporated into society in a way that simultaneously eliminated the visible social effects of their "neediness" while at the same time making them again productive.[194] For Foucault, one of the driving forces behind the different processes of confinement that he describes was the new demands for labor that resulted from the economic crises of the early modern period.[195] This is certainly suggestive for think-ing about *as órfãs d'el Rei*, but, in their case, their potential productivity was narrowly understood in terms of reproductive labor. Indeed, their po-tential value to the colonial state hinged on the state's ability to instrumen-talize their reproductive capacities.

The significance and implications of the case of *as órfãs d'el Rei* is fur-ther clarified when we consider the broader system of forced colonization that developed in tandem with the practice of sending white women to the colonies. As Coates explains, the practice of sending penal exiles to the col-onies developed out of a penal system already in place in Portugal before its overseas expansion. Well before the 15th century, criminals were relocated within Portugal as part of a two-part system that, on the one hand, allowed the Crown to use their forced labor by sending them to the galleys.[196] On the other hand, some criminals were offered asylum in exchange for being sent to border regions that were sparsely populated and needed manpower to defend their frontiers.[197] As Coates explains, the state modified an old tool of penal exile to fashion a method of forced colonization.[198] Geraldo Perioni further discusses how exile (both internal and external) was articulated in Portuguese penal law in relation to the death penalty. As he shows, penal law codified a series of offenses that were followed by the expressions "morra por ello" or "morra por isso."[199] Nevertheless, the punishment that was actually administered was exile, not death, which he reads as a way of formulating exile as a type of civil rather than physical death. Pieronis' insight allows us to think about the way in which exile functioned within a broader economy of crime and punishment where we see a change in emphasis from the expendability of bodies to the economic and political instrumentalization of their use.

The type of offenses punishable by exile spanned a broad range of social and moral issues: including heresy, treason, counterfeiting, and sodomy.[200] The Crown differentiated between internal and external exile—the former being the more lenient form of punishment—but it also actively encouraged the latter since it served its interests overseas.[201] The length of time and the stipulated location for the punishment varied according to the offense, with permanent banishment to the colonies being the highest form of punishment, except for the death penalty.[202] With the establishment of the Inquisition in Portugal in 1536, exile to the colonies became an even more widely practiced form of punishment. As Coates states, "exile was one of the punishments most frequently used by the Inquisition during early modern times."[203] During the 16th century, the colonies were also seen as places for punishment where people could still return from, after a period that allowed them to purge their sins. According to Laura de Mello e Souza, the voyage itself was seen as part of the ritual of exile, and the time spent in the colonies was viewed as a type of purification.[204]

It is also critical to note that the practice of penal exile to the colonies developed in a context of momentous socio-economic transformations that had produced within Europe a category of economically "surplus" populations. Indeed, the crisis of vagrancy during the 16th century that Karl Marx famously discusses in his theorization of Primitive Accumulation is registered in Portuguese discourses about poverty, and this was used as a justification for colonial exile. As Angela Barreto Xavier shows, there are a series of competing discourses that circulated in Portugal during the 16th century on the question of poverty and how to deal with it. On the one hand, the representation of the poor as *pauper chirsti* was a common trope that had been around since the Middle Ages and that greatly influenced the imaginary and policies of mendicant orders.[205] Barreto Xavier characterizes this view as one that emphasized asceticism, corporeal sacrifices, and suffering, and that associated divine salvation with the way destitute individuals endured said challenges.[206] As she points out, however, although the poor were the protagonists of these types of discourses, the majority of texts that disseminated these views targeted the rich as their primary audiences and addressed what they should do in relation to the poor in order to achieve the salvation of their own souls.[207] Barreto Xavier presents this position as one that advocated for a type of welfare (*assistencialismo*), and she argues that this model did not attempt to solve poverty but rather to mitigate its effects while still maintaining existing hierarchies between rich and poor.[208] It was expected that the rich would feel compassion and help the poor, and, within this formulation, women were frequently used as archetypical examples, both as figures in need of assistance, as well as charitable subjects who provided assistance. As Barreto Xavier shows, these discourses also influenced institutional formations. Specifically, she shows how they influenced the creation of the Santa Casa da Misericórdia in Lisbon, which became one of many in Portugal and later also overseas.[209] The first *misericórdia* was founded in Lisbon in 1498, but others were soon established throughout Portugal as well as in the colonies. The *misericórdias* were increasingly institutionalized, and they served the Crown's obligations to fulfill charity on a state level. Their establishment often went hand-in-hand with the founding of a city, and they became an empire-wide institution.[210] It is also important to note that the administrative structure of the *misericórdias* excluded Jews, Moors, and blacks, which points to the type of socio-racial distinction on which the institutions were premised.[211]

Barreto Xavier also points out that legislation from the 16th century made a distinction between voluntary and involuntary poverty, and, accordingly, between those who were deserving of assistance from those who were not.[212] These ideas acquired increasing currency in the course of the 16th century and were increasingly linked to ideas about vagrancy. As Barreto Xavier notes, the association between the poor and the vagabond became frequent in these types of formulations.[213] Pauperism was also represented as a problem for public order and, within this framework, it was the conservation of social order rather than the reciprocity of salvation that was at stake.[214] The explicit codification of these ideas created the distinction between the good behavior of the poor that merited assistance, and bad behavior that led to punishment.[215] Barreto Xavier references Thomas More as a thinker who influenced the broader reflections about poverty and socio-economics change during this period, and she argues that, even though Portugal did not produce anything analogous to the Poor Laws in England, both in representations and institutional practices, the country was certainly influenced by these external developments.[216] For Barreto Xavier, this was not only the result of the crisis that resulted from the transition from feudalism to early mercantile capitalism but, above all, the emergence of increasingly centralized and disciplinary powers.[217]

In the justification of colonial exile for criminals, it is clear that circulating discourses on poverty influenced developing legislation and practices. It is noteworthy, though, that as part of the effort to make penal exiles (or *degredados*) useful to Portugal's empire-building ambitions, these figures first underwent an important discursive transformation. As Coates explains

> [w]ell before the *degredado* left Portugal, the Crown began to refer to him as a soldier rather than the more accurate exile, criminal, or convict....This terminology reflected the Crown's desire that these people, former threats to society and its stability, become useful in the empire.[218]

Coates contends that the Crown deliberately confused these terms, and he shows that practices of impressment for public service systematically targeted the poor.[219] Vagrants in particular were presented as well suited for military service, but other vulnerable groups associated with economic inactivity were also frequently targeted. In 1638, the city council in Lisbon suggested that "the lazy and idle be rounded up and sent to Brazil to serve."[220] As Coates suggests, the Crown was not only eager to round up vagrants, but also to compile lists of their names for future projects.[221] Pieroni discusses the exile of vagrants to the colonies as well, and he highlights the fact that Brazil became a primary destination.[222] It should also be noted that the collection and transportation of *degredados* was part of an intricate system that involved different types of institutions. The Santa Casa de Misericórdia, for instance, assumed some of the financial burdens of feeding and clothing indigent prisoners before they were sent overseas.[223] What all of this suggests is that, similar to the process that Foucault describes in *Discipline and Punish* and the lectures leading up to that book, the development of Portugal's penal legal system evinces the emergences of novel ways of exercising power that go beyond the sovereign's right to take life or let live. These new forms of power linked together a series of state institutions focused on what Foucault termed "the political economy of bodies," that is, the investment of power in the disciplining of productive bodies that can be made to serve the interests of nascent capitalism.[224]

Penal exile to Brazil was prioritized precisely after 1549, once the Crown had assumed a more active stance on the permanent occupation and population of the colony. As Coates recounts, although Brazil was used as a site for exile from the beginning, it was not until 1549 that Brazil was prioritized as a destination over other African colonies.[225] It was also in 1549, at the time of the arrival of the first governor-general and the first Jesuits under Nóbrega's supervision, that the largest shipment of *degredados* was sent to Brazil.[226] Coates challenges the high number of penal exiles that other historians claim first arrived in 1549 (some estimates are as high as 600), but he acknowledges that by that time the Inquisition was already well established and likely contributed to the fact that the number was higher than ever before. It is especially striking that, though Coates is skeptical about these numbers, he speculates that they seem unrealistic unless "it represented a major, coordinated effort by both church and state to populate Portuguese America."[227] Now, while extant evidence on this particular group of *degredados* is inconclusive, there are other supporting facts that suggest that a major coordinated effort to populate the Brazilian colony was certainly assumed as an imperial project.

One way in which we can think about the regulatory biopolitical ambitions implicit in the system of penal exile is by considering the fact that Brazil became the favored location for female convicts. As Laura de Mello e Souza describes, Portuguese women who were seen as "undesirables" in the metropole, enjoyed greater social standing in the colony—where they tended to marry quickly—and thus were seen as helpful in the reproduction of a Portuguese population overseas.[228] The predilection for sending women to the colony is also confirmed by Coates, who shows that women whose crimes would have warranted longer and harsher exiles in places in Africa, were instead increasingly sent to Brazil.[229] This is particularly evident in the case of the Inquisition since the institution sent sixty-two percent of its convicted female sinners to Brazil during the second half of the 17th century.[230] Mello e Souza's analysis focuses specifically on cases of exile ordered by the Inquisition, and she argues that the practice constituted a twofold process of social exclusion and reincorporation.[231] These practices were also overtly politicizing women's reproductive capacity in the interest of the colonial imperative to populate the colony.

The practice of forced and state-sponsored colonization that facilitated a global exchange of *órfãs d'el Rei* and female convicts, when considered in relation to the momentous socio-economic transformations happening in Europe, is illustrative of what feminist theorist Silvia Federici describes as the process through which women's embodied role in reproduction was transformed into a state matter. As part of this process, as Federici argues, a series of power dynamics coalesced around the interrelated objectives of attempting to dispossess women of their knowledge and authority over their own bodies, and of transforming them into a naturalized site of reproductive labor.[232] In the case of Brazil, this practice was inaugurated with Nóbrega, and his writing is critical to understand not only the politicization of racially qualified life in early modern discourses but also how life's politicization helped sanction the instrumentalization and regulation of white women's reproductive capacities while increasingly distinguishing them from differently racialized women.

Conclusion

As shown in this chapter, Nóbrega played a major role in shaping the policy of *aldeamento* during the initial phases of its implementation. In his writing, the project is justified by appealing to a segregationist logic that explicitly differentiates between *brancos* and *índios*, and though his characterization of the latter is not consistently homogenizing—for instance, in cases where he distinguishes between *negros da terra* and *gentios* or *índios da terra*—it nevertheless illustrates the way in which the reorganization of space helped shape processes of racialization in colonial Brazil.

A historically contextualized analysis of Nóbrega's also allows us to trace his role in shaping the system of state-sponsored colonization that institutionalized global traffic in Portuguese women. Both projects decisively influenced early processes of racialization. The first by contributing to the gradual homogenization of *índios* through a practice of spatial concentration, and the second by bringing into focus how processes of racialization are shaped by the ways in which different women's reproductive capacities have been historically regulated. Nóbrega's petition for female orphans is part of a broader trend in which the fostering of life begins to be increasingly politicized as part of a strategy for colonization. Analyzing Nóbrega's role in shaping the course of Brazil's colonization in relation to the history of segregation in Spanish America also calls attention to the differing ways in which racially qualified life was politicized in early modernity: whereas in Spanish America fostering indigenous population growth was explicitly used to justify segregationist measures, in Portuguese America the emphasis was on expanding the size of the Portuguese colonists, who are increasingly depicted as white. A comparative reading of these cases thus offers critical insight to understand how the broader reconfiguration of power's hold over life shaped the colonization of the Americas, and it brings into focus the interrelations between notions of race, sex, and segregation.

Finally, it is important to note that, before Nóbrega even left for São Vicente in 1553 and helped bring about the shift toward the policy of *aldeamento*, he wrote a series of letters that evince the way in which he sought to regulate reproductive relations between differently racialized groups of people. This context has long been described as the basis for Brazil's history of *mestiçagem* or racial mixture, but, as Ronaldo Vainfas argues, the narrative about the presumed lack of racial preconceptions by Portuguese men who engaged in widespread reproductive relations with differently racialized women needs to be revised and contextualized by considering the context of slavery and coerced sexual relations in which these relations developed.[233] In his words: "Colonização exploratória e escravista, eis as coordenadas da suposta 'liberdade sexual' dos séculos passados…. [O] aparente desregramento sexual dos portugueses funcionava, na prática, como condição inerente ao processo colonizatório."[234] In Brazil's case, it is critical to stress that the policy of *aldeamento*, premised as it was on a segregationist logic, not only developed in a context of *mestiçagem*—as did the policy of *congregación* or *reducción* in the context of Spanish America—this context of widespread reproductive relations between differently racialized groups further took place in a colonial context of domination that is often occluded by celebratory narratives of racial mixture in colonial Latin America.

Notes

1 Charlotte de Castelnau-L'Estoile similarly describes aldeamento as a "política de concentração levada a efeito pelos jesuítas," and she argues that "Os jesuítas do Brasil inventaram então o *aldeamento*, isto é, uma aldeia de evangelização onde eram reunidos índios de origens diversas com os quais residiam os missionários." See *Operários de uma vinha estéril: Os Jesuítas e a conversão dos índios no Brasil 1500–1620* (Editorial da Universidade do Sagrado Coração, 2006), 19. Likewise, John Manuel Monteiro describes aldeamentos as "concentrações improvisadas e instáveis de índios provenientes de sociedades distintas." See *Negros da Terra: Índios e Bandeirantes de São Paulo* (Companhia das Letras, 1994), 43.

2 Daniel Nemser, *Infrastructures of Race: Concentration and Biopolitics in Colonial Mexico* (University of Texas Press, 2017); Maria Regina Celestino de Almeida, *Metamorfoses indígenas: identidade e cultura nas aldeias coloniais do Rio de Janeiro* (Arquivo Nacional, 2003).

3 As Charlotte de Castelnau-L'Estoile notes, both *aldeia* and *aldeamento* are used to describe the policy of indigenous sedentarization ushered in by the Jesuits. As she notes, though, the term *aldeia* is also used at times to describe "aldeias 'autenticamente' indígenas (de criação não-jesuíta)." There is thus some ambiguity in discourses from the period, so here I use both terms since in Nóbrega's discourse he uses the term *aldeias. Operários de uma vinha estéril*, 24. For more on the importance that itinerancy had for the Jesuits prior to the move towards *aldeamento* see Charlotte de Castelnau-L'Estoile, *Operários de uma vinha estéril*, 98–99.

4 See John Manuel Monteiro, *Negros da Terra,* 42; José Eisenberg, *As missões jesuíticas e o pensamento político moderno* (Editora EFMG, 2000), 89. There is a slight discrepancy in the date these scholars offer on the foundation of the aldeamento de Piratininga but here I follow Monteiro's periodization. It is also important to note that, although this chapter focuses on Nóbrea's role in shaping aldeamento, as noted, Anchieta also played an important role. For more on Achieta's role see Charlotte de Castelnau-L'Estoile, *Un catholicisme colonial: Le mariage des Indiens et des esclaves au Brésil, XVI-XVIII* (Presses Universitaires de France, 2019), 72; Charlotte de Castelnau-L'Estoile, *Operários de uma vinha estéril*, 103; John Manuel Monteiro, *Negros da Terra,* 41, 42.

5 Alida Metcalf, *Family and Frontier in Colonial Brazil. Santana de Parnaíba, 1580–1822* (University of California Press, 1992), 82. Charlotte de Castelnau-L'Estoile also argues that the Jesuits collaboration with Mem de Sa in founding the aldeamentos was inspired by what the Spaniards were doing in Spanish America. See *Un catholicisme colonial*, 180.

6 See Beatriz Perrone Moises, "Índios livres e índios escravos: Os princípios da legislação indigenista do período colonial (séculos XVI a XVIII)," in *História dos índios no Brasil*, edited by Manuela Carneiro da Cunha (Companhia das Letras, 1992), 118. As Charlotte de Castelnau-L'Estoile and Maria Regina Celestino de Almeida note, although only Jesuits and indigenous groups from different ethnic backgrounds were allowed to live in aldeamentos, other people resided there as well. See Charlotte de Castelnau-L'Estoile, *Operários de uma vinha estéril*, 19, 54, 89; Maria Regina Celestino de Almeida, *Metamorfoses indígenas: identidade e cultura nas aldeias coloniais do Rio de Janeiro* (Arquivo Nacional, 2003), 131–136.

7 Charlotte de Castelnau-L'Estoile, *Operários de uma vinha estéril*, 137, 150; Beatriz Perrone Moises, "Índios livres e índios escravos," 117, 119, 120; John Manuel Monteiro, *Negros da Terra,* 36, 44. For more on the involvement of Jesuits in sugar production see *Operários de uma vinha estéril*, 58, 275.

8 Beatriz Perrone Moises, "Índios livres e índios escravos," 118–119; Charlotte de Castelnau-L'Estoile, *Un catholicisme colonial*, 180.

9 John Manuel Monteiro, *Negros da Terra*, 44–45. See also Charlotte de Castelnau-L'Estoile, *Operários de uma vinha estéril*, 54; Beatriz Perrone Moises, "Índios livres e índios escravos," 119.

10 Charlotte de Castelnau-L'Estoile, *Operários de uma vinha estéril*, 144. For more on the restriction of people's movement see also Maria Regina Celestino de Almeida, *Metamorfoses indígenas*, 131–136.

11 Charlotte de Castelnau-L'Estoile, *Operários de uma vinha estéril*, 115, 274. See also Maria Regina Celestino de Almeida, *Metamorfoses indígenas*, 135.

12 Charlotte de Castelnau-L'Estoile, *Operários de uma vinha estéril*, 54–55.

13 Beatriz Perrone Moises and Charlotte de Castelnau-L'Estoile similarly argue that aldeamento was premised on a segregationist logic. Perrone Moises contends that this is confirmed by the changes implemented by the Marques de Pombal in the 18th century, which, as she says introduced laws to try to incentivize the presence of whites in aldeias to end the "odiosa separação entre uns e outros." See Beatriz Perrone Moises, "Índios livres e índios escravos," 119. Charlotte de Castelnau-L'Estoile similarly argues that "os padres da província procuraram adaptar seus métodos de evangelização e criaram a *aldeia*, agrupamento fundado pelas necessidades de evangelização, no qual os índios são reunidos e isolados das populações europeias." See *Operários de uma vinha estéril*, 89.

14 Manuel da Nóbrega, *Cartas do Brasil e mais escritos do Manuel da Nóbrega*, edited by Serafim Leite (Atlântida, 1955), 154. Letter from São Vicente, March 10, 1553.

15 Beatriz Perrone Moises, "Índios livres e índios escravos," 117, 119. See also Maria Regina Celestino de Almeida, *Metamorfoses indígenas*, 131–132.

16 Beatriz Perrone Moises, "Índios livres e índios escravos," 118, 119.

17 Maria Leônia Chaves de Resende, "Minas mestiças: índios coloniais em busca da liberdade no século do ouro," *Cahiers des Amériques latines* 44, no. 44 (2003): 66; José Eisenberg, "Antonio Vieira and the Justification for Indian Slavery," *Luso-Brazilian Review* 40, no. 1 (2003): 90; Alida Metcalf, "The Entradas of Bahia of the Sixteenth Century," *The Americas* 61, no. 3 (2005): 373–400; Castelnau-L'Estoile, *Un catholicisme colonial*, 164, 271; Beatriz Perrone Moises, "Índios livres e índios escravos," 117.

18 Nóbrega's supported indigenous and African slavery as a necessary means to develop the colony, and yet he still defended the liberty for majority of indigenous. See John Manuel Monteiro, *Negros da Terra*, 41.

19 Castelnau-L'Estoile, *Un catholicisme colonial*, 180, 184; Beatriz Perrone Moises, "Índios livres e índios escravos," 123.

20 Maria Regina Celestino de Almeida, *Metamorfoses indígenas*, 25, 81, 102, 109. See also Beatriz Perrone Moises, "Índios livres e índios escravos," 117.

21 See John Manuel Monteiro, *Negros da Terra*, 33, 35, 42, 155.

22 Beatriz Perrone Moises, "Índios livres e índios escravos," 120.

23 Beatriz Perrone Moises, "Índios livres e índios escravos," 123; Charlotte de Castelnau-L'Estoile, *Operários de uma vinha estéril*, 123.

24 See John Manuel Monteiro, *Negros da Terra*, 45–46, 143; Charlotte de Castelnau-L'Estoile, *Operários de uma vinha estéril*, 143, 144.

25 Beatriz Perrone Moises, "Índios livres e índios escravos," 123; Castelnau-L'Estoile *Un catholicisme colonial*, 205, 236–237, 241; John Manuel Monteiro, *Negros da Terra*, 167. For more on how the Roman legal principle of *partus sequitur ventrem* developed in Brazil in relation to enslaved Africans see Martha S. Santos, "Slave Mothers': Partus Sequitur Ventrem, and the Naturalization of Slave Reproduction in Nineteenth-Century Brazil," *Tempo* 22, no. 41 (2016): 468, 479.

26 On this point it is important to stress that, as Manuela Carneiro da Cunha argues, it is critical to consider indigenous subjects as agents of their own history not simply as victims of destructive politics and practices. See *História dos índios no Brasil* (Companhia das Letras, 1992).

27 Ronaldo Vainfas, *A heresia dos índios: Catolicismo e rebeldia no Brasil colonial* (Companhia das Letras, 1995), 76; Charlotte de Castelnau-L'Estoile, *Operários de uma vinha estéril*, 125, 126.

28 Ronaldo Vainfas, *A heresia dos índios*, 76–83. For additional forms of indigenous resistance see also Ronaldo Vainfas, *A heresia dos indios*, 64–67.

29 Charlotte de Castelnau-L'Estoile, *Operários de uma vinha estéril*, 125, 126.

30 Charlotte de Castelnau-L'Estoile, *Un catholicisme colonial*, 181; Maria Regina Celestino de Almeida, *Metamorfoses indígenas*, 136.

31 See Charlotte de Castelnau-L'Estoile, *Un catholicisme colonial*, 164. As Charlotte de Castelnau-L'Estoile explains, indigenous slavery was temporarily prohibited by a law from 1611 issued by the Spanish monarch during the Iberian Union (150–1640). The law was soon afterwards revoked, however. See Charlotte de Castelnau-L'Estoile, *Un catholicisme colonial*, 271, 345. John Manuel Monteiro also shows that in 1570 the Portuguese crown tried to regulate but not prohibit indigenous slavery. See *Negros da Terra*, 4–42. For more on indigenous slavery in Brazil see John Manuel Monteiro, *Negros da terra*; Maria Leônia Chaves de Resende, "Minas mestiças: índios coloniais em busca da liberdade no século do ouro," *Cahiers des Amériques latines* 44, no. 44 (2003): 66; José Eisenberg, "Antonio Vieira and the Justification for Indian Slavery," *Luso-Brazilian Review* 40, no. 1 (2003): 90; Alexander Marchant "From Barter to Slavery: The Economic Relations of Portuguese and Indians in the Settlement of Brazil 1500–1580," in *The John Hopkins University Studies in Historical and Political Science*, Volume LX (The Jonh Hopkins Press, 1942), 13–160; Stuart Schwartz, "Indian Labor and New World Plantations," 57; Stuart Schwartz, "Indian Labor and New World Plantations," 60; Justin Bucifferro, "A Forced Hand," 291; Alida Metcalf, *Go-Betweens*, 174–175.

32 It is important to also stress that, starting in 1549, Brazil was prioritized as a destination for Portuguese penal exiles, and, in particular, for female convicts (or *degredadas*), who were increasingly sent to the colony. For more on this see Timothy Coates, *Convicts and Orphans. Forced and State-Sponsored Colonizers in the Portuguese Empire, 1550–1755* (Stanford University Press, 2001), 63, 85.

33 Timothy Coates, *Convicts and Orphans*, 3, 187.

34 Dauril Alden, "Changing Jesuit Perceptions of the Brasis during the Sixteenth Century," *Journal of World History* 3, no. 2 (1992): 206. For more on Nóbrega's family relationship with King João III, see also Thomas Cohen, "Who Is My Neighbor?," 212.

35 Manuel da Nóbrega, *Cartas do Brasil e mais escritos*, 79–80. Beginning in 1550, orphan boys from Portugal were also sent to Brazil to aid the missionary efforts. See Alida Metcalf, *Go-betweens*; Dauril Alden, "Changing Jesuit Perceptions," 213. In a letter from August 1551 acknowledges the arrival or orphan boys from Portugal, see *Cartas do Brasil e mais escritos*, 87.

36 Rodolfo Garcia, "As órfas." *Revista do Instituto Histórico e Geográfico Brasileiro* 192 (1946): 138.

37 See Anais da Biblioteca Nacional do Rio de Janeiro, vol. 57 (Ministério da Educação, 1939), 50.

38 Rodolfo Garcia, "As órfas," 142; Timothy Coates, "State-Sponsored Female Colonization in the *Estado da Índia, ca. 1550 1750*," in *Sinners and Saints. The Successors of Vasco da Gama*, edited by Sanjay Subrahmanyam (Oxford University Press, 1995), 40–56. For the only record on the orphans who arrived

in Brazil sometime in 1608 and 1609 see also *Anais da Biblioteca Nacional do Rio de Janeiro*, vols. 57, 50.

39 Stuart B. Schwartz, *Early Brazil a Documentary Collection to 1700* (Cambridge University Press, 2010), 13.

40 Antonio Carlos Robert Moraes, *Bases da Formação Territorial do Brasil. O Território colonial brasileiro no 'longo' século XVI* (Editora Hucitec, 2000), 293; Pasquale Petrone, *Aldeamentos Paulistas* (Editora da Universidade de Sao Paulo, 1995), 22–23.

41 Pasquale Petrone, *Aldeamentos Paulistas*, 22. For more on indigenous slavery in Brazil see also Alida Metcalf "The Entradas of Bahia of the Sixteenth Century," *The Americas* 61, no. 3 (2005): 373–400.

42 Justin Bucifferro, "A Forced Hand: Natives, Africans, and the Population of Brazil, 1545–1850," *Revista de História Económica* 31, no. 2 (2013): 287.

43 Carlos Alberto de Moura Ribeiro Zeron, *Linha de fé. A companhia de Jesus e a Escravidão no Processo de Formação da Sociedade Colonial. Brasil, Séculos XVI e XVII* (Editora da Universidade de São Paulo, 2011), 49; Stuart B. Schwartz, *Early Brazil a documentary collection to 1700* (Cambridge University Press, 2010), 13.

44 Stuart B. Schwartz, *Early Brazil*, 13.

45 Antonio Carlos Robert Moraes, *Bases da Formação*, 300.

46 Edson Carneiro, *A cidade do Salvador: uma reconstituição histórica* (Edição da 'Organização Simões,' 1954), 15.

47 Stuart B. Schwartz, "Indian Labor and New World Plantations: European Demands and Indian Responses in Northeastern Brazil," *The American Historical Review* 83, no. 1 (1978): 48; Antonio Carlos Robert Moraes, *Bases da Formação*, 299.

48 Antonio Carlos Robert Moraes, *Bases da Formação*, 301.

49 Pasquale Petrone, *Aldeamentos Paulistas*, 24–25; Edson Carneiro, *A cidade do Salvador*, 17, 20, 23.

50 Carlos Alberto de Moura Ribeiro Zeron, *Linha de fé. A companhia de Jesus e a Escravidão no Processo de Formação da Sociedade Colonial. Brasil, Séculos XVI e XVII* (Editora da Universidade de São Paulo, 2011), 47. See also letter from Gouveia to the King in Luiz Norton, "A colonização Portuguesa do Brasil (1500–1550)," *Revista de Historia de America* no. 138 (2007): 192.

51 See Carlos Alberto de Moura Ribeiro Zeron, *Linha de fé. A companhia de Jesus e a Escravidão no Processo de Formação da Sociedade Colonial. Brasil, Séculos XVI e XVII* (Editora da Universidade de São Paulo, 2011), 47.

52 Carlos Alberto de Moura Ribeiro Zeron, *Linha de fé*, 46–47, 52.

53 Maria Regina Celestino de Almeida, *Metamorfoses indígenas: identidade e cultura nas aldeias coloniais do Rio de Janeiro* (Arquivo Nacional, 2003), 58.

54 Carlos Alberto de Moura Ribeiro Zeron, *Linha de fé*, 52–54; Stuart B. Schwartz, *Early Brazil*, 37.

55 The beginning of the new colonizing tactics adopted in Brazil after 1549 are described by Antonio Hespanha as formal colonization, see *Filhos da terra: Identidades mestiças nos confins da expansão portuguesa* (Edições Tinta da China, 2019), 25. Hespanha also briefly discusses what he calls the "Repúblicas Indias dos jesuítas no Brasil," see *Filhos da terra*, 69.

56 Carlos Alberto de Moura Ribeiro Zeron, *Linha de fé*, 55.

57 For more on the construction of Salvador da Bahia see Edson Carneiro, *A cidade do Salvador: uma reconstituição histórica* (Edição da 'Organização Simoes,' 1954). See also Stuart B. Schwartz, "Cities of Empire: Mexico and Bahia in the Sixteenth Century," *Journal of Inter-American Studies* 11, no. 4 (1969): 618, 631.

58 Carlos Alberto de Moura Ribeiro Zeron, *Linha de fé*, 56; Serafim Leite, *Breve itinerário para uma biografia do P. Manuel da Nóbrega, fundador da província do Brasil e da cidade de São Paulo* (Edições Brotéria, 1955), 52. Says they arrived in April of 1549. Says with them arrived also some Portuguese women. 42 IN all, she says, a 1,000 people, among them six missionaries. Casteleneu Un Catholicisme, 42.

59 See Guillermo Ignacio Vitali, "Escenas de Evangelización: Verdad y Archivo en las Cartas de Manuel da Nóbrega," *Alea Estudos Neolatinos* 22, no. 2 (2020): 42.

60 Alida Metcalf, *Go-Betweens and the Colonization of Brazil 1500–1600* (University of Texas Press, 2006), 91.

61 Thomas Cohen, "Who Is My Neighbor? The Missionary Ideals of Manuel da Nóbrega," in *Jesuit Encounters in the New World: Jesuit Chroniclers, Geographers, Educators and Missionaries in the Americas, 1549–1767,* edited by Joseph A. Gagliano and Charles E. Ronan (Institutum Historicum, 1997), 211, 213; Dauril Alden, "Changing Jesuit Perceptions of the Brasis during the Sixteenth Century," *Journal of World History* 3, no. 2 (1992): 206.

62 Manuel da Nóbrega, *Cartas do Brasil e mais escritos*, 51. For additional examples see also 47, 48, 51, 61.

63 Manuel da Nóbrega, *Cartas do Brasil e mais escritos*, 61.

64 Nóbrega himself earned a degree in cannon law after studying four years at the University of Salamanca, and three years at the University of Coimbra. Both universities were at the forefront of some of the most important juridical debates from the period—including over the legitimacy of the Iberian conquest, the nature and rights of indigenous groups, and slavery—and Nóbrega's writings not only reflect his educational background they further show that he actively contributed to ongoing debates. See Thomas Cohen, "Who Is My Neighbor?," 212; Virginia Rau, "Review of *Cartas do Brasil e mais escritos do P. Manuel da Nóbrega (Opera Omnia) by Serafim Leite,*" *The Hispanic American Historical Review* 36, no. 3 (1956): 390. For more on the University of Coimbra and Salamanca and their influence on juridical debates about the Americas see Anthony Pagden, *The Fall of Natural Man* (Cambridge University Press, 1982), 60–69; José Eisenberg, "A escravidao voluntária dos índios do Brasil e o pensamenot politico moderno," *Análise Social* 39, no. 170 (2004): 7.

65 Manuel da Nóbrega, *Cartas do Brasil e mais escritos*, 19, 20. See also Edson Carneiro, *A cidade do Salvador*, 17. For more on the number of colonists living in Bahia at the time see Maria Luiza Marcílio, "The Population of Colonial Brazil," in *The Cambridge History of Latin America. Volume II,* edited by Leslie Bethell (Cambridge University Press, 1984), 37–58; Justin Bucifferro, "A Forced Hand: Natives, Africans, and the Population of Brazil, 1545–1850," *Revista de História Económica* 31, no. 2 (2013): 290.

66 Manuel da Nóbrega, *Cartas do Brasil e mais escritos*, 19, 20.

67 Manuel da Nóbrega, *Cartas do Brasil e mais escritos*, 21, 23.

68 Alida Metcalf, *Go-Betweens,* 91.

69 Manuel da Nóbrega, *Cartas do Brasil e mais escritos*, 36–37.

70 Manuel da Nóbrega, *Cartas do Brasil e mais escritos*, 50, 51.

71 Alida Metcalf, "'Harvesting Souls': The Society of Jesus and the first Aldeias (Mission Villages) of Bahia," in *Native Brazil: Beyond the Convert and the Cannibal, 1500–1900,* edited by Hal Langfur (The University New Mexico Press, 2014), 31–32.

72 Hal Langfur, "Recovering Brazil's Indigenous Pasts," in *Native Brazil: Beyond the Convert and the Cannibal, 1500–1900,* edited by Hal Langfur (The University New Mexico Press, 2014), 7.

73 Alida Metcalf, "'Harvesting Souls,'" 32. See also Maria Regina Celestino de Almeida, *Metamorfoses indígenas*, 50.
74 Manuel da Nóbrega, *Cartas do Brasil e mais escritos*, 98–100. See also Manuel da Nóbrega, *Cartas do Brasil e mais escritos*, 87.
75 Alida Metcalf, "'Harvesting Souls,'" 40. For more on the Bishop's arrival Charlotte de Castelnau-L'Estoile, *Un catholicisme colonial*, 43.
76 Manuel da Nóbrega, *Cartas do Brasil e mais escritos*, 149.
77 Serafim Leite, *Breve itinerário para uma biografia do P. Manuel da Nóbrega, fundador da província do Brasil e da cidade de São Paulo* (Edições Brotéria, 1955), 93.
78 Manuel da Nóbrega, *Cartas do Brasil e mais escritos*, 154.
79 Manuel da Nóbrega, *Cartas do Brasil e mais escritos*, 160–161.
80 Manuel da Nóbrega, *Cartas do Brasil e mais escritos*, 162.
81 Alida Metcalf, "'Harvesting Souls,'" 40.
82 Manuel da Nóbrega, *Cartas do Brasil e mais escritos*, 157.
83 Manuel da Nóbrega, *Cartas do Brasil e mais escritos*, 170.
84 José Eisenberg, *As missões jesuíticas*, 90.
85 Manuel da Nóbrega, *Cartas do Brasil e mais escritos*, 166. As Alida Metcalf explains in reference to this passage, though, this was precisely the type of incursions into "the wilderness" that governor Tomé de Sousa explicitly proscribed, not least of all because of because it also involved entering disputed territories with Spaniards, see *Go-Betweens*, 105.
86 Manuel da Nóbrega, *Cartas do Brasil e mais escritos*, 167, 190.
87 José Eisenberg, *As missões jesuíticas*, 92.
88 Manuel da Nóbrega, *Cartas do Brasil e mais escritos*, 332.
89 José Eisenberg, *As missões jesuíticas*, 93.
90 Manuel da Nóbrega, *Cartas do Brasil e mais escritos*, 270–271.
91 Thomas Cohen, "Who Is My Neighbor?," 220–221; José Eisenberg, *As missoes jesuíticas*, 91. Anchieta also wrote a poem in Latin praising Mem de Sa's military campaigns, see Alida Metcalf, *Go-Betweens*, 112.
92 Rafael Chambouleyron, "A evangelização do Novo Mundo: o Plano do Pe. Manuel da Nóbrega," *Revista de História* 134 (1996): 37, 39, 40.
93 José Eisenberg, *As missões jesuíticas*, 93. Notably, the *Diálogo* has received fairly limited academic attention. Existin studies include Castelneau's reading, lists Thomas Cohen, and Mecenas Dourado only. Later also adds that Carlos Zeron studies in in his thesis. Operarios 103, later 106.
94 José Eisenberg, *As missões jesuíticas*, 94.
95 Ibid.
96 José Eisenberg, *As missões jesuíticas*, 96.
97 José Eisenberg, *As missões jesuíticas*, 95. For additional analyses of the *Diálogo* see also Thomas Cohen, "Who Is My Neighbor? The Missionary Ideals of Manuel da Nóbrega," in *Jesuit Encounters in the New World: Jesuit Chroniclers, Geographers, Educators and Missionaries in the Americas, 1549–1767*, edited by Joseph A. Gagliano and Charles E. Ronan (Institutum Historicum, 1997), 220–228; Charlotte de Castelnau-L'Estoile, *Operários de uma vinha estéril*, 103–116.
98 Manuel da Nóbrega, *Diálogo sobre a conversão do gentio*, edited by Serafim Leite (Comissão do IV Centenário da Fundação de São Paulo, 1954), 73–74.
99 Manuel da Nóbrega, *Diálogo sobre a conversão do gentio*, 75.
100 Manuel da Nóbrega, *Diálogo sobre a conversão do gentio*, 85.
101 Ibid.
102 Manuel da Nóbrega, *Diálogo sobre a conversão do gentio*, 86.

103 For more on the pogrom against *conversos* in 1506 in Portugal see Angus MacKay, "Popular Movements and Pogroms in Fifteenth-Century Castile," *Past & Present* 55 (May 1972): 33–67; Renee Levine Melammed, *A Question of Identity: Iberian Conversos in Historical Perspective* (Oxford University Press, 2004), 60.
104 Manuel da Nóbrega, *Diálogo sobre a conversão do gentio*, 73–74.
105 Manuel da Nóbrega, *Diálogo sobre a conversão do gentio*, 89–90.
106 Manuel da Nóbrega, *Diálogo sobre a conversão do gentio*, 91.
107 Manuel da Nóbrega, *Diálogo sobre a conversão do gentio*, 93.
108 Ibid.
109 For more on the curse of Ham (in Portuguese, "a maldição de Cam"), see Brian Connolly, "The Curse of Canaan; or, A Fantasy of Origins in Nineteenth-Century America," in *Connexions: Histories of Race and Sex in North America*, edited by Jennifer Brier, Jim Downs, Jennifer Morgan (University of Illinois Press, 2016), E-book; James Sweet, "The Iberian Roots of American Racist Thought," *The William and Mary Quarterly* 54, no. 1 (1997): 148, 149, 158.
110 María Elena Martínez, "Space, Order, and Group Identities in a Spanish Colonial Town: Puebla de los Angeles," in *The Collective and the Public in Latin America: Cultural Identities and Political Order*, edited by Luis Roniger, Tamar Herzog (Sussex Academic Press, 2000), 15.
111 María Elena Martínez, "Space, Order, and Group Identities," 16.
112 José Eisenberg, *As missões jesuíticas*, 108.
113 Manuel da Nóbrega, *Diálogo sobre a conversão do gentio*, 97.
114 Ibid.
115 Manuel da Nóbrega, *Diálogo sobre a conversão do gentio*, 98.
116 Manuel da Nóbrega, *Diálogo sobre a conversão do gentio*, 99.
117 Serafim Leite, *Breve itinerário*, 129.
118 José Eisenberg, *As missões jesuíticas*, 110.
119 Manuel da Nóbrega, *Cartas do Brasil e mais escritos*, 333.
120 Manuel da Nóbrega, *Cartas do Brasil e mais escritos*, 334.
121 Manuel da Nóbrega, *Cartas do Brasil e mais escritos*, 335.
122 As Alida Metcalf, *Go-Betweens*, note 64, 299.
123 José Eisenberg, *As missões jesuíticas*, 111.
124 Ibid.; Stuart B. Schwartz, "Indian Labor and New World Plantations: European Demands and Indian Responses in Northeastern Brazil," *The American Historical Review* 83, no. 1 (1978): 54.
125 Stuart B. Schwartz, "Indian Labor," 54.
126 Alida Metcalf, "'Harvesting Souls,'" 42.
127 Alida Metcalf, "'Harvesting Souls,'" 44.
128 Carlos Alberto de Moura Ribeiro Zeron, *Linha de fé. A companhia de Jesus e a Escravidão no Processo de Formação da Sociedade Colonial. Brasil, Séculos XVI e XVII* (Editora da Universidade de São Paulo, 2011), 122–123.
129 Carlos Alberto de Moura Ribeiro Zeron, *Linha de fé*, 335.
130 José Eisenberg, *As missões jesuíticas*, 111.
131 Stuart B. Schwartz, "Indian Labor," 57.
132 José Eisenberg, *As missões jesuíticas*, 110. For more on the Jesuits' jurisdiction see Charlotte de Castelnau-L'Estoile, *Un catholicisme colonial*, 84–86.
133 Alida Metcalf, *Go-Betweens*, 111.
134 José Eisenberg, *As missões jesuíticas*, 111.
135 Manuel da Nóbrega, *Cartas do Brasil e mais escritos*, 278, 280.
136 José Eisenberg, *As missões jesuíticas*, 171.
137 Manuel da Nóbrega, *Cartas do Brasil e mais escritos*, 280.

138 Manuel da Nóbrega, *Cartas do Brasil e mais escritos*, 290.
139 Manuel da Nóbrega, *Cartas do Brasil e mais escritos*, 279.
140 Manuel da Nóbrega, *Cartas do Brasil e mais escritos*, 281.
141 Manuel da Nóbrega, *Cartas do Brasil e mais escritos*, 282.
142 Ibid.
143 Alida Metcalf, "'Harvesting Souls,'" 44–45; Charlotte de Castelnau-L'Estoile, *Un Catholicisme Colonial*, 70.
144 Alida Metcalf, "'Harvesting Souls,'" 44–45.
145 Ibid.
146 Manuel da Nóbrega, *Cartas do Brasil e mais escritos*, 282; José Eisenberg, *As missões jesuíticas*, 113.
147 Manuel da Nóbrega, *Cartas do Brasil e mais escritos*, 282–283.
148 José Eisenberg, *As missões jesuíticas*, 115.
149 Ronaldo Vainfas, *Trópico dos pecados: Moral, Sexualidade e Inquisicao no Brasil* (Editora Campus, 1989), 22.
150 Alida Metcalf, "'Harvesting Souls,'" 45. For an additional contextualization and analysis of the 155 letter see Charlotte de Castelnau-L'Estoile, *Operários de uma vinha estéril*, 126–127.
151 Alida Metcalf, "'Harvesting Souls,'" 49.
152 Alida Metcalf, "'Harvesting Souls,'" 51.
153 See the 1566 debate between Nóbrega and Caxas about indigenous enslavement. For more on this, see Carlos Alberto de Moura Ribeiro Zeron, *Linha de fé*, 111, 112, 327; José Eisenberg, "A escravidao voluntária dos índios do Brasil e o pensamenot politico moderno," *Análise Social* 39, no. 170 (2004): 7–35.
154 Hal Langfur, "Recovering Brazil's Indigenous Pasts," in *Native Brazil: Beyond the Convert and the Cannibal,* 1500–1900, edited by Hal Langfur (The University New Mexico Press, 2014), 7; Stuart B. Schwartz, "Indian Labor," 60.
155 Ibid. Schawartz also shows While it is true that African slaves were present from the earliest days of Portugal's colonization of Brazil, as Schwartz argues and other scholars confirm, it was only after the 1570s that the African slave trade expanded dramatically—partly because, by then, the spread of epidemics had decimated indigenous groups. See "Indian Labor and New World Plantations," 60; Justin Bucifferro, "A Forced Hand," 291; Alida Metcalf, *Go-Betweens,* 174–175.
156 See Charlotte de Castelnau-L'Estoile, *Operários de uma vinha estéril*, 276.
157 Manuel da Nóbrega, *Cartas do Brasil e mais escritos*, 114.
158 Manuel da Nóbrega, *Cartas do Brasil e mais escritos*, 19.
159 Though the wording is ambitious, Serafim Leite confirms that, in this passage, Nóbrega uses the expression "gente da terra" to talk about the Portuguese colonists and *negras* to describe indigenous women. See footnotes 4 and 5 in Manuel da Nóbrega, *Cartas do Brasil e mais escritos*, 19.
160 Manuel da Nóbrega, *Cartas do Brasil e mais escritos*, 29, 30.
161 Manuel da Nóbrega, *Cartas do Brasil e mais escritos*, 30.
162 Manuel da Nóbrega, *Cartas do Brasil e mais escritos,* 79–80.
163 See Nóbrega's letter from September 13, 1551, in *Cartas do Brasil e mais escritos*, 94–95. For an analysis of the letter see also Carlos Alberto de Moura Ribeiro Zeron, *Linha de fé*, 79.
164 Manuel da Nóbrega, *Cartas do Brasil e mais escritos*, 101.
165 For more on amancebamento and marriage practices in Brazil see Charlotte de Castelnau-L'Estoile, *Un catholicisme colonial: Le mariage des Indiens et des esclaves au Brésil, XVI–XVIII* (Presses Universitaires de France, 2019).
166 Manuel da Nóbrega, *Cartas do Brasil e mais escritos*, 102.

167 Though in the letter above Nóbrega does not use the term *mestiças* to describe the women that, in his words, were helping alleviate the alleged shortage in marriageable women, he does use the term *mestiços* in later letters, which suggests that the term was gradually consolidating as a marker of group identity. In a letter from 1556, for instance, speaking about the indigenous custom that permitted sexual unions between uncles and nieces—which Nóbrega strictly condemns as being against papal bulls and canon law, as well as contrary to the "impedimento de consanguinidade"—he states that on this issue "[os] mestiços da terra ... nisto são iguais com o gentio." Similarly, in a letter from 1561 addressed to Diego Laynez, Nóbrega concludes by asking whether recent marriage stipulations will be applicable to the descendants of Christian *mestiços* since, as he adds "alguns deles são tais, que deles aos mesmos gentios há pouca diferença." It is unclear what specific marriage reforms Nóbrega is referring to but, in the copy of his letter found in Rome, a side note indicates that the same marriage rules do apply to *mestiços*. As each of these letters indicate, Nóbrega remained doubtful that *mestiços*—even the descendants of Christian *mestiços*—could indeed be considered as equal to the Portuguese. As he repeatedly states, in many ways they continued to be almost the same as the natives, as if something about their genealogical heritage carried with it a type of impurity that even conversion to Christianity could not expunge. In this sense, Nóbrega appeals to notions of purity of blood, but he re-configures them within the context of emerging colonial processes of racialization. See Manuel da Nóbrega, *Cartas do Brasil e mais escritos*, 206, 394.

168 See Manuel da Nóbrega, *Cartas do Brasil e mais escritos*, 206, 394.

169 Manuel da Nóbrega, *Cartas do Brasil e mais escritos*, 114.

170 This is not to minimize the cultural importance that was ascribed to the presence of white women in the colonies, for, as Charles Boxer argues, in many of the settlements that had little or no Portuguese women, the metropolitan language, religion, and culture were severely diluted. Charles Boxer, *Women in Iberian Expansion Overseas 1415–1815* (Oxford University Press, 1975), 35. Yet, as John R. Russell-Wood suggests, white women were also seen as an "instrument for populating the vast expanses of Portuguese America." John R. Russell-Wood, "Women and Society in Colonial Brazil," *Journal of Latin American Studies* 9, no. 1 (1977): 33.

171 Drawing on Lévi-Strauss's work on kinship, she argues that a critical interpretation of his theories can provide a general framework for thinking about the organization of human sexuality and the ways this affects large-scale political processes like state-making, the accumulation of wealth, and the maintenance of differential access to political and economic resources. To develop this argument, she begins by discussing anthropological theories on the role of reciprocal gift giving in the development of early social formations. As she explains, and as Kojin Karatani has argued more recently, both Marcel Mauss and Lévi-Strauss argue that "the principles of social formation in archaic societies can be located in the gift-countergift reciprocal system, under which various items are given and reciprocated, including food, property, women, land, service, labor, and ritual." Lévi-Strauss adds to the theory of primitive reciprocity the idea that marriages are for the most basic form of gift exchange in which women are the most precious of gifts. The "gift" of women, as Rubin notes, establishes not only a relation of reciprocity, but, more significantly, one of kinship.

172 Gayle Rubin, "The Traffic in Women," 169, 207.

173 Gayle Rubin, "The Traffic in Women," 174.

174 Gayle Rubin, "The Traffic in Women," 175–176.

175 Antônio de Jaboatão, *Catálogo genealógico das pricipaes famílias: que pro-cederam de Albuquerques e Cavalcantes em Pernamubuco e Caramurús na Bahia* (Imprensa Oficial, 1950), 177; Rodolfo Garcia, "As órfãs," 138. Rodolfo Garcia, "As órfãs," 138. Though ultimately Catarina did not marry—despite a special provision from 1555 increasing the prestige of the colonial post that would be granted to her husband as part of her dowry—her two sisters did.

176 Rodolfo García, whose study on the groups of orphans that arrived between 1551 and 1608/1609, continued to be the most comprehensive study on the subject regarding Brazil, obliquely suggests that the orphans that arrived sometime in 1608/1609 were most likely sexually assaulted. See "As órfãs," 143.

177 On a symbolic level, the case of *as órfãs d'el Rei* can be read as a kind of prosthetic extension of the king's imperial sovereignty. King João III had fathered nine children of his own with Queen Catarina, but every one of them died within their parents' lifetime. Their only child to have survived childhood, João Manuel, died in 1554, not long after he had fathered his only child: Sebastião I. Though the birth of Sebastião resolved the succession problem that would have doubtlessly preoccupied João III, we can see how the case *as órfãs d'el Rei*—when read in light of the king's own family tragedy—takes on added significance as a biopolitical scheme designed to physically reproduce the sovereign's symbolic heirs. By nominally adopting the orphans, and by backing the institutions that sponsored their voyage and marriage overseas, the king was helping advance a colonial project designed to increase the size of the Portuguese population abroad, and, on a symbolic register, the king's own figurative family. For more on this aspect of King João III's biography see Ana Isabel Buescu, *D. João III. 1502–1557* (Printer Portuguesa Ind. Gráfica Lta, 2008), 191.

178 Timothy Coates, *Convicts and Orphans,* 144.

179 Timothy Coates, *Convicts and Orphans,* 3.

180 I use the expression "traffic in women" following Gayle Rubin's early work in "The Traffic in Women: Notes on the 'Political Economy' of Sex," in *Towards and Anthropology of Women,* edited by Rayna R. Reiter (Monthly Review Press, 1975), 157–210. She later refines these arguments in "The Trouble with Trafficking: Afterthoughts on 'The traffic in women',", in *Deviations: A Gayle Rubin Reader* (Duke University Press, 2011), 33–65. See also the Interview "Sexual Traffic," which features a conversation between Judith Butler and Gayle Rubin, published in *A Journal of Feminist Cultural Studies* 6.2, no. 3 (1994).

181 Timothy Coates, "State-Sponsored Female Colonization," 40.

182 Timothy Coates, "State-Sponsored Female Colonization," 41. See also Timothy Coates, *Convicts and Orphans,* 138–139.

183 Timothy Coates, "State-Sponsored Female Colonization," 42–43.

184 Ana Isabel Marques Guedes, "Tentativas de controle da reprodução da população colonial: As órfas d'El Rei," in *O Rosto feminino da expansão portuguesa* (Comissão para a Igualdade e para os Direitos da Mulher, 1994), 665.

185 Timothy Coates, *Convicts and Orphans,* 3, 142, 144.

186 Ana Isabel Marques Guedes, "Tentativas de controle da reprodução," 666; Suely Creusa Cordeiro de Almeida, *O sexo devoto: normatização e resistência feminina no Império Português XVI – XVIII* (Imprensa Universitária da UFRPE, 2005), 181–183.

187 Suely Creusa Cordeiro de Almeida, *O sexo devoto,* 185. Hebe Mattos also shows that, beginning in the seventeenth century, the socio-racial label *mulato* started to be included in purity of blood regulations in Portugal and shows hos this was then used in Brazil. See "'Pretos' and 'Pardos' between the Cross and

the Sword: Racial Categories in Seventeenth Century Brazil," *Revista Europea de Estudios Latinoamericanos y del Caribe* 80 (2006): 43–55.

188 Suely Creusa Cordeiro de Almeida, *O sexo devoto*, 179.

189 Suely Creusa Cordeiro de Almeida, *O sexo devoto*, 180.

190 Suely Creusa Cordeiro de Almeida, *O sexo devoto*, 183.

191 Timothy Coates, *Convicts and Orphans*, 131.

192 Judith Butler, *Undoing Gender* (Routledge, 2004), 15.

193 Suely Creusa Cordeiro de Almeida, *O sexo devoto*, 182–183.

194 Paul Rabinow and Nikolas Rose, "Biopower Today," *BioSocieties* 1 (2006), 135.

195 Paul Rabinow and Nikolas Rose, "Biopower Today," *BioSocieties* 1 (2006), 128, 131.

196 Timothy Coates, *Convicts and Orphans*, 42.

197 Timothy Coates, *Convicts and Orphans*, 42; Geraldo Pieroni, *Os excluídos do Reino: A Inquisição portuguesa e o degredo para o Brasil Colônia* (Editora Universidade de Brasília, 2000), 25–26.

198 Timothy Coates, *Convicts and Orphans*, 188.

199 Geraldo Pieroni, *Os excluídos do Reino*, 45.

200 Timothy Coates, *Convicts and Orphans*, 25.

201 Timothy Coates, *Convicts and Orphans*, 23.

202 Geraldo Pieroni, *Os excluídos do Reino*, 50.

203 Timothy Coates, *Convicts and Orphans*, 25.

204 Laura de Mello e Souza, *Inferno Atlântico: Demonologia e Colonização séculos XVI-XVIII* (Companhia das Letras, 1993), 89.

205 Angela Barreto Xavier, "Imagens de pobres, pobreza e assistência entre os século XV e XX," in *Portugaliae Monumenta Misericordiarum*, Vol. 10, edited by José Pedro Paiva (União das Misericórdias Portuguesas, 2017), 16.

206 Ibid.

207 Barreto Xavier, "Imagens de pobres," 17.

208 Barreto Xavier, "Imagens de pobres," 19.

209 Barreto Xavier, "Imagens de pobres," 20. For more on *misericórdias,* and child abandonment in Portugal also see Isabel dos Guimarães Sá, "Child Abandonment in Portugal: Legislation and Institutional Care," *Continuity and Change* 9, no. 1 (1994): 69–89; Isabel dos Guimarães Sá, "Managing Social Inequality: Confraternal Charity in Portugal and Its Overseas Colonies," *Social Science History* 41, no. 1 (2017): 121–135.

210 Timothy Coates, *Convicts and Orphans*, 12–14; Barreto Xavier, "Imagens de pobres," 20; Isabel dos Gimaraes sá, "Managing Social Inequality," *Social Science History* 41, no. 1 (2017): 121–135.

211 Suely Creusa Cordeiro de Almeida, *O sexo devoto: normatização e resistência feminina no Império Português XVI – XVIII* (Imprensa Universitária da UFRPE, 2005), 160.

212 Barreto Xavier, "Imagens de pobres," 20.

213 Ibid.

214 Barreto Xavier, "Imagens de pobres," 21.

215 Ibid.

216 Barreto Xavier, "Imagens de pobres," 22.

217 Barreto Xavier, "Imagens de pobres," 20–21.

218 Timothy Coates, *Convicts and Orphans*, 65.

219 Timothy Coates, *Convicts and Orphans*, 66.

220 Ibid.

221 Timothy Coates, *Convicts and Orphans*, 207.

222 Geraldo Pieroni, *Os excluídos do Reino*, 43.

223 Timothy Coates, *Convicts and orphans*, 32.
224 Michel Foucault, *Discipline and Punish. The Birth of the Prison* (Vintage Books, 1995), 25; Stuart Elden, *Foucault: The Birth of Power* (Polity, 2017), 58–59, 97–98.
225 Timothy Coates, *Convicts and Orphans*, 63.
226 Timothy Coates, *Convicts and Orphans*, 78–79.
227 Timothy Coates, *Convicts and Orphans*, 79.
228 Timothy Coates, *Convicts and Orphans*, 99.
229 Timothy Coates, *Convicts and Orphans*, 85.
230 Ibid.
231 Laura de Mello e Souza, *Inferno Atlântico: Demonologia e Colonização séculos XVI–XVIII* (Companhia das Letras, 1993), 100.
232 Silvia Federici, *Caliban and the Witch* (Automedia, 2004), 16, 86–89, 181.
233 Ronaldo Vainfas, *Trópico dos pecados*, 50–51.
234 Ronaldo Vainfas, *Trópico dos pecados*, 52.

Conclusion
Historicizing Race

> Arguing that racial discourses took a particular form in the nineteenth century is one thing; contending that they did not operate in the early modern period, quite another.
>
> María Elena Martínez[1]

Over the past decades, there has been a growing interest in historicizing notions of race. As a social construct, the concept of race has a historical trajectory that sheds light on the formation of hierarchically codified social relations, on various processes of violence and material dispossession, and on the changing epistemological foundations that have provided racism's conditions of possibility. Historicizing notions of race, moreover, allows us to question racism as a linear, transhistorical process while accounting for the specificities of its functioning in relation to concrete moments and processes. As part of ongoing efforts to historicize notions of race, an increasing number of scholars have challenged the view that it is anachronistic to use race as an analytical category prior to the 19th century when racial doctrine solidified in relation to theories about human difference grounded on enlightenment science.[2] In particular, scholars have called attention to three key processes that, in the course of the early modern period, helped shape the historical trajectory of race as a social construct with concrete material effects.

First, the institutionalization of purity of blood statutes in Iberia in the middle of the 15th century has long been the focal point for arguments about the emergence of notions of race.[3] Among others, the work of María Elena Martínez has helped establish that the notion of purity of blood was predicated on deterministic ideas about heredity premised on the idea that "Jewishness" was transmitted in the blood, that is, that it was a natural, inheritable condition.[4] For her, examining the ideology of purity of blood and its effects—among them, the establishment of the Inquisition—is critical because it allows us a major shift whereby notions of difference previously grounded on religion were superseded by increasingly naturalized forms of hierarchical differentiation premised on the belief that genealogy had a

DOI: 10.4324/9781003145196-6

deterministic role in shaping a person's character and behavior. Martínez further shows that increasing awareness and concerns about genealogy had particular implications for women, partly because women's embodied role in childbirth and the production of breast milk led to increasing associations of female bodies with impurity. She also compellingly argues that ideas about purity of blood influenced the system of socio-racial classification that developed in Spanish America known as the *sistema de castas*, which appealed to notions of blood proportions to categorize the various groups of people that Spanish colonization brought into contact and the reproductive relations that ensued.[5]

The rise and expansion of the Atlantic slave trade has likewise been identified by scholars as a second key process that can help us historicize the emergence and development of notions of race. Enslaved Africans first arrived in Portugal in the 1440s, and, over the next centuries, the slave trade steadily increased to various parts of Europe and then dramatically expanded with Europe's colonization of the Americas. The racializing implications of the African slave trade have, in turn, been the object of numerous studies, many of which consider how the development of notions of race are tied to the advancement of capitalism and the consolidation of Atlantic slavery.[6] James Sweet, for instance, argues that 15th-century Iberian discourses associated black skin color with infidelity and inferiority, and he shows that discriminatory attitudes and policies toward enslaved Africans pre-existed the expansion of the Atlantic slave trade in the 16th century.[7] While Sweet emphasizes that the "racist ideology" that sanctioned the commodification of human beings in the 15th century operated without a stable concept of race, he nevertheless suggests that race is a useful analytical tool to understand the dynamics of power relationships in the early modern period.[8] He further contends that economic factors like the emergence of capitalism cannot on their own account for the establishment and perpetuation of Atlantic slavery; instead, he insists on the need to consider how the cultural discourses that were used to justify the commodification of human beings influenced the development of notions of race.[9]

In contrast to Sweet, Jennifer Morgan has argued more recently that the history of Atlantic slavery is intricately interconnected with both the rise of European capitalism and the development of notions of race.[10] One of Morgan's major conceptual interventions turns precisely on the need to consider the interconnections between, on the one hand, the development of notions of racial difference that sanctioned the commodification of human beings, and, on the other, the emergence of capitalist economic frameworks that determined the value of human beings as commodities.[11] According to her, economics and race are best understood as "mutually constitutive," and, for her, the history of Atlantic slavery cannot be dissociated from the emergence and development of racial capitalism.[12] Notably, Morgan also contends that the origins of notions of race precede the rise of the Atlantic slave trade; as she puts it, "The idea of race emerged out of the older notion of 'the other' rooted in religion, language, wealth, and sovereignty historically grounded in medieval Europe."[13] Nonetheless, as she argues, "the transatlantic slave trade...indelibly shaped notions of race."[14]As mentioned in the introduction, moreover, Morgan also underscores the fact that Atlantic slavery rested on a notion of heritability that had particular implications for enslaved women. This is why, for her, motherhood—and, more specifically, what she calls "racialized maternity"—is one of the key vectors that allow us to trace the interconnections between capitalist economics and emerging notions of racial difference.

Another key process that is regularly invoked in scholarship on the history of race concerns Europe's colonization of the Americas. Both the development of notions of purity of blood and the rise of the Atlantic slave trade are critically tied to Europe's colonial expansion in the Americas. Yet, in addition to underscoring how these processes shaped colonial systems of racialization, scholars have also called attention to other important developments, including juridical debates over the "nature" and rights of indigenous peoples. Scholars like Anibal Quijano and George M. Fredrickson, for instance, argue in differing ways that the well-known debates between Bartolomé de las Casas and Juan Ginés de Sepúlveda—which ultimately led to the prohibition of indigenous slavery in Spanish America—are illustrative of the consolidation of racializing distinctions in the early modern period.[15] In his analysis of said debates, Quijano contends that Sepúlveda's views represented an "extreme position" premised on the presumed inferiority of indigenous groups, and he suggests that, although his position was ultimately sidelined in laws that prohibited indigenous enslavement in Spanish America, he asserts that "the idea of basic biological differences among humans was never questioned."[16] Similarly, George M. Fredrickson characterizes Sepúlveda's position as "a classic statement of sixteenth-century racism," and he argues that Spanish colonization is "critical to the history of Western racism because its attitudes and practices served as a kind of segue between the religious intolerance of the Middle Ages and the naturalistic racism of the modern era."[17]

While the different arguments outlined above help establish the need to consider how early modern processes shaped the historical trajectory of notions of race, research on these topics is ongoing. *Race, Sex, and Segregation in Colonial Latin America* contributes to ongoing efforts to historicize notions of race and works to expand this scholarship. It does so by showing that the emergence and early development of segregationist policies in Spanish and Portuguese America decisively shaped colonial processes of racialization. The book draws from existing scholarship and seeks to intervene in ongoing discussions by, on the one hand, contributing to arguments about the periodization of notions of race, and on the other, by proposing a theory of racialization that develops existing conceptual frameworks.

In terms of periodization, the book advances two main claims. First, it shows that notions of purity of blood informed segregationist projects in Spanish and Portuguese America. As shown in Chapter 1, both Vasco de Quiroga and Bartolomé de las Casas appealed to notions of purity of blood as they drew out paternalistic plans for spatial reorganization based on their shared goal of conserving and fostering indigenous demographic growth. In Quiroga's case, notions of purity of blood were also evoked to help justify his call for the creation of separate indigenous communities, and his views and actions played a critical role in shaping the transition toward the segregationist dual republic model. Chapter 2 further shows that the emphasis on maintaining indigenous women in "Indian towns" can be contextualized by considering how discourses about the perceived dangers of breastmilk—which were linked to ideas about purity of blood—influenced segregationist laws. In Chapter 3, I also demonstrate that Felipe Guaman Poma de Ayala made marked distinctions between the different socio-racial groups that constituted Andean colonial society, and I contend that his insistence that Spaniards, Indians, and blacks should not be "mixed" is partly justified by appealing to a discourse about purity of blood. Finally, in Chapter 4, I argue that notions of purity of blood inform Manuel da Nóbrega's views in *Diálogo sobre a conversão do gentio*, and I point out that one of the most important institutions that were set up in Portugal to facilitate the transportation of white women to the colonies required proof of blood purity for admission. Each of these instances helps corroborate María Elena Martínez's argument about the need to consider how notions of purity of blood influenced processes of racialization in both Iberia and its colonies, and it helps expand her work by considering additional ways in which we can trace these processes.

A second claim about the periodization of notions of race that I advance in the book pertains to the topic of slavery. On the one hand, the monograph shows that, while in Spanish America segregationist projects developed in a context following the abolition of indigenous slavery in 1542, in colonial Brazil, the policy of *aldeamento* was established in a setting in which the enslavement of diverse indigenous groups was massively—if unevenly—practiced until the mid-18th century. As discussed in Chapter 4, this created a critical juridical distinction between *índios aldeados* and *negros da terra*, and this in turn established an important difference in terms of how diverse native groups were racialized in Brazil. In turn, this history helps foreground that scholarship on the development of notions of race that focuses on how juridical debates over the "nature" and rights of indigenous people in the 16th century helped shape processes of racialization tends to elide both the long history of indigenous slavery in Brazil and the implications this has for thinking about the presumed "biological differences" that Quijano suggests were grafted onto the indigenous as a supposedly undifferentiated population group.[18] On the other hand, the book emphasizes the significance that Atlantic slavery has for tracing the development of notions of race. It does so by considering the way in which reproductive sex between enslaved Africans and other groups was politicized by nascent colonial states, by pointing out ways in which segregation contributed to this politicization, and by signaling to ways in which laws governing hereditary slavery in Spanish and Portuguese America can be productively developed considering Morgan's arguments and conceptual framework.

On a conceptual level, *Race, Sex, and Segregation in Colonial Latin America* advances a theory of racialization. It shows that the notion of race, as a social construct with concrete material effects, operates in law and cultural discourses, was used to demarcate a person's social status as free or enslaved, was evoked to regulate people's movement based on racial ascription, and was consistently articulated in relation to discourses about reproduction. The articulation of notions of race to reproduction, in turn, has a series of conceptual implications that I delineate in the book. In Chapter 1, I consider how notions of population begin emerging in the early modern period in relation to depopulation crises that happened concurrently in Europe, as part of the transition to early capitalism, and in the Americas, as an effect of colonizing violence and the spread of disease. I argue that the growing awareness of populations as a political and economic problem brings into focus the way in which the politicization of life at the level of collectivities is tied to a process of differentiation that contributed to the composition of differently racialized groups, and I suggest that these processes can be productively analyzed in dialogue with Foucault's theory of biopolitics. In Chapter 2, I trace how the politicization of life—and, more specifically, the politicization of indigenous life, that is, racially qualified life—was used to justify segregationist projects, and I contend that legal discourses that sought to regulate reproductive relations between differently construed groups of people helped solidify racializing distinctions between increasingly homogenizing conceptions of Africans, indigenous, and Europeans as distinct population groups. In Chapter 3, I further emphasize Guaman Poma's consistent plea for fostering indigenous population growth, I show that his endorsement of segregation is explicitly articulated in relation to this issue, and I consider the implications that this formulation has for how the author politicizes, and seeks to regulate, indigenous women's reproductive capacities. Finally, in Chapter 4, I argue that Nóbrega's repeated petition that white Portuguese women be sent to Brazil—as well as the institutional mechanisms that were used to facilitate the transportation of Portuguese women to the colonies—foregrounds a broader pattern of colonial governance increasingly staked on the regulatory management of life. I also highlight the implications this has for tracing how racializing distinctions are mapped onto women's bodies and what this entails for thinking about how racializing distinctions are tied to the historically differential ways in which women's reproductive capacities have been historically regulated.

The monograph also advances a theory of racialization that aims to reformulate the way in which notions of mestizaje or *mestiçagem* have been invoked to dismiss the effectiveness of segregationist efforts in Spanish and

Portuguese America. By showing that segregationist laws, practices, and discourses developed in a context in which reproductive sex between differently racialized groups became increasingly regulated, I offer a different interpretive approach that foregrounds the way in which notions of racial mixture work to reify, rather than undermine, ideas about racial difference. The history of racial mixture in Latin America has long been informed by celebratory narratives that developed in the aftermath of independence movements, but by tracing the origins of this history and by reframing it as a history of racialized sexuality, I show that it offers unique insights to understand the conceptual links between race, sex, and reproduction. The account of this history that I lay out in the book further shows that the context of widespread reproductive relations between differently racialized groups took place in a context of colonial domination that is often occluded by celebratory narratives, and it cannot be dissociated from a much broader restructuration of power's hold over life that begins to take shape in early modernity, both at the level of individual bodies and in the general sense of the population.

Notes

1 Maria Elena Martínez, *Genealogical Fictions: Limpieza de Sangre, Religion, and Gender in Colonial Mexico* (Stanford University Press, 2008), 11.
2 For more on the development of notions of race in the 19th century, see Robert J.C. Young, *Colonial Desire: Hybridity in Theory, Culture and Race* (Routledge, 1995), 6–19. Some scholars of colonial Latin America still question the periodization of race during the early modern period. Robert Schwaller, for instance, argues that although his book "describes the evolution of race, the categories of difference under analysis were not yet 'races.'" He goes on to argue that "Nevertheless, during the sixteenth century, categories of difference had begun to undergo a process of racialization." See *Géneros de Gente in Early Colonial Mexico: Defining Racial Difference* (Norman: University of Oklahoma Press, 2016), 6. Similarly, Joanne Rappaport contends that "The epistemological basis of racial differentiation in the sixteenth and seventeenth centuries revolved around the notion that external characteristics were mutable, quite the opposite of modern notions of racial fixity." Not until the 19th century, she argues, did an epistemological shift occur that allowed for "the emergence of what came to be viewed as a stable system of racial classification." See *The Disappearing Mestizo: Configuring Difference in the Colonial New Kingdom of Granada* (Duke University Press, 2014), 37.
3 For additional studies on purity of blood see Robert Wald Sussman (Harvard University Press, 2014), Francisco Bethencourt, *Racisms: From the Crusades to the Twentieth Century* (Princeton University Press, 2013); Angela Barreto Xavier, "Purity of Blood and Caste Identity Narratives among Early Modern Goan Elites," in *Race and Blood in the Iberian World*, edited by Max S. Hering Torres, María Elena Martínez, David Niremberg (Lit Verlag, 2012), 125–149; George M. Fredrickson, *Racism: A Short History* (Princeton University Press, 2002); Max S. Hering Torres, "Purity of Blood. Problems of Interpretation," in *Race and Blood in the Iberian World*, edited by Max S. Hering Torres, María Elena Martínez, David Niremberg (Lit Verlag, 2012), 11–38; David Niremberg, "Race and the Middle Ages. The Case of Spain and Its Jews," in *Rereading*

the *Black Legend. The Discourses of Religious and Racial Difference in the Renaissance* Empires, edited by Margaret R. Greer, Walter D. Mignolo, Maureen Quilligan (University of Chicago Press, 2007), 71–87, and Verena Stolke, "O enigma das interseções: classe, 'raça,' sexo, sexualidade. A formação dos impérios transatlânticos do século XVI ao XIX," *Estudos Feministas* 14, no. 1 (2006): 15–42.

4 Maria Elena Martínez, *Genealogical Fictions,* 28.

5 Maria Elena Martínez, *Genealogical Fictions,* 56. This idea of blood proportions was also later used to think about heredity in enslaved African populations, as clearly illustrated in a passage by the Benedictine priest and bishop of Pamplona, Prudencio Sandoval (1533–1620) who argued that there was a resemblance between *conversos'* impurity of blood and the black skins of Africans:

> No condeno la piedad cristiana que abraza a todos; que erraría mortalmente, y sé que en el acatamiento divino no hay distinción del gentil al judío; porque uno solo es el Señor de todos. ¿Mas quién podrá negar que en los descendientes de judíos permanece y dura la mala inclinación de su antigua ingratitud y mal conocimiento, como en los negros el accidente inseparable de su negrura? Que si bien mil veces se juntan con mujeres blancas, los hijos nacen con el color moreno de sus padres. Así el judío no le basta [ser] por tres partes hidalgo, o cristiano viejo, que solo una raza lo inficiona y daña, para ser en sus hechos, de todas maneras, judíos dañosos por extremo en las comunidades.

See *Historia de la vida y hechos del emperador Carlos V.Biblioteca de Autores Españoles.* [1606]. Vol. 82 of *Biblioteca de AutoresEspañoles*, (Ediciones Atlas, 1955), 319.

6 A classic study on the subject is Eric Williams' *Capitalism and Slavery* (University of North Carolina Press, 1994 [1944]). Sweet engages and critiques William's thesis. For additional analyses see Russell Menard, *Sweet Negotiations: Sugar, Slavery, and Plantation Agriculture in Early Barbados* (University of Virginia Press); Francisco Bethencourt, *Racisms: From the Crusades to the Twentieth Century* (Princeton University Press, 2013), 83–100.

7 James Sweet, "The Iberian Roots of American Racist Thought," *The William and Mary Quarterly* 54, no. 1 (Jan 1997): 143–165.

8 James Sweet, "The Iberian Roots of American Racist Thought," 143, 144.

9 James Sweet, "The Iberian Roots of American Racist Thought," 143.

10 Jennifer Morgan, *Reckoning with Slavery: Gender, Kinship, and Capitalism in the Early Black Atlantic* (Duke University Press, 2021), 12, 56, 237.

11 Jennifer Morgan, *Reckoning with Slavery,* 12, 16–17.

12 Jennifer Morgan, *Reckoning with Slavery,* 15.

13 Jennifer Morgan, *Reckoning with Slavery,* 59.

14 Jennifer Morgan, *Reckoning with Slavery,* 3.

15 David T. Goldberg similarly argues that after the colonization of West Africa and later the New World, a racial consciousness appears and is explicitly expressed in 16th-century politico-philosophical and economic debates, where, as he puts it, there materializes an "unquestioned *racial* difference between European, American Indian, and Negro." See *Racist Culture* (Blackwell, 1993), 24–26.

16 See Aníbal Quijano, "Questioning 'Race'," *Socialism and Democracy* 21, no. 1 (2007): 51. For more on debates over the "nature" and enslavement of indigenous groups see Lewis Hanke, *The Spanish Struggle for Justice in the Conquest of America* (Little Brown and Company, 1965).

17 George Fredrickson, *Racism: A Short History* (Princeton University Press, 2002), 36–37. In his history of race, Fredrickson also contends that the Spanish doctrine of purity of blood was "undoubtedly racist." See *Racism: A Short History*, 33. He also argues that the conquest and colonization of the Canary Islands is another important process to theorize notions of race. See *Racism: A Short History*, 35–40.

18 Daniel Nemser also discusses other limitations of Quijano's theorization of race. See Nemser, *Infrastructures of Race: Concentration and Biopolitics in Colonial Mexico* (University of Texas Press, 2017), 5–7.

Bibliography

Archives

Archivo General de la Nación (AGN), Mexico City, Mexico.

Published Materials

Acosta, Abraham. "Unsettling Coloniality: Readings and Interrogations." *Journal of Commonwealth and Postcolonial Studies* 6, no.1 (Spring 2018): 3–16.

Adorno, Rolena. "A Witness unto Itself: The Integrity of the Autograph Manuscript of Felipe Guaman Poma de Ayala's *El primer nueva corónica y buen gobierno*." In *New Studies of the Autograph Manuscript of Felipe Guaman Poma de Ayala's 'Nueva corónica y buen gobierno,'* edited by Rolena Adorno and Ivan Boserup, 7–106. Museum Tusculanum Press, 2003.

———. *Guaman Poma. Writing and Resistance in Colonial Peru.* University of Texas Press, 2000.

———. "Introduction." In *Unlocking the Doors to the Worlds of Guaman Poma and His* Nueva corónica, edited by Rolena Adorno and Ivan Boserup, 10–11. The Royal Library Museum Tusculanum Press, 2015.

———. "Los textos manuscritos de Guaman Poma (I) La preparación de la *Nueva corónica* para la imprenta." In *La memoria del mundo inca: Guaman Poma y la escritura de la* Nueva corónica, edited by Jean-Philippe Husson, 41–60. Fondo Editorial de la Pontifica Universidad Católica del Perú, 2016.

——— and John V. Murra. "Notas Aclaratorias." In *El primer nueva corónica y buen gobierno,* edited by John V. Murra and Rolena Adorno, 1126–1161. Siglo Veintiuno, 2006.

———. "Racial Scorn and Critical Contempt: Review of *Nueva corónica y buen gobierno.*" *Diacritics* 4, no. 4 (1974): 2–7.

———. "Textos imborrables: Posiciones simultaneas y sucesivas del sujeto colonial." *Revista de Crítica Literaria Latinoamericana* 21, no. 41 (1995): 33–49.

———. "The Depiction of Self and Other in Colonial Peru." *Art Journal* 49, no. 2 (1990): 110–118.

———. *The Polemics of Possession in Spanish-American Narrative.* Yale University Press, 2007.

Agamben, Giorgio. *Homo Sacer: Sovereign Power and Bare Life.* Stanford University Press, 1998.

Aguayo Spencer, Rafael. *Don Vasco de Quiroga, taumaturgo de la organización social seguido de apéndide documental.* Editorial Polis, 1939.

Alden, Dauril. "Changing Jesuit Perceptions of the Brasis during the Sixteenth Century." *Journal of World History* 3, no. 2 (1992): 205–218.

Anais da Biblioteca Nacional do Rio de Janeiro. Vol. 57. Serviço Gráfico do Ministério da Educação, 1939.

Annaes da Biblioteca Nacional do Rio de Janeiro. Vol. 27. Officina Typographica da Biblioteca Nacional, 1906.

Ares Queija, Berta. "Mestizos, mulatos y zambaigos (Virreinato del Perú, siglo XVI)." In *Negros, mulatos, zambaigos: derroteros africanos en los mundos ibéricos*, edited by Berta Ares Queija and Alessandro Stella, 75–88. Escuela de Estudios Hispano-Americanos, 2000.

Balasopoulos, Antonis. "Dark Light: Utopia and the Question of Relative Surplus Population." *Utopian Studies* 27, no. 3 (2016): 615–629.

Baptiste, Victor N. *Bartolomé de las Casas and Thomas More's Utopia.* Labyrinthos, 1990.

Barreto Xavier, Angela. "Imagens de pobres, pobreza e assistência entre os século XV e XX." In *Portugaliae Monumenta Misericordiarum.* Vol. 10, edited by José Pedro Paiva, 15–41. União das Misericórdias Portuguesas, 2017.

———. "Purity of Blood and Caste Identity Narratives among Early Modern Goan Elites." In *Race and Blood in the Iberian World*, edited by Max S. Hering Torres, María Elena Martínez and David Niremberg, 125–149. Lit Verlag, 2012.

Bauer, Ralph. "'EnCountering' Colonial Latin American Indian Chronicles: FelipeGuaman Pomade Ayala's History of the 'New' World." *American Indian Quarterly* 25, no. 2 (2001): 274–312.

Bennett, Herman L. *Africans in Colonial Mexico: Absolutism, Christianity, and Afro-Creole Consciousness, 1570–1640.* Indiana University Press, 2005.

———. *Colonial Blackness: A History of Afro-Mexico.* Indiana University Press, 2009.

Benoist, Valerie. "La conexión entre casta y familia en la representación de los negros dentro de la obra de Guarnan Poma." *Afro-Hispanic Review* 29, no. 1 (2010): 35–54.

Bentancor, Orlando. "La disposición de la materia en la *Información en derecho* de Vasco de Quiroga." In *Estudios transatlánticos postcoloniales II: Mito, archivo, disciplina: Cartografías culturales*, edited by Ileana Rodríguez and Josebe Martínez, 171–207. Anthropos Editorial, 2011.

———. *The Matter of Empire. Metaphysics and Mining in Colonial Peru.* University of Pittsburg Press, 2017.

Benton, Lauren. *A Search for Sovereignty: Law and Geography in European Empires 1400 1900.* Cambridge University Press, 2014.

Bergmann, Emilie L. "Milking the Poor: Wet-nursing and the Sexual Economy of Early Modern Spain." In *Marriage and Sexuality in Medieval and Early Modern Iberia*, edited by Eukene Lacarra Lanz, 90–114. Routledge, 2002.

Bernasconi, Robert. "Crossed Lines in the Racialization Process: Race as a Border Concept." *Research in Phenomenology* 42 (2012): 206–228.

Bethencourt, Francisco. *Racisms: From the Crusades to the Twentieth Century.* Princeton University Press, 2013.

Boserup, Ivan. "Los textos manuscritos de Guaman Poma (II): Las etapas de la evolución del manuscrito *Galvin* de la *Historia general del Perú* de Martín de Murúa." In *La memoria del mundo inca: Guaman Poma y la escritura de la Nueva corónica*, edited by Jean Philippe Husson, 61–116. Fondo Editorial de la Pontifica Universidad Católica del Perú, 2016.

Boxer, Charles. *Women in Iberian Expansion Overseas 1415–1815.* Oxford University Press, 1975.

Brewer-García, Larissa. *Beyond Babel: Translations of Blackness in Colonial Peru and New Granada.* Cambridge University Press, 2020.

———. "Bodies, Texts, and Translators: Indigenous Breast Milk and the Jesuit Exclusion of Mestizos in Late Sixteenth-Century Peru." *Colonial Latin American Review* 21, no. 3 (2012): 369–390.

Brier, Jennifer, Jim Downs, and Jennifer Morgan, eds. *Connexions: Histories of Race and Sex in North America.* University of Illinois Press, 2016. E-book.

Brokaw, Galen. "The Poetics of Khipu Historiography: Felipe Guaman Poma de Ayala's 'Nueva corónica' and the 'Relación de los quipucamayos." *Latin American Research Review* 38, no. 3 (2003): 111–147.

Bucifferro Justin. "A Forced Hand: Natives, Africans, and the Population of Brazil, 1545–1850."*Revista de História Económica* 31, no. 2 (2013): 285–317.

Buescu, Ana Isabel. *D. João III. 1502–1557.* Printer Portuguesa Ind. Gráfica Lta, 2008.

Burns, Kathryn. "Gender and the Politics of Mestizaje: The Convent of Santa Clara in Cuzco." *The Hispanic American Historical Review* 78, no. 1 (1998): 5–44.

———. "Unfixing Race." In *Rereading the Black Legend: The Discourses of Religious and Racial Difference in the Renaissance Empires*, edited by Margaret Greer, Walter Mignolo and Maureen Quilligan, 188–202. University of Chicago Press, 2007.

Butler, Judith. *Precarious Life: The Powers of Mourning and Violence.* Verso, 2004.

———. "Sexual Traffic," interview with Gayle Rubin, *A journal of Feminist Cultural Studies* 6.2, no. 3 (1994).

———. *Undoing Gender.* Routledge, 2004.

Cardenas Bunsen, José. "Manuscript Circulation, Christian Eschatology, and Political Reform: Las Casas's *Tratado de las doce dudas* and Guaman Poma's *Nueva corónica.*" In *Unlocking the Doors to the Worlds of Guaman Poma and His* Nueva corónica, edited by Rolena Adorno and Ivan Boserup, 65–86. The Royal Library Museum Tusculanum Press, 2015.

Carneiro, Edson Carneiro. *A cidade do Salvador: uma reconstituição histórica.* Edição da 'Organização Simões,' 1954.

Casey, James. *Early Modern Spain: A Social History.* Routledge, 1999.

Castelnau-L'Estoile, Charlotte de. *Operários de uma vinha estéril: Os Jesuítas e a conversão dos índios no Brasil 1500–1620.* Editorial da Universidade do Sagrado Coração, 2006.

———. *Un catholicisme colonial: Le mariage des Indiens et des esclaves au Brésil, XVI–XVIII.* Presses Universitaires de France, 2019.

Castilleja, Aida. "La configuración del espacio local en tres pueblos de la laguna de Pátzcuaro. El componente político-administrativo de la diferenciación del espacio: articulación e integración." In *Del territorio a la Arquitectura en el Obispado de Michoacán*, edited by Carlos Paredes Martínez and Catherine Ross Ettinger, 275–301. Consejo Nacional Para la Ciencia y Tecnología, 2008.

Castro, Daniel. *Another Face of Empire. Bartolome de las Casas, Indigenous Rights, and Ecclesiastical Imperialism.* Duke University Press, 2007.

Castro-Klaren, Sara. "Dancing and the Sacred in the Andes: From the 'Taqui-Oncoy' to 'Rasu Niti.'" *Dispositio* 14, no. 36/38 (1989): 169–185.

Celestino de Almeida, Maria Regina. *Metamorfoses indígenas: identidade e cultura nas aldeias coloniais do Rio de Janeiro.* Arquivo Nacional, 2003.

Chambouleyron, Rafael. "A evangelização do Novo Mundo: o Plano do Pe. Manuel da Nóbrega." *Revista de História* 134 (1996): 37–47.

Chang-Rodriguez, Raquel. "Coloniaje y conciencia nacional: Garcilaso de la Vega Inca y Felipe Guamán Poma de Ayala." *Cahiers du monde hispanique et luso-brésilien*, no. 38 (1982): 29–43.

Chaves de Resende, Maria Leônia. "Minas mestiças: índios coloniais em busca da liberdade no século do ouro." *Cahiers des Amériques latines* 44, no. 44 (2003): 61–76.

Chavez Carvajal, Maria Guadalupe. *Propietarios y esclavos negros en Valladolid de Michoacán, 1600–1650.* Universidad Michoacana de San Nicolás de Hidalgo, 1994.

Coates, Timothy. *Convicts and Orphans. Forced and State-Sponsored Colonizers in the Portuguese Empire, 1550–1755.* Stanford University Press, 2001.

———. "State-Sponsored Female Colonization in the *Estado da India, ca. 1550 1750.*" In *Sinners and Saints. The Successors of Vasco da Gama*, edited by Sanjay Subrahmanyam, 40–56. Oxford University Press, 1995.

Cohen, Thomas. "Who Is My Neighbor? The Missionary Ideals of Manuel da Nóbrega." In *Jesuit Encounters in the New World: Jesuit Chroniclers, Geographers, Educators and Missionaries in the Americas, 1549–1767*, edited by Joseph A. Gagliano and Charles E. Ronan, 209–228. Institutum Historicum, 1997.

Colectivo Emancipaciones. https://colectivoemancipaciones.org

Connolly, Brian. "The Curse of Canaan; or, a Fantasy of Origins in Nineteenth-Century America." In *Connexions: Histories of Race and Sex in North America*, edited by Jennifer Brier, Jim Downs and Jennifer Morgan. University of Illinois Press, 2016. E-book.

Cook, Noble David. *Born to Die. Disease and New World Conquest, 1492–1650.* Cambridge University Press, 1998.

Cordeiro de Almeida, Suely Creusa. *O sexo devoto: normatização e resistência feminina no Império Português XVI–XVIII.* Imprensa Universitária da UFRPE, 2005.

Covarrubias Reyna, Miguel. "Santa Fé. Utópico pueblo absorbido por la ciudad de México." *Arqueología Mexicana*, no. 134 (2015): 74–79.

Cushman, Gregory. "The Environmental Contexts of Guaman Poma: Interethnic Conflict over Forest Resources and Place in Huamanga, 1540–1600." In *Unlocking the Doors to the Worlds of Guaman Poma and His* Nueva corónica, edited by Rolena Adorno and Ivan Boserup, 87–140. The Royal Library Museum Tusculanum Press, 2015.

De Mello e Souza, Laura. *Inferno Atlântico: Demonologia e Colonização séculos XVI–XVIII.* Companhia das Letras, 1993.

Del Valle, Ivonne. "A New Moses: Vasco de Quiroga's Hospitals and the Transformation of Indians from 'Bárbaros' to 'Pobres.'" In *Iberian Empires and the Roots of Globalization*, edited by Ivonne del Valle, Anna Moore and Rachel Sarah O'Toole, 47–73. Vanderbilt University Press, 2020.

Dillon, Michel. "Cared to Death. The Biopoliticised Time of Your Life." *Foucault Studies* 2 (2005): 37–46.

Dos Guimarães Sá, Isabel. "Child Abandonment in Portugal: Legislation and Institutional Care." *Continuity and Change* 9, no. 1 (1994): 69–89.

———. "Managing Social Inequality: Confraternal Charity in Portugal and Its Overseas Colonies." *Social Science History* 41, no. 1 (2017): 121–135.

Durantaye, Leland. *Giorgio Agamben: A Critical Introduction.* Stanford University Press, 2009.

Duviols, Pierre. "Cristóbal de Albornoz. Instrucción." In *Fábulas y mitos de los incas,* edited by Henrique Urbano and Pierre Duviols. Editorial Historia 16, 1989.

Eisenberg, José. "A escravidao voluntária dos índios do Brasil e o pensamenot politico modern." *Análise Social* 39, no. 170 (2004): 7–35.

———. "Antonio Vieira and the Justification for Indian Slavery." *Luso-Brazilian Review* 40, no. 1 (2003): 89–95.

———. *As missões jesuíticas e o pensamento político moderno.* Editora EFMG, 2000.

Elden, Stuart. *Foucault: The Birth of Power.* Polity, 2017.

Encina, Diego. *Cedulario Indiano.* https://babel.hathitrust.org/cgi/pt?id=inu.3200 0004954873&view=1up&seq=372&q1=569

Escobedo Mansilla, Ronald. "El tributo de los zambaigos, negros y mulatos libres en el virreinato peruano." *Revista de Indias* 41 (1981): 43–46.

Espinosa, Aurelio. *The Empire of the Cities. Emperor Charles V, the Comunero Revolt, and the Transformation of the Spanish System.* Koninklijke Brill NV, 2009.

Estenssoro Fuchs, Juan Carlos. "Los colores de la plebe: razón y mestizaje en el Perú colonial." In *Los cuadros del mestizaje del virrey Amat y la representación etpnografica en el Perú colonial,* edited by Natalia Majluf, 66–107. Museo de Arte de Lima, 2000.

Federici, Silvia. *Caliban and the Witch. Women, the Body and Primitive Accumulation.* Automedia, 2014.

Feros, Antonio. *Speaking of Spain: The Evolution of Race and Nation in the Hispanic World.* Harvard University Press, 2017.

Foucault, Michel. *Discipline and Punish. The Birth of the Prison.* Vintage Books, 1995.

———. *The History of Sexuality: An Introduction, Volume I.* Translated by Robert Hurley. Vintage Books, 1990 [1976].

Fredrickson, George M. *Racism: A Short History.* Princeton University Press, 2002.

García, Rodolfo. "As órfãs." *Revista do Instituto Histórico e Geográfico Brasileiro* 192 (1946): 137–142.

Garofalo, Leo J. "The Shape of a Diaspora: The Movement of Afro-Iberians to Colonial Spanish America." In *Africans to Spanish America: Expanding the Diaspora,* edited by Sherwin K. Bryant, Rachel Sarah O'Toole, and Ben Vinson. University of Illinois Press, 2012.

Gates Jr., Henry Louis. *Black in Latin America.* NYU Press, 2012.

Goldberg, David Theo. *Racist Culture.* Blackwell, 1993.

Gómez, Fernando. *Good Places and Non-Places in Colonial Mexico. The Figure of Vasco de Quiroga (1470–1565).* University Press of America, 2001.

Graubart, Karen. "Competing Spanish and Indigenous Jurisdictions in Early Colonial Lima." *Latin American History: Oxford Research Encyclopedias.* Published online 2016.

———. "Containing Law within Walls: The Protection of Customary Law in Santiago del Cercado, Peru." In *Protection and Empire: A Global History,* edited by Lauren Benton, Adam Clulow, and Bain Attwood, 13–28. Cambridge University Press, 2017.

————. "Learning from the Qadi: The Jurisdiction of the Local Rule in the Early Colonial Andes." *Hispanic American Historical Review* 95, no. 2 (2015): 195–228.

Guamán Poma de Ayala, Felipe. *El primer nueva corónica y buen gobierno*, edited by John V. Murra and Rolena Adorno. Siglo Veintiuno, 2006.

Haliczer, Stephen. *The Comuneros of Castile. The Forging of a Revolution, 1475–1521*. The University of Wisconsin Press, 1981.

Hanke, Lewis. *All Mankind is One. A Study in the Disputation Between Bartolomé de las Casas and Juan Ginés de Sepúlveda in 1550 on the Intellectual and Religious Capacity of the American Indians*. Northern Illinois University Press, 1974.

————. *The Spanish Struggle for Justice in the Conquest of America*. Little, Brown and Company, 1965.

Harrison, Regina. "Guaman Poma: Law, Land, and Legacy." In *Unlocking the Doors to the Worlds of Guaman Poma and His* Nueva corónica, edited by Rolena Adorno and Ivan Boserup, 141–161. The Royal Library Museum Tusculanum Press, 2015.

Hering Torres, Max. "Purity of Blood. Problems of Interpretation." In *Race and Blood in the Iberian World*, edited by Max S. Hering Torres, María Elena Martínez, and David Niremberg, 11–38. Lit Verlag, 2012.

Hernández Cendejas, Gerardo Alberto. "El liderazgo y la ideologia communal de Elpidio Dominguez Castro en Santa Fe de la Laguna, Michocan, 1979–1988." *Tzintzun. Revista de Estudios Históricos*, no. 39 (2004): 113–140.

Hespanha, Antonio. *Filhos da terra: Identidades mestiças nos confins da expansão portuguesa*. Edições Tinta da China, 2019.

Hill, Ruth, "*Casta* as Culture and the *Sociedad de Castas* as Literature." In *Interpreting Colonialism*, edited by Byron Wells and Philip Stewart, 231–259. Oxford University Press, 2004.

Holland, Augusta. "Importancia de los enanos y corcovados en la *Nueva corónica*." In *La memoria del mundo inca: Guaman Poma y la escritura de la* Nueva corónica, edited by Jean-Philippe Husson, 273–300. Fondo Editorial de la Pontifica Universidad Católica del Perú, 2016.

Husson, Jean-Philippe. "A Little Known but Essential Element of the Cultural Context of the *Nueva corónica*: Felipe Guaman Poma de Ayala's Native Sources." In *Unlocking the Doors to the Worlds of Guaman Poma and His* Nueva corónica, edited by Rolena Adorno and Ivan Boserup, 163–187. The Royal Library Museum Tusculanum Press, 2015.

————. "Prólogo." In *La memoria del mundo inca: Guaman Poma y la escritura de la* Nueva corónica, edited by Jean-Philippe Husson, 9–40. Fondo Editorial de la Pontifica Universidad Católica del Perú, 2016.

Jaboatão, Antônio de. *Catálogo genealógico das pricipaes famílias: que procederam de Albuquerques e Cavalcantes em Pernamubuco e Caramurús na Bahia*. Imprensa Oficial, 1950.

Jameson, Fredric. *Archaeologies of the Future: The Desire Called Utopia and Other Science Fictions*, 34–35. Verso, 2007.

JanMohamed, Abdul. "Sexuality on/of the Racial Border: Foucault, Wright, and the Articulation of 'Racialized Sexuality.'" In *Discourses of Sexuality: from Aristotle to AIDS,* edited by Domma Stanton, 94–116. University of Michigan Press, 1993.

Juchari eratsikua, Cherán K'eri: retrospective histórica, territorio e identidad étnica. Casimiro Leco Tomás, Alicia Lemus Jimenez and Ulrike Keyser Ohrt (cords). Consejo Mayor de Gobierno Comunal de Cherán, 2018.

Karatani, Kojin. The *Structure of World History: From Mods of Production to Modes of Exchange.* Translated by Michael K. Bourdaghs. Duke University Press, 2014.

Khaimovich, Gregory. "In Search of the Background for the Bilingualism of *El primer nueva corónica y buen gobierno.*" In *Unlocking the Doors to the Worlds of Guaman Poma and His* Nueva corónica, edited by Rolena Adorno and Ivan Boserup, 189–210. The Royal Library Museum Tusculanum Press, 2015.

Klohn, Alex M. and Philippe Chastonay. "Guaman Poma de Ayala's 'New Chronicle and Good Governmnet: A Testimony on the Health of the Indigenous Populations in XVIth Century Peru." *Hygiea Internationalis: An Interdisciplinary Journal of the History of Public Health* (2015): 147–161.

Konetzke, Richard. *Colección de Documentos para la Formación Social de Hispanoamérica 1493–1810,* Volumen I (1493–1592). Consejo Superior de Investigaciones Científicas, 1953.

———. *Colección de Documentos para la Formación Social de Hispanoamérica 1493–1810,* Volumen II, Primer Tomo. Consejo Superior de Investigaciones Científicas, 1953.

Krippner Martínez, James. "Invoking 'Tata Vasco': Vasco de Quiroga Eighteenth Twentieth Centuries." *The Americas* 56, no. 3 (2000): 1–28.

Lacarra Lanz, Eukene. "Changing Boundaries of Licit and Illicit Unions: Concubinage and Prostitution." In *Marriage and Sexuality in Mediaeval and Early Modern Iberia,* edited by Eukene Lacarra Lanz, 158–194. Routledge, 2002.

Landers, Jane G. "Cimarrón and Citizen: African Ethnicity, Corporate Identity, and the Evolution of Free Black Towns in the Spanish Circum-Caribbean." In *Slaves, Subjects, and Subversives: Blacks in Colonial Latin America,* edited by Jane G. Landers and Barry M. Robinson, 111–145. University of New Mexico Press, 2006.

Langfur, Hal. "Recovering Brazil's Indigenous Pasts." In *Native Brazil: Beyond the Convert and the Cannibal,* 1500–1900, edited by Hal Langfur, 1–28. The University New Mexico Press, 2014.

Las Casas, Bartolomé. "Memorial de denuncias." In *Biblioteca de autores españoles. Obras Escogidas de Bartolomé de las Casas. Opúsculos, Cartas y Memoriales,* Tomo110, edited by Juan Perez de Tuleda Bueso. Real Academia Española, 1958.

———. "Memorial de remedios para las Indias." In *Biblioteca de autores españoles. Obras Escogidas de Bartolomé de las Casas. Opúsculos, Cartas y Memoriales,* Tomo110, edited by Juan Perez de Tuleda Bueso. Real Academia Española, 1958.

Lavrín, Asunción. "Sexuality in Colonial Mexico: A Church Dilemma." In *Sexuality and Marriage in Colonial Latin America,* edited by Asunción Lavrín, 47–95. University of Nebraska Press, 1992.

Lee, Christina H. and Ricardo Padrón. "Introduction." In *The Spanish Pacific, 1521–1815: A Reader of Primary Sources.* Amsterdam University Press, 2020.

Leite Serafim. *Breve itinerário para uma biografia do P. Manuel da Nóbrega, fundador da província do Brasil e da cidade de São Paulo.* Edições Brotéria, 1955.

León, Nicolás. *Documentos inéditos referentes al ilustrísimo señor Don Vasco de Quiroga. Existentes en el Archivo General de Indias.* José Miguel Quintana, intr. Mexico: José Porrúa e Hijos, 1940.

Lisi, Francesco Leonardo. *El tercer concilio limense y la aculturación de los indígenas sudamericanos.* Ediciones Universidad de Salamanca, 1990.

Livi Bacci, Massimo. *Conquest and the Destruction of the American Indios.* Polity Press, 2008.

Lohmann Villena, Guillermo "Una carta inédita de Huamán Poma de Ayala." *Revista de Indias* 6 (1945): 325–327.

López-Baralt, Mercedes. *Ícono y conquista: Guamán Poma de Ayala.* Ediciones Hiperión, 1988.

———. "Un ballo in maschera: Hacia un Guaman Poma multiple." *Revista de Crítica Literaria Latinoamericana* 21, no. 41 (1995): 69–93.

Lund, Joshua. *The Impure Imagination. Toward a Critical Hybridity in Latin American Writing.* University of Minnesota Press, 2006.

———. *The Mestizo State. Reading Race in Modern Mexico.* University of Minnesota Press, 2012.

Lynch, John. "The Institutional Framework of Colonial Spanish America." *Journal of Latin American Studies* 24 (1994): 69–81.

MacCormack, Sabine. "Pachacuti: Miracles, Punishments, and Last Judgment: Visionary Past and Prophetic Future in Early Colonial Peru." *The American Historical Review* 93, no. 4 (1988): 960–1006.

Macera, Pablo, "Introducción." In *Phelipe Gvaman Poma de Aiala. Y no ay remedio*, edited by Elías Prado Tello y Alfredo Prado Prado, 25–80. CIPA Centro de Investigación y Promoción Amázonica, 1991.

Málaga Medina, Alejandro. "Las reducciones en el Perú durante el gobierno del Virrey Toledo." *Kollasuyo: revista de estudios bolivianos* 87 (1974): 43–71.

Mamani Macedo, Mauro. "Introducción." In *Guamán Poma de Ayala: las travesias culturales,* edited by Mauro Mamani Macedo, 9–14. Facultad de Letras y Ciencias Humanas Universidad Mayor de San Marcos, 2016.

Marcílio, Maria Luiza. "The Population of Colonial Brazil." In *The Cambridge History of Latin America. Volume II,* edited by Leslie Bethell, 37–58. Cambridge University Press, 1984.

Marques Guedes, Ana Isabel. "Tentativas de controle da reprodução da população colonial: As órfas d'El Rei." In *O Rosto feminino da expansão portuguesa,* 665–673. Comissão para a Igualdade e para os Direitos da Mulher, 1994.

Martínez, María Elena. *Genealogical Fictions: Limpieza de Sangre, Religion, and Gender in Colonial Mexico.* Stanford University Press, 2008.

———. "Space, Order, and Group Identities in a Spanish Colonial Town: Puebla de los Angeles." In *The Collective and the Public in Latin America: Cultural Identities and Political Order,* edited by Luis Roniger and Tamar Herzog, 13–36. Sussex Academic Press, 2000.

Martínez Baracs, Rodrigo. *Convivencia y utopía. El gobierno indio y español de la 'ciudad de Mechuacan, 1521–1580.* Instituto Nacional de Antropología e Historia, 2005.

Martz, Linda. *Poverty and Welfare in Habsburg Spain.* Cambridge University Press, 1983.

Marx, Karl. *Capital Volume I.* Penguin Classics, 1990.

Massey, Doreen. *Space, Place and Gender.* University of Minnesota Press, 2009.

Mbembe, Achille. *Necropolitics.* Trans. Steven Corcoran. Duke University Press, 2019.

McKinley, Michelle A. "Such Unsightly Unions Could Never Result in Holy Matrimony: Mixed-Status Marriages in Seventeenth-Century Colonial Lima." *Yale Journal of Law and the Humanities* 217 (2010): 217–255.

McWorther, Ladelle. "Sex, Race, and Biopower: A Foucauldian Genalogy." *Hypatia* 19, no. 3 (2004): 38–62.

Menard, Russell. *Sweet Negotiations: Sugar, Slavery, and Plantation Agriculture in Early Barbados.* University of Virginia Press, 2006.

Metcalf, Alida. *Family and Frontier in Colonial Brazil. Santana de Parnaíba, 1580–1822.* University of California Press, 1992.

———. *Go-Betweens and the Colonization of Brazil. 1500–1600.* University of Texas Press, 2006.

———. "'Harvesting Souls': The Society of Jesus and the First Aldeias (Mission Villages) of Bahia." In *Native Brazil: Beyond the Convert and the Cannibal,* 1500–1900, edited by Hal Langfur, 29–61. The University New Mexico Press, 2014.

———. "The Entradas of Bahia of the Sixteenth Century." *The Americas* 61, no. 3 (2005): 373–400.

Mignolo, Walter. "Delinking." *Cultural Studies* 21, no. 2–3 (2007): 449–514.

———. "El pensamiento decolonial: desprendimiento y apertura. Un manifiesto." In *El giro decolonial. Reflexiones para un diversidad epistémica más allá del capitalismo global,* edited by Santiago Castro-Gómez and Ramón Grosfoguel, 25–46. Siglo del Hombre Editores, 2007.

———. "Preamble: The Historical Foundation of Modernity/Coloniality and the Emergence of Decolonial Thinking." In *Companion to Latin American Literature and Culture,* edited by Sara Castro Klaren, 12–32. Wiley-Blackwell Publishing, 2008.

Monteiro, John Manuel. *Negros da Terra: Índios e Bandeirantes de São Paulo.* Companhia das Letras, 1994.

Moore, Jason W. *Capitalism and the Web of Life.* Verso, 2015.

Moraes, Antonio Carlos Robert. *Bases da Formação Territorial do Brasil. O Território colonial brasileiro no 'longo' século XVI.* Editora Hucitec, 2000.

Morales, Mónica. *Reading Inebriation in Early Colonial Peru.* Ashgate, 2012.

More, Anna. *Baroque Sovereignty: Carlos Sigüenza y Góngora and the Creole Archive of Colonial Mexico.* University of Pennsylvania Press, 2013.

More, Thomas. *Utopia.* [1516] 1518 Latin Copy. Nettie Lee Benson Library in Austin.

———. *Utopia.* Translated by Robert Adams. W. W. Norton & Company, 1991.

Moreno, Juan Joseph. *Fragmentos de la vida y virtudes del V. Illmo. y Rmo. Sr. Dr. D. Vasco de Quiroga, Primer Obispo de la Santa Iglesia Cathedral de Michoacan y fundador del Real, y Primitivo Colegio de San Nicolás Obispo de Valladolid.* Imprenta del Real, y más antiguo Colegio de San Ildefonso, 1766.

Morgan, Jennifer. "Partus sequitur ventrem: Law, Race, and Reproduction in Colonial Slavery." *Small Axe* 22, no. 55 (2018): 1–17.

———. *Reckoning with Slavery: Gender, Kinship, and Capitalism in the Early Black Atlantic.* Duke University Press, 2021.

Mörner, Magnus. *La corona Española y los foráneos en los pueblos de indios de América.* Almqvist & Wiksell, 1970.

———. *Race Mixture in the History of Latin America.* Little, Brown and Company, 1967.

Mumford, Jeremy. *Vertical Empire. The General Resettlement of Indians in the Colonial Andes.* Duke University Press, 2012.

Mundy, Barbara. *The Death of Aztec Tenochtitlan, the Life of Mexico City.* University of Texas Press, 2015.

Murra, John V. "Waman Puma, Etnógrafo del mundo Andino." In *El primer nueva corónica y buen gobierno,* edited by John V. Murra and Rolena Adorno, xiii–xix. Siglo Veintiuno, 2006.

Myers, Kathleen. *Fernández de Oviedo's Chronicle of America: A New History for a New World.* University of Texas Press, 2007.

Nagel, Joane. "Ethnicity and Sexuality." *Annual Review of Sociology* 26 (2000): 107–133.

Nemser, Daniel. *Infrastructures of Race: Concentration and Biopolitics in Colonial Mexico.* University of Texas Press, 2017.

———. "Primitive Accumulation, Geometric Space, and the Construction of the Indian." *Journal of Latin American Cultural Studies* 24, no. 3 (2015): 335–352.

Nielsen, Jesper and Mettelise Fritz Hansen. "Dedications and Devils: Comparing Visual Representations of in Early Colonial Mesoamerican Sources and Guaman Poma's *Nueva corónica.*" In *Unlocking the Doors to the Worlds of Guaman Poma and His* Nueva corónica, edited by Rolena Adorno and Ivan Boserup, 233–268. The Royal Library Museum Tusculanum Press, 2015.

Niremberg, David. "Race and the Middle Ages. The Case of Spain and Its Jews." In *Rereading the Black Legend: The Discourses of Religious and Racial Difference in the Renaissance Empires,* edited by Margaret Greer, Walter Mignolo and Maureen Quilligan, 71–87. University of Chicago Press, 2007.

Nóbrega, Manuel da. *Cartas do Brasil e mais escritos do Manuel da Nóbrega,* edited by Serafim Leite. Atlântida, 1955.

———. *Diálogo sobre a conversão do gentio,* edited by Serafim Leite. Comissão do IV Centenário da Fundação de São Paulo, 1954.

Norton, Luiz. "A colonização Portuguesa do Brasil (1500–1550)." *Revista de Historia de America* no. 138 (2007): 177–210.

Ossio, Juan M. "Inca Kings, Queens, Captains, and *Tocapus* in the Manuscripts of Martín de Murúa and Guaman Poma." In *Unlocking the Doors to the Worlds of Guaman Poma and His* Nueva corónica, edited by Rolena Adorno and Ivan Boserup, 291–328. The Royal Library Museum Tusculanum Press, 2015.

———. "Mito e historia en torno a la fecha de nacimiento de Guaman Poma de Ayala." In *La memoria del mundo inca: Guaman Poma y la escritura de la* Nueva corónica, edited by Jean-Philippe Husson, 147–164. Fondo Editorial de la Pontifica Universidad Católica del Perú, 2016.

O'Toole, Rachel Sarah. *Bound Lives: African, Indians, and the Making of Race in Colonial Peru.* University of Pittsburgh Press, 2012.

Oviedo, Gonzálo Fernández y Valdes. *Historia General y Natural de las Indias.* Tomo I. Editorial Guarania, 1535.

Pagden, Anthony. *The Fall of Natural Man.* Cambridge University Press, 1982.

Paredes Martínez, Carlos. *Historia de los pueblos indígenas de México.* Centro de Investigaciones y Estudios Superiores en Antropología Social, 2017.

——— and Marta Terán. *Autoridad y gobierno indígena en Michoacán.* Vol. 1. El Colegio de Michoacán, 2003.

Penyak, Lee M. "Incestuous Natures: Consensual and Forced Relations in Mexico, 1740–1854." In *Sexuality and the Unnatural in Colonial Latin America,* edited by Zeb Tortorici, 162–187. University of California Press, 2016.

Perrone Moises, Beatriz. "Índios livres e índios escravos: Os princípios da legislação indigenista do período colonial (séculos XVI a XVIII)." In *História dos índios no Brasil*, edited by Manuela Carneiro da Cunha, 115–132. Companhia das Letras, 1992.

Petrone, Pasquale. *Aldeamentos Paulistas*. Editora da Universidade de São Paulo, 1995.

Pieroni, Geraldo. *Os excluídos do Reino: A Inquisição portuguesa e o degredo para o Brasil Colônia*. Editora Universidade de Brasília, 2000.

Prado Tello, Elías and Alfredo Prado Prado. "Presentación." In *Phelipe Gvaman Poma de Aiala. Y no ay remedio*, edited by Elías Prado Tello and Alfredo Prado Prado, 13–22. CIPA Centro de Investigación y Promoción Amázonica, 1991.

Prevotel, Audrey. "A Central Aspect of the Intellectual, Religious, and Artistic Context of the *Nueva corónica: Lives of Saints.*" In *Unlocking the Doors to the Worlds of Guaman Poma and His* Nueva corónica, edited by Rolena Adorno and Ivan Boserup, 331–353. The Royal Library Museum Tusculanum Press, 2015.

Proctor, Frank Trey. "African Diasporic Ethnicity in Mexico City to 1650." In *Africans to Spanish America: Expanding the Diaspora*, edited by Sherwin K. Bryant, Rachel Sarah O'Toole, and Ben Vinson, 50–72. University of Illinois Press, 2012.

Puente Luna, José Carlos de la. "El capitán, el ermitaño y el cronista. Claves para establecer cuándo nació el autor de la *Nueva corónica y buen gobierno.*" In *La memoria del mundo inca: Guaman Poma y la escritura de la* Nueva corónica, edited by Jean-Philippe Husson, 117–146. Fondo Editorial de la Pontífica Universidad Católica del Perú, 2016.

———. "That Which Belongs to All: Khipus, Community, and Indigenous Legal Activism in the Early Colonial Andes." *The Americas* 72, no. 1 (2015): 19–54.

Quijano, Aníbal. "Questioning 'Race.'" *Socialism and Democracy* 21, no. 1 (2007): 45–53.

Quiroga, Vasco. "Carta al Consejo de Indias." In *Don Vasco de Quiroga. Taumaturgo de la organización social,* edited by Rafael Aguayo Spencer, 77–83. Ediciones Oasis, S.A., 1970.

———. *Información en derecho del licenciado Quiroga sobre algunas provisiones del real consejo de Indias.* [1535]. Carlos Herrejón Peredo. Secretaría de Educación Pública, 1985.

———. "Reglas y Ordenanzas para el Gobierno de los Hospitales de Santa Fe de México y de Michoacán." In *Don Vasco de Quiroga. Taumaturgo de la organización social*, edited by Rafael Aguayo Spencer, 245–269. Editorial Polis, 1940.

———. "Testamento." In *Don Vasco de Quiroga. Taumaturgo de la organización social*, edited by Rafael Aguayo Spencer, 273–292. Ediciones Oasis, S.A., 1970.

Quispe Agioli, Rocío. "Escribirlo es nunca acabar: cuatrocientos cinco años de lecturas y silencios de una *Opera Aperta* colonial andina." *Letras: Revista de Investigacion de la Facultad de Letras y Ciencias Humanas* 91, no. 133 (2020): 5–34.

———. "Mestizos (in)deseables en el Perú colonial temprano." *Revista de Crítica Literaria Latinoamericana* XLIII, no. 86 (2017): 127–150.

———. "Yo y el otro: identidad y alteridad en la 'Nueva Corónica y Buen Gobierno.'" *MLN* 119, no. 2 (2004): 226–251.

Rabinow, Paul. *The Foucault Reader*. Pantheon Books, 1984.

Rabinow, Paul and Nikolas Rose. "Biopower Today." *BioSocieties* 1 (2006): 195–217.

Rama, Angel. *La ciudad letrada*. Ediciones del Norte, 1984.

Rappaport, Joanne. *The Disappearing Mestizo: Configuring Difference in the Colonial New Kingdom of Granada*. Duke University Press, 2014.

Rau, Virginia. "Review of *Cartas do Brasil e mais escritos do P. Manuel da Nóbrega (Opera Omnia) by Serafim Leite*." *The Hispanic American Historical Review* 36, no. 3 (1956): 390–391.

Recopilación de Leyes para las Indias, 1681. https://home.heinonline.org

Rosenthal, Olimpia. "*As órfãs d'el rei*: Racialized Sex and the Politicization of Life in Manuel da Nóbrega's Letters from Brazil." *Journal of Lusophone Studies* 1, no. 2 (2016): 72–97.

———. "Guamán Poma and the Genealogy of Decolonial Thought." *Journal of Commonwealth and Postcolonial Studies* 6, no. 1 (2018): 64–85.

———. "La figura abyecta del mestizo en *El primer nueva corónica y buen gobierno*." *Letras: Revista de Investigacion de la Facultad de Letras y Ciencias Humanas* 85, no. 121 (2014): 31–46.

Ruan, Felipe E. "Andean Activism and the Reformulation of Mestizo Agency and Identity in Early Colonial Peru." *Colonial Latin American Review* 21, no. 2 (2012): 209–237.

Rubin, Gayle. "The Traffic in Women: Notes on the 'Political Economy' of Sex." In *Towards and Anthropology of Women*, edited by Rayna R. Reiter, 157–210. Monthly Review Press, 1975.

———. "The Trouble with Trafficking: Afterthoughts on 'The Traffic in Women.'" In *Deviations: A Gayle Rubin Reader*, edited by Gayle Rubin. Duke University Press, 2011.

Russell-Wood, John R. "Women and Society in Colonial Brazil." *Journal of Latin American Studies* 9, no. 1 (1977): 1–34.

Salomon, Frank. "Guaman Poma's *Sapci* in Ethnographic Vision." In *Unlocking the Doors to the Worlds of Guaman Poma and His* Nueva corónica, edited by Rolena Adorno and Ivan Boserup, 355–396. The Royal Library Museum Tusculanum Press, 2015.

Sánchez-Albornoz, Nicolás. "The Population of Colonial Spanish America." In *The Cambridge History of Latin America. Volume II,* edited by Leslie Bethell, 3–34. Cambridge University Press, 1984.

Santos, Martha S. "Slave Mothers': Partus Sequitur Ventrem, and the Naturalization of Slave Reproduction in Nineteenth-Century Brazil." *Tempo* 22, no. 41 (2016): 467–487.

Schwaller, Robert C. *Géneros de Gente in Early Colonial Mexico: Defining Racial Difference*. University of Oklahoma Press, 2016.

———. "Mulata, Hija de Negro y India": Afro-Indigenous Mulatos in Early Colonial Mexico." *Journal of Social History* 44, no. 3 (2011): 889–914.

Schwartz, Stuart B. "Cities of Empire: Mexico and Bahia in the Sixteenth Century." *Journal of Inter-American Studies* 11, no. 4 (1969): 616–637.

———. *Early Brazil a Documentary Collection to 1700*. Cambridge University Press, 2010.

———. "Indian Labor and New World Plantations: European Demands and Indian Responses in Northeastern Brazil." *The American Historical Review* 83, no. 1 (1978): 43–79.

———. "Pecar en colonias: Mentalidades populares, inquisición y actitudes hacia la fornicación simple en España, Portugal y las colonias americanas." *Cuadernos de Historia moderna* no. 18 (1997): 51–68.

Seijas, Tatiana. "Asian Migrations to Latin America in the Pacific World, 16th–19th Centuries." *History Compass* 14 (2016): 573–581.

———. *Asian Slaves in Colonial Mexico: From Chinos to Indians.* Cambridge University Press, 2014.

Serrano Gassent, Paz. *Vasco de Quiroga. Utopía y derecho en la conquista de América.* FCE (Política y Derecho), 2002.

Silverblatt, Irene. "Family Values in Seventeenth-Century Peru." In *Native Traditions in the Postconquest World,* edited by Elizabeth Hill Boone and Tom Commins, 63–89. Dumbarton Oaks, 1998.

———. *Moon, Sun, and Witches: Gender Ideologies and Class in Inca and Colonial Peru.* Princeton University Press, 1987.

Socolow, Susan Migden. *The Women of Colonial Latin America.* Cambridge University Press, 2000.

Solórzano Pereira, Juan de. *Política Indiana,* Libro II, Tomo I. Ediciones Atalas 1972 [1647].

Stolcke, Verena. "Los mestizos no nacen sino que se hacen." *Avá* 14 (2009).

———. "O enigma das interseções: classe, 'raça,' sexo, sexualidade. A formação dos impérios transatlânticos do século XVI ao XIX." *Estudos Feministas* 14, no. 1 (2006): 15–42.

Stoler, Ann Laura. *Along the Archival Grain. Epistemic Anxieties and Colonial Common Sense.* Princeton University Press, 2009.

———. *Duress: Imperial Durabilities in Our Times.* Duke University Press, 2016.

———. *Race and the Education of Desire: Foucualt's History of Sexuality and the Colonial Order of Things.* Duke University Press, 1995.

Stolke, Verena. "O enigma das interseções: classe, 'raça,' sexo, sexualidade. A formação dos impérios transatlânticos do século XVI ao XIX." *Estudos Feministas* 14, no. 1 (2006): 15–42.

Sweet, James H. "The Iberian Roots of American Racist Thought." *The William and Mary Quarterly* 54, no. 1 (1997): 143–166.

Talavera Ibarra, Oziel Ulises. "El dominio racial de los no indígenas en Uruapan: ocupación del espacio y del territorio." In *Del Territorio a la Arquitectura en el Obispado de Michoacán,* edited by Carlos Salvador Paredes Martínez, Guadalupe Salazar González, Catherine Rose Ettinger, and Luis Alberto Torres Garibay, 115–135. Universidad Michoacana de San Nicolás de Hidalgo, 2008.

Tena Ramírez, Felipe. *Vasco de Quiroga y sus pueblos de Santa Fe en los siglos XVIII y XIX.* Editorial Porrúa, 1977.

Vaccarella, Eric. "Estrangeros, uellacos, santos y rreys: la representación de los negros en la obra de Felipe Guamán Poma de Ayala." *Revista Iberoamericana* LXVIII, no. 198 (2002): 13–26.

Vainfas, Ronaldo. *A heresia dos índios: Catolicismo e rebeldia no Brasil colonial.* Companhia das Letras, 1995.

———. *Trópico dos pecados: Moral, Sexualidade e Inquisicao no Brasil.* Editora Campus, 1989.

Van Deusen, Nancy. *Between the Sacred and the Worldly: The Institutional and Cultural Practice of Recogimiento in Colonial Lima.* Stanford University Press, 2001.

———. *Global Indios: The Indigenous Struggle for Justice in Sixteenth-Century Spain.* Duke University Press, 2015.

Vicuña Guengerich, Sara. "Virtuosas y corruptas: Las mujeres indígenas en las obras de Guamán Poma de Ayala y el Inca Garcilaso de la Vega." *Hispania* 96, no. 4 (2013): 672–683.

Vieira Powers, Karen. "Conquering Discourses of 'Sexual Conquest': Of Women, Language, and Mestizaje." *Colonial Latin American Review* 11, no. 1 (2002): 7–32.

———. *Women in the Crucible of Conquest: The Gendered Genesis of Spanish American Society, 1500–1600*. University of New Mexico Press, 2005.

Vinson III, Ben. *Before Mestizaje: The Frontiers of Race and Caste in Colonial Mexico*. Cambridge University Press, 2017.

Vitali, Guillermo Ignacio. "Escenas de Evangelización: Verdad y Archivo en las Cartas de Manuel da Nóbrega." *Alea Estudos Neolatinos* 22, no. 2 (2020): 41–58.

Warren, J. Benedict. *Vasco de Quiroga en África*. Fimax Publicistas, 1998.

———. *Vasco de Quiroga y sus Hospitales-Pueblo de Santa Fe*. Ediciones de la Universidad Michoacana, 1977.

Williams, Eric. *Capitalism and Slavery*. University of North Carolina Press, 1994 [1944].

Wolfe, Patrick. *Traces of History: Elementary Structures of Race*. Verso, 2016.

Yannakakis, Yanna and Martina Schrader-Kniffki. "Between the 'Old Law' and the New: Christian Translation, Indian Jurisdiction, and Criminal Justice in Colonial Oaxaca." *Hispanic American Historical Review* 96, no. 3 (2016): 517–548.

Young, Robert C. *Colonial Desire: Hybridity in Theory, Culture and Race*. Routledge, 1995.

———. "Foucault on Race and Colonialism." *New Formations* 25 (1995): 57–65.

Zavala, Silvio A. "La 'utopia' de Tomás Moro en la Nueva España." In *La utopia mexicana del siglo XVI. Lo bello, lo verdadero y lo bueno*. Tovar de Teresa, Guillermo, dir. Grupo Azabache, 1992.

———. *Las instituciones jurídicas en la conquista de América*. 3 ed. Editorial Porrúa, 1988.

———. *Recuerdo de Vasco de Quiroga*. Editorial Porrua, 1965.

Zeron, Carlos Alberto de Moura Ribeiro. *Linha de fé. A companhia de Jesus e a Escravidão no Processo de Formação da Sociedade Colonial. Brasil, Séculos XVI e XVII*. Editora da Universidade de São Paulo, 2011.

Index

Note: Page numbers followed by "n" denote endnotes.

enslavement 7, 9, 31, 32, 40–42, 50,
53, 58–60, 91, 97, 99, 116, 128,
129, 131, 133, 137, 142, 144–146,
148–152, 156, 163n25, 169n153,
175–178, 180n5, 180n16
equity 26
escriuanos 94
españoles/as 54, 56, 57, 59, 61, 71, 76,
77, 80
Espelho de casados (Barros) 155
"Estatuto das aldeias" (Mem de Sá) 127
estupro 111
European colonialism 49
exchange of women 153, 154
exile (or banishment) 10, 16n64, 38, 39,
60, 93, 103, 120n37, 130, 133, 154,
156–160, 164n32

failure of dual republic 51, 52, 83n23
familias 37
Federici, Silvia 6, 8, 160
female orphan (*órfãs d'el Rei*) 154–160,
171n177
Feros, Antonio 55
fortified trading posts (*feitorias*) 131
Foucault, Michel 7, 87n84, 156;
biopolitics, theory of 7, 8, 178;
biopower, theory of 4–5, 15n39,
25, 34, 81; *Discipline and Punish*
159; *History of Sexuality* 4; political
economy of bodies 159; on
race–sexuality relationship 5–6
Fredrickson, George M. 176, 181n17
free marriage choice 55
free womb (*vientre libre*) 53, 60
free womb laws 60

Gassent, Paz Serrano 38
gender 70, 103, 107, 150: oppression 153
gente de razón 143
gentios 133, 161
gíbaro 51
Giles, Peter 30
Góis, Luís de 132
Goldberg, David T. 180n15
Gouveia, Diego 132–133
group identity 1, 4, 10, 126, 170n167
Guaman Poma de Ayala, Felipe 178;
*El primer nueva corónica y buen
gobierno* 116; *Historia general del
Pirú* 92; *Nueva corónica* 90–96, 99,
104–106, 109, 112, 115, 116, 118n7;
segregation, endorsement of 90–117
Guedes, Ana Isabel Marques 155

Harvey, David 45
Henriques, Dom Leão 145
heritability 7, 176
Hespanha, Antonio 165n55
Hispaniola island: Spanish-indigenous
marriage in 54
Historia general del Pirú (Guaman
Poma de Ayala) 92
History of Sexuality (Foucault) 4
Holland, Augusta 91
homogenization 1, 3, 10, 14n20, 23, 28,
105, 108, 126, 127, 129, 137, 160,
161, 178
hospital town 17–20, 28, 34–42, 47n90,
47n110, 47n115, 49

idleness 37, 71, 99
Ignatious of Loyola 140
Inca rule 95
Indian towns (*pueblos de indios*):
40-42, 49–51, 67, 68, 76–78, 80,
93-95, 97, 99-104, 110, 112, 113,
123n89, 177
índias da terra/índios da terra 133, 152,
161, 177
indigenous labor power 49, 68, 97, 98,
101, 126, 128
indigenous life, politicization of
25–34, 42–43
indigenous segregation, justification and
regulation of 62–70
indios (*indias, yndios*) 1, 10, 27,
53–55, 59, 61, 62, 65, 66, 70, 71, 76,
96, 103, 105, 107, 108, 126, 137,
160, 161
indios aldeados 126–129, 177
indios chinos 50
Información en derecho (Quiroga) 20,
22–26, 28, 33, 39
instrumentalization of women's
reproductive capacities 10, 12, 130,
131, 151, 153, 160

Jameson, Fredric 28
Jesuit missionaries ("coadjutores
temporais") 140
juridical discourses 9, 10, 53–62, 65,
79–81, 116
juridico-political power
106, 109
jurisdiction 3, 9, 10, 11, 20, 21, 34, 36,
39, 42, 50, 56, 66, 73, 93, 94, 99,
108, 115, 132
justice 26